Lambert Simnel
and the
Battle of Stoke

Untuk Adinda Fatimah dan Anakanda Masni

Lambert Simnel

and the

Battle of Stoke

Michael Bennett

ALAN SUTTON · Gloucester

ST. MARTIN'S PRESS · New York

First published in the United State of America in 1987 by
St. Martin's Press, Inc.,
175 Fifth Avenue,
New York, NY 10010

Library of Congress Cataloging in Publication Data

Bennett, Michael J. (Michael John), 1949–
    Lambert Simnel and the Battle of Stoke.

    Bibliography: P
    Includes index.
    1. Simnel, Lambert.   2. Stoke, Battle of, England, 1487.
    3. Great Britain—History—Henry VII, 1485–1509.
    4. Imposters and imposture—Great Britain—Bibliography.
    i Title DA330.8.S55B46   1987   942.05′1   87-14666
    ISBN 0-312-01213-6

First published in Great Britain in 1987 by
Alan Sutton Publishing,
30 Brunswick Road,
Gloucester, GL1 1JJ

British Library Cataloguing in Publication Data

Bennett, Michael J.
    Lambert Simnel and the Battle of Stoke.
    1. Great Britain—History—Richard III,
    1483–1485   2. Great Britain—
    History—Henry VII, 1485–1509
    I. Title
    942.04′6   DA260

    ISBN 0-86299-334-2

Typesetting and origination by
Alan Sutton Publishing Limited
Printed in Great Britain

CONTENTS

ACKNOWLEDGEMENTS   vii

1   Prologue: Whitsuntide 1487   1

2   Blood and Roses   15

3   The Tudor Interlude   27

4   The Lambert Simnel Mystery   41

5   The Gathering Storm   57

6   The Struggle for the Kingdom   69

7   The Battle of Stoke   89

8   The Significance of 1487   105

APPENDIX   121

LIST OF ABBREVIATIONS   139

NOTES   141

INDEX   153

LIST OF ILLUSTRATIONS

1	Henry VII, (died 1509), showing him in late middle age	2
2	Christchurch Cathedral, Dublin, where Lambert Simnel was crowned	5
3	Groat attributed to Lambert Simnel, struck in Dublin, 1487	8
4	Italian sword of about 1460	12
5	North German sallet of about 1480	20
6	Elizabeth of York, (died 1503)	28
7	Garter stall plate of Francis, Lord Lovell	34
8	'Herald's report' of the battle of Stoke, showing Lambert Simnel's real name	46
9	Medieval chapel of Magdalen College, Oxford, possibly connected with Lambert Simnel	49
10	Margaret of York, Duchess of Burgundy, (died 1503)	52
11	Seal of John de la Pole, Earl of Lincoln	55
12	German mercenaries of the 15th century	62
13	Irish warriors of the early 16th century, engraved by Durer	67
14	Keep of Kenilworth Castle, Warwickshire, where Henry VII stayed, summer 1487	70
15	Furness Abbey, Lancashire	72
16	Bootham Bar, York, besieged by the Lords Scrope in the name of 'Edward VI'	80
17	Sir John Savage, (died 1492), Macclesfield, Cheshire	83
18	Newark church, Nottinghamshire	90
19	Ballock dagger, North German, 15th century	93
20	Mace, Italian, late 15th century	93
21	Composite Gothic field armour, made in North Italy *c.* 1480	96
22	John de Vere, Earl of Oxford, (died 1513), drawing of his tomb effigy	98
23	The Red Gutter, scene of many deaths after the battle	100
24	Spur found on the battlefield at Stoke	102
25	Seal of Jasper Tudor, Duke of Bedford	110
26	Sir Reginald Bray, (died 1503) from the stained glass at Great Malvern Priory	114
27	Sir Richard Edgecombe, (died 1489), painting in his home Cotehele Manor Cornwall, of his tomb at Morlaix, Brittany	117
28	The 'Burrand Bush' stone	118

MAPS

The Road to Stoke Field 4–16 June 1487   87
Stoke Field 16 June 1487   88

Photographs and illustrations were supplied by, or are reproduced by kind permission of the following: Society of Antiquaries of London (1, 10); British Museum (3, 8); Burrell Collection, Glasgow Museums and Art Galleries (5, 19, 20); Clive Hicks (15); National Gallery of Ireland (13); National Portrait Gallery, London (6); Newark Museum, Nottingham and Sherwood District Council (18, 23, (photographs by Francis Welch), 24, 28); Board of Trustees of the Armouries, H.M. Tower of London, Crown Copyright (21); Trustees of the Wallace Collection, London (4); Geoffrey Wheeler (9, 11, 12, 14, 16, 17, 26, 27).

Picture research by Carolyn and Peter Hammond

Jacket: Henry VII from a peinting by Michiel Sittow, inscribed and dated 1505; courtesy of the National Portrait Gallery, London. Border incorporates a contemporary royal crown with a symbolic representation of Lambert Simnel as 'the King's monkey'. Jacket concept and illustrations: Geoffrey Wheeler. Design: Martin Latham.

ACKNOWLEDGMENTS

When I wrote about the battle of Bosworth two years ago, I believed that quincentenaries only happened every five hundred years. The exercise could not possibly be habit-forming. To follow now with a study of the rebellion of 1487 might appear to observers to be the sure sign of an addiction, which could see me bound to the remorseless regimen of Henry VII for a quarter of a century. All I can plead is that when, at the solicitation of Alan Sutton, I undertook this project I did so in the belief that there was an interesting and significant episode of English history which deserved more extended and serious treatment than it had been previously afforded. If the story of Lambert Simnel were not told in 1987, there was a danger that it would not be taken up again for another half millenium. Since embarking on the book I have received help from a number of quarters. Among the scholars, archivists and librarians who passed on information are M. Condon, C.S.L. Davies, Ralph Griffiths, Alison Hanham, C. Harper-Bill, Peter Poggioli, Colin Richmond, David Smith, R.L. Storey and H. Tomlinson. I would like especially to thank Peter Clifford and his colleagues for production, Peter and Carolyn Hammond for the picture research, Hugh Aixill for sharing his thoughts on the battlefield with me, and Anne Bishop, my sister, for her sleuthing around Newark. I incurred many debts of gratitude in Hobart: Rod Thomson shouldered an extra teaching burden; Annette Sumner arranged interlibrary loans; Ian Smith, Bob Develin and Peter Davis helped on points of translation; Airlie Alam prepared the maps; Louise Gill offered criticisms of the first draft; and Em Underood proof-read against the clock. For her work on the index, and for so much more besides, I thank my mother, Vera Bennett. For her initial encouragement and continuous support in what was a short but exacting enterprise, I am most grateful to my wife, Fatimah.

M.B.

Hobart, Tasmania
May, 1987

The House of Plantagenet

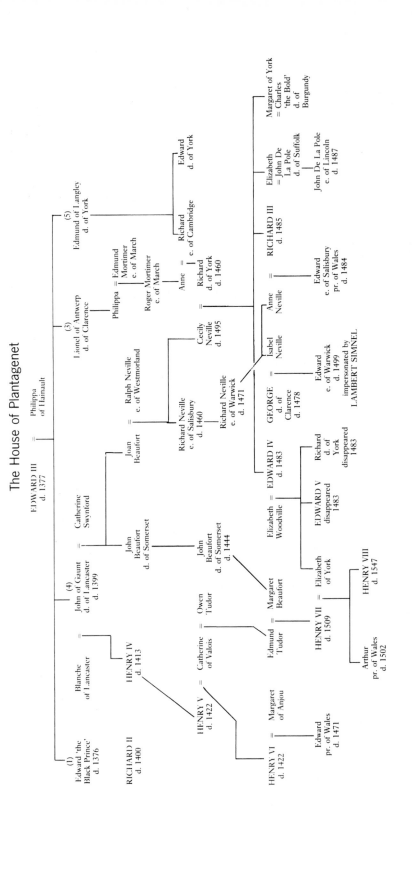

1 Prologue: Whitsuntide 1487

The old battlefield to the south of Market Bosworth lay convalescent, its ruddy clay soil no longer red with blood and its scars now covered with a second spring growth. It was now the end of spring in 1487, and it would soon be difficult to trace the site of the battle. Nonetheless there were still many people in the neighbourhood who could still see in their mind's eye the army of Richard III arrayed on the brooding eminence of Ambien hill, the awesome spectacle of the breakneck charge down the western slopes, the bloody encounter among the scrub and mire, the hacking down of the king at Sandeford. The villagers of Dadlington, or at least the bolder spirits among them, probably had the fullest view of the action as well as the subsequent acclamation of Henry VII on Crown hill.[1] Though the dead king was carried to Leicester, and later buried in the Greyfriars convent, it was to their little church that most of the slain were brought. There was still talk of the endowment of a proper battlefield chapel. Pilgrim traffic and well-lined offertory boxes might yet reconcile the villagers to their grisly legacy. It was not to happen this year. Piety must wait on peace.

For the people around Bosworth, the warmer and longer days of May held no promise of carefree repose. As the weeks slipped by between Easter and Pentecost, there was more to think about than the 'smoke farthings' or chimney tax that householders had to pay as their Pentecostal offering to the mother-church at Leicester.[2] Throughout the realm, but perhaps more especially in the counties of Leicester and Warwick, the spectre of civil war loomed larger and more menacing. It was no longer news that in Ireland there was a boy who claimed to be a scion of the house of York, and that some Yorkist lords were attempting to raise an army in the Netherlands to invade England. What did become apparent at this time was that the challenge from Ireland was acquiring considerable support and that there was a chance that it would be supported from the continent. The precipitate arrival at Coventry of Henry VII late in April obviously signalled that this was what the government suspected. By the end of May it was clear that far from the king leading an expedition to Ireland to suppress the rebellion, the Yorkist lords and their allies looked set to launch an invasion of England.

By Ascension Day Market Bosworth and other towns and villages within a day's ride of Coventry were drawn into a theatre of war. For some time the roads around had buzzed with the movements of royal messengers, careering across

Henry VII, (died 1509), showing him in late middle age.

the countryside with letters for the king's friends and reports on the king's enemies. In ever widening circuits Henry VII's harbingers and scourers moved around the midlands buying up supplies at bargain prices. Local larders were emptied to provide for the royal household as it grew into the nucleus of a large army. The human resources of the region were culled for transport and other duties. William Altoft of Atherstone, whose medical work after Bosworth must have impressed the right people, was one local man whose services were to be greatly appreciated.[3] Above all, of course, there was the mobilisation of the fencible men of the region, under such local commanders as Edward Grey, Viscount Lisle, constable of Kenilworth, and Edward, Lord Hastings from nearby Kirkby Muxloe. Soon the roads were full of cavalrymen, footsoldiers and camp-followers. Since the king lay at Kenilworth, and the perceived threat lay to the north and northwest, the Leicestershire farmers had reason to be anxious that their pastures would again see passages of arms.

*   *   *

As Whitsuntide approached, Henry VII could not immure himself from the atmosphere of confusion and alarm that was building up around the land. Although only thirty years old, he had long ago learned the virtues of vigilance and caution. Half his life, from 1471 until the battle of Bosworth less than two years ago, had been lived in exile, rarely more than a Lancastrian mascot and a pawn in a diplomatic game, and always a target for Yorkist intrigue. Looking northwards from Kenilworth, in the direction of the scene of his triumph, he, like many others, must have wondered what the bloodshed at Bosworth had achieved. Of course, in public the king and his supporters stressed the providential nature of his triumph over a parricidal tyrant. In the toppling and slaughter of Richard III, the battle had indeed been decisive, but the rather shoddy circumstances of the battle made it a little hard to see any sort of vindication of his title. More positively, he presented himself as the kinsman and, more tendentiously, the heir general, of his saintly half-uncle, Henry VI, but it is doubtful whether either claim carried much weight with more than a small faction. More crucial in the winning of hearts and minds was his promise to marry Elizabeth of York, the eldest daughter and, assuming the deaths of her brothers, the heir of Edward IV. It was a promise renewed at the close of his first session of parliament in December 1485, and fulfilled early in the following year. Its significance for public opinion stretched far beyond sentiment. The union of the roses offered the best prospect for an end to discord and the restoration of stability in the body politic. When the marriage bore immediate fruit with the birth of a son nine months later, many people found real comfort in the thought that the new line was properly grafted onto the old stock, and hoped that the end was in sight to the dynastic strife of the previous generation.[4]

It had been a real struggle for Henry VII to broaden his power-base. Even in 1487, there were still few people he could absolutely trust, save his paternal uncle, Jasper Tudor, now duke of Bedford, and the small circle of friends who had shared his exile. He recognised well enough his dependence at Bosworth and in the establishment of his regime, on the tactical genius of the old

Lancastrian warhorse, John de Vere, earl of Oxford, and on the immense military following of his stepfather, Thomas Stanley, now earl of Derby, but he could never take their loyalty and commitment wholly for granted. Arrayed against him in the early days, were not only the many lords, gentlemen and communities who had cause to be loyal to the memory of Richard III, but also the many people who understandably found it hard to accept the accession of the largely unknown Welsh adventurer, Henry Tudor. It was certainly the case that although magnates like Henry Percy, earl of Northumberland, had not lifted a finger to save Richard III in 1485, they could not for that reason be regarded as supporters of the Tudor regime. In seeking to win the allegiance of a wider section of the political nation, Henry had perforce shown great circumspection, overlooking as much as he could overlook in the past records of peers, county notables and royal servants. In his first year or so, at least, he acted with generosity and magnanimity towards men whose commitment to him he had every reason to doubt, and indeed his policies had borne some fruit. His progresses through the realm, including his visits to towns like Nottingham and York, where the late king had been well regarded, had been public relations successes. Yet, even in Warwickshire and Leicestershire, the very heart of his kingdom, Henry had faced first smouldering discontent, and then open insurrection. He could not but feel that there was an incurable giddiness in the body politic. Many simple folk, doubtless encouraged by some who should have known better, saw the 'sweating sickness', which ravaged the realm from autumn 1485 through 1486, as a sign that his rule would be unusually harsh and deleterious. At the same time, the royal marriage, on which much popular hope was pinned, was not progressing as smoothly as had been hoped. By the summer of 1487, it was widely felt that the king was remiss in not arranging for the coronation of the queen, who eight months after the birth of the prince of Wales remained uncrowned.

Waiting at Kenilworth for news of his adversaries, Henry VII might even have felt some empathy with the man whom he had supplanted. Though he had summoned to his side, for relaxation and emotional support, his mother, Lady Margaret Beaufort, and his wife, Elizabeth of York, he must have felt all the crushing loneliness of supreme power. Anxiously watching for signs of anxiety and dissembling among his counsellors, he knew that at any moment he must set out once more to submit his title to the crown to ordeal by battle. Like Richard III before him, he would then himself have the daunting task of holding together and ensuring the loyalty of men, whose commitment in the crucial hour could not be forced. Like the challenge he presented to his predecessor, the challenge he had now to face came from an unexpected quarter, and by its very preposterousness it was deeply unnerving. A determined group of malcontents, supported by a formidable force of German mercenaries, had established themselves in Dublin, and were threatening to invade England, doubtless with promises of powerful assistance from as yet undeclared traitors in the realm. They had with them a young boy, whom they claimed was Edward, earl of Warwick, the last male Plantagenet, and whom they had crowned as Edward VI. What real intelligence Henry VII had about the enterprise is unclear. There were certainly a great many points which awaited clarification. On one point,

Christchurch Cathedral, Dublin, where Lambert Simnel was crowned.

however, the normally taciturn and secretive king was vocal and unequivocal, at least in his public utterances. The puppet-king was no Plantagenet, but an impostor called Lambert Simnel.

The cathedral of Christchurch, Dublin, had staged many spectacles in the three centuries since its construction, but none more remarkable than the coronation ceremony on Ascension day, 24 May 1487. The old and commodious church, normally so dank and eerily hollow, glowed and throbbed as the large and curious congregration waited expectantly on this summer day. Most of the normal points of reference were obscured or overlooked. For the moment the miracle-working relics of the staff of Jesus and the cross of the Holy Trinity were unattended. The battered effigy of Richard 'Strongbow', the progenitor of Anglo-Irish society and a founder of Christchurch, lay redundantly in its alcove in the nave, walled in by the backs of the great crowd. In the chapel of St Loo, the bronze-cased heart of St Lawrence O'Toole, his partner in the re-founding of the church in the late twelfth century, was temporarily forgotten as an object of veneration. All eyes were turned to the procession of splendidly robed prelates and cathedral clergy, richly accoutred noblemen and knights, and in their midst the ten year old youth who was to be crowned in Dublin as Edward VI, king of England and France.[5]

Presiding over the proceedings, never far from centre stage, was Gerald Fitzgerald, the 'great' earl of Kildare, governor of Ireland. Around him were gathered the chief officers of the lordship of Ireland and an impressive array of

Anglo-Irish lords. The ecclesiastical establishment was well represented by the archbishop of Dublin and four other bishops. A rarer sight was the knot of distinguished-looking strangers, who included John de la Pole, earl of Lincoln, a nephew of the Yorkist kings, and Francis Lovell, viscount Lovell, a former confidant of Richard III. As representatives of the house of Plantagenet and the English peerage, this pair probably escorted the fresh-faced child to his place before the high altar. John Payne, bishop of Meath gave the sermon, and outlined the claims of the boy to the throne. It all seemed so indisputable: as Edward, earl of Warwick, the son of the late duke of Clarence, he was the next male heir of Edward IV and Richard III, and indeed the last surviving Plantagenet. The ceremony proceeded with dignity, though not without a measure of improvisation. A coronet was taken for the occasion from the head of a locally revered statue of the Virgin Mary. Once the crown had been placed on his young brow, the boy was lustily acclaimed by the congregation as King Edward. The cheers of acclamation were soon echoing through the streets of Dublin, where large crowds gathered along the road to the castle. So difficult was it for the loyal townspeople to see their diminutive lord that he was borne aloft on the broad and high shoulders of Lord Darcy of Platen. The celebrations were completed in grand style at Dublin castle with a state banquet and lavish entertainments.

Over the preceding weeks the young king had become well known in Anglo-Irish society. He was a handsome and well-proportioned youth, graceful in manner and alert in conversation. There had been many sceptics and secret spies who had talked to him about his past, but he had responded with facility and assurance. In his tale he had needed no prompting. He was indeed a prince of the house of Plantagenet. He was Edward, earl of Warwick, Clarence's son and heir. His mother, who had died when he was a baby, was Isabel Neville, daughter and heiress of Warwick the Kingmaker. He had been totally orphaned in 1478 when his father was falsely charged with treason and secretly put to death. Since then he had lived in straitened circumstances, first as the ward of the grasping marquis of Dorset, and then during Richard III's time as a virtual prisoner at Sheriff Hutton castle. After the accession of Henry Tudor, he had been transferred to the Tower of London, the very place where his father had met his end. Daily he had feared for his life, but eventually well-wishers had effected his escape. With God's assistance he had managed to reach Ireland, where he trusted to find men who honoured his father and grandfather, and who would support his cause against the 'Welsh milksop' who had usurped his throne.

The boy could not have been better schooled to win Irish hearts. From the outset the solemn but plucky youth had brought tears to the eyes of the people of Dublin. The outlines of his tragic story were already well-known, but gained considerable emotional charge from being related in the first person. The appeals of a friendless orphan are never easy to resist, but such appeals had special force for many people in the Irish Pale coming from a scion of the house of York. The memory of the boy's grandfather, Richard, duke of York, who had held office as lieutenant of Ireland from the late 1440s to 1460, was cherished among most Anglo-Irish. During his firm but even-handed rule, the Irish Pale had known a degree of political stability and constitutional progress which in retrospect took on the glow of a golden age. Not surprisingly, the Anglo-Irish establishment welcomed the accession of his son to the throne in 1461, and through the brokerage of the earl of Kildare its support for the Yorkist monarchy brought the colony important privileges from Edward IV and more latterly Richard III. It was never forgotten, however, that the duke of York had another son, George, duke of Clarence, who was actually born in Ireland, and whose destiny might have been seen to lie in the lordship. Like the two previous dukes of Clarence, he had served for a while as lieutenant of Ireland, though he had not been permitted to take up office in person. He certainly seems to have had credit and connections in the colony. At the time of his arrest and imprisonment he was apparently considering having his infant son dispatched to Ireland for safe-keeping.[6] It was this man's son who was now appealing to them for assistance.

What made the cause of the young pretender compelling even to the most hard-headed in the Irish colony, however, was the arrival in Dublin, at the head of an impressive force of German mercenaries, of John de la Pole, earl of Lincoln. He was a twenty-five year-old young man of impeccable credentials. The eldest son of the duke of Suffolk, he was the heir to a noble house, which though only dating back to Edward III's time, was unusually illustrious and well-endowed. He counted among his ancestors on his father's side not only grandees with impressive records of service to the crown, but also the famous poet, Geoffrey Chaucer. The lineage of his mother, Elizabeth, was even more portentous. She was the daughter of Richard, duke of York, and the sister of Edward IV and Richard III, and her sons could thus regard themselves as princes of the house of York. Lincoln's special status was clearly acknowledged by his royal uncles. After the death of his only legitimate son in 1484, King Richard not only appointed him to the lieutenancy of Ireland, but also seems to have regarded him as his heir to the throne. Manifestly, the circumstance that in 1487 the earl of Lincoln was acknowledging the pretender in Dublin as his cousin, and offering himself as his champion, must have carried great weight with many people. Even though he was apparently a late recruit to the movement, few could doubt that he would be the real leader of the enterprise, and Henry VII's chief adversary. It is a pity that so little is known about his character, save for conventional statements affirming his nobility, gallantry and wisdom. Anecdotal evidence about him suggests a rather more complex character. According to later tradition, he was rather circumspect, especially in what he said, adopting such circumlocutions as, 'I will not confidently aver it; but it is so and so, if men may be credited in their mortality' or; 'The number amounts to so many, if men fail not in their computations'.[7] Perhaps with an uncle like Richard III it was wise to choose your words carefully, and with Geoffrey Chaucer as an ancestor, words came easily.

Needless to say, for the power-élite in Dublin it was not merely a combination of sentiment and fair-minded appraisal of Yorkist claims that drove the enterprise forward. In securing the coronation of the young claimant to the kingdom of England and the lordship of Ireland, the earl of Kildare and his faction thought not in terms of sacrifice but in terms of consolidating their own position and securing constitutional privileges. As the lieutenant of the boy-king, Kildare assumed vice-regal powers, and exploited his position to entrench the Fitzgerald ascendancy. For the English colony as a whole it offered a unique opportunity to properly establish the liberties and autonomy which had been the promise of Yorkist rule. It is not known what grand declarations were made in the parliament summoned on Edward VI's behalf, but the government seems to have had no hesitation in striking coins in the new king's name. Of course, it is the case that the new regime was regarded with at least some scepticism in Dublin, and actively resisted in Waterford and some other towns. Yet it cannot be assumed that it was wholly without significance for the Gaelic chieftains beyond the Pale. Kildare was already a force to be reckoned with beyond Leinster and Meath, extending his overlordship into Munster, Connacht and Ulster. None since Brian Boru, the last high king, had wielded such power and authority in Ireland.[8]

*   *   *

In the summer of 1487 England was awash with rumours. The king issued, on Whitsunday, a stern proclamation that all tale-tellers unable to name their sources in court were to be pilloried.[9] It was impossible for people to know what to credit about the identity of the pretender, the men who were supporting him, the aims of the movement, and the degree of support it enjoyed. There was so much that was mysterious about the whole affair, so much that, for all his informers and spies, and despite having sent a herald to Dublin for an audience with the alleged prince, even Henry VII did not know. Needless to say, even what the government knew, perhaps including the 'coronation' in Dublin, it did not necessarily wish to be bruited abroad. Conversely, what the government condescended to tell the people might well have been less than the truth. The king might have put on display in London the 'real' earl of Warwick, and declared the boy in Dublin to be an impostor named Lambert Simnel, but predictably the rebels, for their part, insisted that it was the Tudor regime that, in desperation, had resorted to trickery. This state of uncertainty was bound to persist, to some degree at least, until the challenge to Henry VII came to some final resolution. Even then, many crucial points could be deliberately obscured

Groat attributed to Lambert Simnel, struck in Dublin, 1487.

or lost to human memory. In his final comment on the affair, Francis Bacon astutely described the king 'as loving to seal up his own dangers'.[10]

The historian, five hundred years later, thus has precious few trustworthy sources for this episode in English history. The most reliable forms of documentation, generally speaking, are government and church records, especially when produced, as part of routine administration, close to the events in question. The chancery rolls, the exchequer accounts, court records, bishops' registers and municipal memoranda, for example, all provide much hard information on people, places and dates, and generally offer firm footholds in historical enquiry. Of their very nature, however, such records tend to be formal and terse, explaining little or nothing of the background to the recorded action. While waiting for news of the invasion, for example, the king instructed his officers to deliver the revenues of land held by his mother-in-law, Elizabeth Woodville, to his wife, the new queen. Later commentators associated the disendowment of the dowager queen with the troubles of the time, implying some involvement in the conspiracy. The record itself, however, simply noted laconically that the king was acting 'for diverse considerations'.[11] Of course, there are some classes of material, most notably official letters, proclamations and judicial proceedings, that are a little more forthcoming. The register of the archbishop of Canterbury contains a record of the 'exposure' of Simnel's imposture made during convocation in February 1487. A letter from the king to the pope, written shortly after the rebellion, described the circumstances of a miracle that had powerfully assisted the royal cause in London. The act of attainder against Lincoln and his associates, entered in the parliament rolls in November, offers a brief narrative account of their treason.[12] Yet the more communicative, the less routinely bureaucratic, official documents appear, the more the historian needs to be on guard. All too obviously, such sources might testify more to what the powers-that-were wanted people to believe, than to what was actually the case.

At the very least administrative records of various sorts help to establish firmly crucial benchmarks in the drama of 1487. The pretender's presence in Dublin was clearly known at the time of the great council and convocation in February, and perhaps even in the previous December, when summonses were sent for the meeting. The king's itinerary, from his departure from Sheen early in Lent through to his arrival at Coventry on St George's eve, can be charted from the workings of the privy seal office. In the lead up to and in the aftermath of the king's confrontation with the rebels, a series of proclamations and letters offer a guide to the process of mobilisation and to the re-establishment of order. The records of chancery and exchequer provide details of pardons granted to and fines exacted from rebels in the months following the battle of Stoke.[13] Incidentally, administrative records provide unimpeachable evidence that within a short time, Henry Tudor's second victory, unlike his first, had a generally accepted name. The initial reports of the battle simply referred to its taking place near Newark. An inquisition held at Rugeley in Staffordshire late in August, however, related to a horse stolen in the battle called 'Stokefield', while in the autumn the mercers of London recorded the appointment of thirty men of their company to wait on the king 'coming from Stoke field'.[14]

Some of the most illuminating records are the more informal and personalised letters written at the time, whether by the king, prominent noblemen, officials or country gentlemen. A few valuable items, touching on the drama of 1487, have survived, including correspondence of the king and the pretender, and the earls of Oxford and Northumberland.[15] When the government records and extant letters are set in sequence, a narrative framework can be established, and some casual relationships can perhaps be inferred. In the case of the conspiracy and rebellion of 1487, this task is made a little easier by the happy chance that the main collection of surviving correspondence also includes a sort of commentary on it. In the house book of the city of York, some conscientious clerk, not only minuted the major decisions of the mayor and aldermen, but also made copies, in sequence, of important letters received and sent. From his arrangement, it becomes clear, for example, that it was the city of York, rather than the government, that took the initiative in preparing itself to resist the rebels. Even more interestingly, the clerk decided to connect up some of the entries with explanatory detail, and in this fashion provided the earliest extant narrative of the rising in the north and what he termed 'the process of the battle beside Newark'.[16]

In the case of another important source, the report of a herald attending the court in the late 1480s, the distinction between a record and a chronicle is also hard to draw. From the reign of Edward IV, if not earlier, it became the practice for heralds to keep journals of events at court and on campaign, presumably to serve as books of precedents as well as records of achievement in the complex and contentious world of ceremony and chivalry. Though wholly devoid of any pretension to literary style, some reports inevitably assumed a crude narrative form. This is the case with the report, or 'brief memory', surviving in the British Library, Cotton MS. Julius B.XII. It covers the king's activities from the early 1486, with short interruptions when the author was rostered on leave, until the beginning of 1490, when the whole account was perhaps written up from notes. The form in which it is most often consulted is based on John Leland's copy, which with the exception of one crucial alteration is remarkably faithful. The report certainly provides an important source of court life in the first years of Henry VII's reign, and provides an eye-witness account of the weeks leading up to the battle of Stoke. Although it was produced by someone well-versed in court affairs, the report was written 'by licence' and is disappointingly bland on matters of state. Rather more surprisingly, it is better on the details of the muster and campaign than on the actual combat.[17]

The events of 1487 are otherwise rather poorly recorded by contemporary or near-contemporary narrative sources. The annals compiled at London and elsewhere do not offer much information beyond the basic details about the battle. It is most unfortunate that neither the second continuator of the *Crowland Chronicle* nor John Rous of Warwick extended their accounts to cover the affair, because both in their own ways could have offered fascinating insights.[18] Even by the end of Henry VII's reign precious little had been written on the affair. The *Great Chronicle of London* merely provided a slightly more elaborate account of the battle, adding only a few details to the earlier annals. Bernard André, the poet laureate and court historiographer, wrote a poem to commemorate the victory and, of course, later treated the episode in his biography of the king.[19] Yet his verse sheds little or no historical light, and his later prose account of the conspiracy and battle is somewhat confused and lacking in conviction. More impressive is the report of his Burgundian counterpart, Jean Molinet. While he is obscure on some points and mistaken on others, he clearly had access to a fair amount of information, apparently from a number of independent sources, including perhaps German mercenaries who had fought in the rebel army.[20]

The standard account of the rising of 1487 comes from the pen of Polydore Vergil.[21] He was the first to attempt a connected and coherent version of the whole affair, and his narrative of the conspiracy, the rebellion and the battle of Stoke became, almost immediately, the dominant tradition. It seems to have been known, for example, to the author of the *Book of Howth*, which otherwise might be viewed as independent testimony on some points. It is incorporated with little more than the occasional gloss, into the English histories of Edward Hall and Raphael Holinshead, the life of Henry VII produced by Francis Bacon, and indeed most modern historical writings.[22] The major problem, therefore, is the reliability of Polydore Vergil's account, and therefore the quality of his sources. It is known that this distinguished humanist scholar only arrived in England around 1502, and thus it seems likely that he did not embark on a narration of the events of 1487 until some twenty years after the affair. Even more worrying is that there is no evidence that he had access to any written sources, whether government records or earlier narratives. The long list of knights and squires who joined the royal host, incorporated in the printed version of his *Anglica Historia*, was in all probability an editorial contribution.[23] More than for most episodes in his history, Vergil seems to have relied on what he learned from talking to people at court, most especially, it would seem, Christopher Urswick. Given the informal nature of his sources, however, it is rather a pity that his smooth and stylish narrative has left few rough edges of circumstantial detail.

Independent traditions regarding the events of 1487 faded in the course of the sixteenth century as Polydore Vergil's attractive, lucid and informed account gained lustre and the appearance of authority through its being repeated and re-worked by other writers. It is certainly the case that information about the affair was preserved in oral tradition for some time. A ballad on the battle of Stoke was in circulation in the early years of Henry VIII's reign.[24] If it took the form of the ballad of Bosworth Field it might have supplied the list of knights and squires fighting for the king that was incorporated into the *Anglica Historia*. The colourful Martin Schwartz and his German mercenaries survived in folk memory, though perhaps only as rather ludicrous 'bogey-men'.[25] Snippets of information were preserved, presumably by families and friends, about quite a number of the other actors in this drama, including the earl of Lincoln, viscount Lovell, Richard Harleston and, perhaps most notably, Nicholas, Lord Howth, who cast himself as the only Irish lord who was not taken in by the imposture.[26] Oral tradition was particularly strong in districts figuring prominently in the affair, most especially the loyalist town of Waterford. The villages around Stoke have their own traditions, some based on the unearthing of bones and artifacts.[27] All told, however, it is surprising

Italian sword of about 1460.

how little can be added to the story from sources later than the reign of Henry VIII.

* * *

The source materials available for Lambert Simnel and the battle of Stoke are limited and generally poor in quality. From this cursory review of the evidence, it is also clear that some of what seem to be the best sources often present the greatest problems of assessment and interpretation. Polydore Vergil's *Anglica Historia*, the fullest and most coherent account, requires particularly careful handling. Apart from its being written late, perhaps as much as a quarter of a century after the events described, it necessarily reflects, to some degree, the official view of events in 1487. Of course, it is possible, on some points of detail, to check his account against earlier records, but this sort of exercise is scarcely reassuring. While Vergil is quite clear, for example, that Simnel's priest–mentor was captured at Stoke in the summer of 1487, the archbishop of Canterbury's register records that he was in custody from the beginning of the year.[28] If Vergil cannot be relied on for important facts, it is difficult to know what reliance to place on his general picture of the conspiracy and its progress. On a number of aspects of the affair, unfortunately, he remains the sole guide. The records alone are rarely informative enough to provide the basis for an alternative view, and on crucial affairs of state might be deliberately misleading. The memoranda written by the royal herald and by the clerk at York are patchy and unenterprising, while the chronicle of Jean Molinet is uneven and a little muddled, but these early narratives must be regarded as more authentic witnesses to the mood of 1487 than Vergil, and in some significant respects allow a different reconstruction and interpretation of events.

A great deal about the conspiracy and rising of 1487 will necessarily remain obscure. From the evidence available, it is hard to escape the impression that there was much about the whole business that was mysterious at the time. All the writers were, to some degree, reliant on government information or misinformation, and popular rumour and gossip. Even if the historian can feel sure that the boy in

Dublin was an impostor, he cannot know who at the time, from Henry VII downwards, had any firm knowledge on the matter. Unless he were writing tongue-in-cheek, Jean Molinet assumed that the lad was the earl of Warwick, and there are grounds for supposing that many people in Ireland believed in their prince. To confuse matters further, the intrigue itself emerged from a miasma of scandal and mystery that dated back to Richard III's reign and beyond. The crux of the problem, needless to say, is that impersonation is necessarily corrosive of truth and certainty. To compound the confusion for historians, Lambert Simnel was followed by Perkin Warbeck and other impostors. Some early chroniclers, most notably Bernard André, anticipated later generations of English school-children, in conflating or otherwise confusing the two episodes.

In seeking an understanding of the events of 1487, it is vital to keep as close as possible to the evidence. For the most part, it will be a matter of crawling on the ground, groping in the gloom for safe footholds, and exploring every nook and cranny for possible leads. Nevertheless, in an enterprise of this sort, it will not be possible to make progress without occasionally climbing above the swirling mist to seek a wider vista. It is the broad perspective that makes sense of the detail, suggests patterns and informs the imagination. In a study of Lambert Simnel and the battle of Stoke, it seems sensible to start by briefly surveying relevant features of the fifteenth-century landscape. In this fashion it is planned to set the scene genealogically and politically, to trace the ramifications and rivalries of the dominant families in Lancastrian and Yorkist England, and to see how dynastic uncertainty and civil strife created a political culture in which imposture briefly but banefully flourished.

2 Blood and Roses

It is no longer fashionable to discern in fifteenth-century English life the 'mixed smell of blood and roses'. In seeking to evoke the early summer of 1487, however, it is hard to dismiss Johan Huizinga's haunting image from the mind.[1] In the literal sense, it was most certainly a time of blood and roses, at a time when on the banks of the river Trent flowers bloomed amid the carnage. In more figurative senses, as well, images of 'blood' and 'roses' loomed large in the consciousness of English people in the mid-1480s. A central concern was with the fate of the house of Plantagenet, which had ruled England for over three centuries, with the extinction or survival of its blood-line, and with the contending claims of princes and pretenders to represent and embody it. The two main branches of the ruling dynasty, which over the previous three decades had disputed the crown, had lately become more and more identified with roses: the red rose of Lancaster and Beaufort and the white rose of York. More recently, the fledgling regime of Henry VII had actively promoted this symbolism, and elaborated on it for propagandist purposes. The marriage of Henry Tudor and Elizabeth of York, a union of the blood-lines of the rival dynasties, was appropriately depicted as two roses entwined. The new royal house of Tudor would adopt as its best known emblem the double rose.[2]

Huizinga did not write for the literal-minded or even the emblematically-minded, nor for that matter with England in mind. What he sought to express in the image were the contrasts and paradoxes of European life and culture in later middle ages. For this noted Dutch historian, the 'mixed smell of blood and roses' epitomised the contrasts in experience – between suffering and joy, adversity and prosperity, war and peace – which were then more keenly felt, and the oscillations in mood – between tenderness and cruelty, love and hate, piety and worldliness – which then seemed more violent and striking. Even if alongside the rich and ebullient tapestry of continental experience, the fabric of English life appears a little bland and colourless, this sort of duality is nonetheless strikingly apparent. English men and women of the late fifteenth century felt and acted with a directness and a passion that even some foreign observers found disconcerting. In the theatre of English public life, most especially, the contrasts and upheavals were notoriously overdrawn and precipitate.

In perceptions of their age, there was among people in England at this time, and remains among historians studying this era, a deep-seated ambivalence. In celebrations of the Tudor triumph, apologists for the new order painted up the contrasts between the horrors of civil war that lay in the past, and the blessings of peace brought in by Henry VII. It was an old refrain, repeating a great deal of the rhetoric used by the Yorkists against the Lancastrians. A mixture of propaganda and pious hope, it belied the present, which in the first years of the Tudor era looked fraught with danger, but also misrepresented the past. The civil strife of the last thirty years had indeed been disruptive. Political dissension had fed on dynastic instability to produce a series of crises, resolved only through battle, execution and murder. Yet images of wholesale carnage and destruction need to be set in a larger frame. Contemporary lamentations about the state of England need to be seen in relation to expectations, and the truth was that the English, well accustomed to fighting in foreign lands, were unused to war, however limited, in their own land. Certainly it is misleading to depict the country as embattled and ravaged by war. In most parts of the realm it was hard even to come across evidence of recent fortification, save of the ornamental sort. In the late fifteenth century there were widespread signs of depopulation, decay of tillage and urban decline, but all of these developments must be attributed to the plague and structural economic changes over a longer time-span. Foreign visitors to England are better guides to the condition of the country, and judging from their reports the dominant impression was of a pleasant, prosperous and peaceful land.[3]

Within an easy day's ride of London there were certainly places which seemed wholly unruffled by the commotions of the time. The copse-lined Chilterns, through which all the traffic between the metropolis and the midlands passed, were studded with sleepy hamlets and bucolic villages. Even the towns of the district had a serene beauty which belied their importance as markets and communication-centres. Where land had been set aside as park or game-reserve, the countryside could be positively arcadian. In a place like Berkhamstead it would be easy to forget the troubles of the time. Though a royal lordship, its castle had no military importance. For a quarter of a century it had been the home of a remarkable lady who had become more withdrawn and devout with the years. For her the days passed in a carefully regulated round of prayers, devotional reading and works of charity. Though a widow since 1460, and increasingly reclusive, she would never succeed quite in losing her public identity. Around the realm there were still old men who could recall her in the prime of her womanhood as the 'rose of Raby'. More generally, she was known as Cecily, dowager duchess of York, the mother of kings, the grandmother of princes and pretenders.[4]

The serenity of her ambience seems a far cry from the hurling world in which Henry Tudor was forced to defend his crown against invasion and insurrection. After the tragedies of her own life, the perturbations of 1487 were doubtless of little moment to her. Nonetheless, in important respects, the lady at Berkhamstead is a natural focus of attention. With her quiet and circumscribed routine, she can be presented as the still centre of a great storm, which after lashing the realm for a generation and violently overthrowing kings and noble houses, seemed now to be approaching its final crisis. No one alive at this time had been so closely involved in the internecine strife of the previous thirty years, and the grand old lady thus provides the most convenient reference-point from which to consider its complex course. At the same time her status as the matriarch of the house of York makes her life-story the simplest way to introduce many of the people involved directly or indirectly in the crisis of 1487, to trace the intricate interlacing of family and politics at this time, and to gain some impression of the problems that arose when the destinies of nations were tied to blood-lines.

*   *   *

Strictly speaking, the house of Neville was not of the old aristocracy. Though it could trace its descent back to the Norman Conquest, and it had a respectable lineage through into the early fourteenth century; it was only at the end of the fourteenth century that Ralph Neville, lord of Raby, emerged as a major force in northern society, was appointed warden of the west march and given the title of earl of Westmorland. His advancement was remarkably rapid, and indicates a man of considerable acumen. Growing up in the last years of Edward III's reign, and first winning his spurs in France at around the age of sixteen, he subsequently applied his martial skills exclusively to border warfare. The royal favour he enjoyed under Richard II owed not a little to the king's concern to establish a counterweight in the north to the house of Percy. Yet the quality of the man and the solidity of his achievement are clear from his ability to continue the process of dynastic aggrandisement in more difficult times. He made all the right moves in 1399, when Richard II was overthrown by Henry of Bolingbroke, and success-fully rode out the storms of 1403–5, when the Percys tried to overthrow the Lancastrian dynasty that they had helped establish. Thenceforward, his credit at the Lancastrian court guaranteed by his marriage to Henry IV's half-sister, Joan Beaufort, his position in the north was uncontested. During the reign of Henry V he was at the height of his reputation. At the time of his death in 1425, he was one of the council of regency for the infant Henry VI, an honoured elder statesman of the Lancastrian regime.[5]

He was a prodigiously successful dynast in a more obvious sense. By his first wife he sired nine children, including a son and namesake who succeeded him as earl of Westmorland. His second wife, Joan Beaufort, the daughter of John of Gaunt, bore him another fourteen children, all with royal blood flowing in their veins. It was this branch of the house of Neville whose aggrandisement was to be one of the most remarkable and disruptive political developments of the fifteenth century. The eldest of the sons was Richard, who through marriage to the heiress of the Montagu's, became the earl of Salisbury. His son in turn was to marry the heiress of the Beauchamps, earls of Warwick, and was to be known in later ages as Warwick the Kingmaker. The old earl of Westmorland was no less active in arranging advantageous matches for his daughters as well as his sons. Among his sons-in-law were to be Humphrey Stafford, duke of Buckingham and Henry Percy, earl of Northumberland. The life of his youngest and, by all accounts, fairest daughter, Cecily, was to be transformed by the most glorious alliance of all. Shortly before her father's death, and though still a child, she married Richard of York, a prince of the blood royal.

Despite the youth and innocence of both bride and groom, it was a heady match from the outset. While she was kin to the house of Lancaster, his lineage had wholly different implications. In important respects the events of 1399 still loomed large in the political consciousness of the nation. The relevance of the deposition of Richard II to the dynastic instability of the fifteenth century is well enough known. The seizure of power by Henry of Bolingbroke, however politically necessary, involved the setting aside, and probably the murder of an anointed ruler. To add to the violence done to the moral order, his accession could be seen to override the arguably superior claim of the Mortimers to the throne. While Henry IV was the son of John of Gaunt, fourth son of Edward III, the Mortimers were heirs of Lionel, duke of Clarence, third son of the old king. Henry of Bolingbroke indirectly acknowledged the point in basing his title on his right of conquest, his 'election' by the lords and commons, and the royal descent of both his father and mother. Most interestingly, a great deal of weight was placed on the bizarre tale that Edmund 'Crouchback', earl of Lancaster, whose heir he was through his mother, had actually been the eldest son of Henry III, displaced by Edward I on account of his bodily infirmity. Far from tampering with the proper order of succession, Henry IV was claiming to restore it.[6]

The significance of this preposterous claim is that it was felt necessary at all. Obviously people at the time were highly sensitive to matters of proper heredity. The deposition of Edward II in 1327 had been easier to handle, because the lawful succession could be preferred. Even then the old king had to be put to death, or at least his death had to be announced and a burial organised. In so far as the fate of Edward II was well-known in the reign of Richard II, it must also have been remembered that according to some reports Edward had not been killed, but had escaped to the continent, ending his days in a monastery in northern Italy.[7] It was to be expected that Richard II, too, would have his after-life. The conspiracy hatched on his behalf by his half-brothers early in 1400 seems to have sealed his fate, but the lack of any proper information on the circumstances of his death inevitably fuelled speculation and loyalist mischief-making. Rumours were soon circulating that Richard II had escaped to Scotland. The major rebellion launched against Henry IV in 1403 drew strength from the rumour that Richard would reappear to claim the crown. The Cheshire gentry who rose in arms at this time were certainly promised that their king would be there to lead them. The Ricardians took to impersonation to support their enterprise. An impostor was maintained at the Scottish court for some time, certainly until after the death of Henry IV. Though in important respects he took pains to lay the ghost of Richard II, Henry V was still troubled by dynastic intrigue. Shortly before his departure for France in 1415, he had to deal with an aristocratic plot which involved negoti-ations to bring the pseudo-Richard to England.[8] Its chief protagonist was the king's cousin, Richard, earl of Cambridge, the younger son of Edmund, duke of York, the fifth son of Edward III. At the same time, Cambridge was seeking to promote the title of his childless brother-in-law, Edmund Mortimer, though no doubt his thoughts were more on the prospects of his son, Richard, heir to the Mortimers and their claim on the throne.

By birth and indeed by baptism, Richard of York was thus the unwitting heir to the Ricardian tradition. His father had been godson of Richard II, and the treason for which he was executed in 1415, however self-interested, probably drew on this connection. Inevitably his youth was spent under the shadow of his father's attainder. His first guardian was Sir Robert Waterton, the former gaoler of Richard II, a man obviously chosen for his commitments to the house of Lancaster rather than for the comforts he provided to princely guests. Yet there seems to have been no intention of denying the boy his due: he was recognised as heir to his father's brother, Edward, duke of York, who was slain at Agincourt in 1415, and to his mother's brother, Edmund Mortimer, who died in 1425. By this stage, too, he was more honourably placed as the ward of the earl and countess of Westmorland. In all likelihood he spent his adolescence at the great northern castle of Raby, and married there the youngest daughter of the house, Cecily, the 'rose of Raby'. Still in his teens, Richard was demonstrably a man with prospects. As well as the duchy of York, the Mortimer earldoms of March and Ulster now descended to him. In 1426 he was knighted in the company of the young Henry VI, and in 1432, in his twenty-first year, he was given livery of his far-flung estates.[9]

In the 1430s Richard, duke of York embarked on the distinguished career in public life for which his royal blood and landed wealth so amply qualified him. In 1430 he led a small retinue to France, where the king's uncle, John, duke of Bedford, was battling to secure the conquests made by Henry V. In 1431 he attended the show-piece coronation of Henry VI in Paris. After Bedford's death in 1435, York was chosen, despite his youth and inexperience, as the king's lieutenant-general in France, serving in this capacity from 1436–7 and from 1440–6. During the early 1440s, however, relations with the king, now himself growing to manhood, soured. York had reason to be slighted by the honours heaped upon the king's Beaufort cousins: in 1443 John, earl of Somerset was given a commission in Gascony which detracted from York's own command, while in 1446 Edmund, later second duke of Somerset and York's great rival, was appointed to succeed him as lieutenant-general. A crucial, though largely unspoken fact was, of course, that after the death of Humphrey, duke of Gloucester in 1447, York was heir presumptive of Henry VI, whose own marriage was childless until 1453. Seen in this light, the promotion of the Beauforts and other noblemen with Lancastrian blood seemed an attempt to redefine the royal family in such a way as to diminish York's own standing and prospects. When in 1449 he resolved to take up personally his appointment as lieutenant of Ireland, he had reason to feel very bitter towards the king and the courtiers who ruled in his name.[10]

By this stage the Lancastrian regime had alienated wider sections of the political nation. Rather remarkably, the king himself was not immune from adverse comment, but his ministers naturally bore the brunt of popular criticism engendered by the collapse of the war-effort in France and corruption and lawlessness at home. The main target was William de la Pole, duke of Suffolk, leader of the court party and close ally of the Beauforts. In the parliament of 1449 steps were taken to impeach him, and early in 1450 he was sent into exile, only to be murdered on board ship. Over the summer tensions mounted as the popular unrest continued and as the ruling faction threatened to take revenge on its opponents. The men of Kent rose in rebellion, calling for the reform of government and demanding that the king should take into his council York and other magnates from outside the court clique. To focus further attention on York, the rebel leader Jack Cade, who was thought to have come from Ireland, took as a pseudonym the name of Mortimer. From 1450 the dynastic issue, at least the issue of the succession to Henry VI, was firmly on the agenda. Richard of York returned from Ireland to press his claims as the senior prince of the blood, and with the mental collapse of Henry VI in 1453–4 he acquired, first, a position of leadership on the council and, then, the protectorate of the realm. When the king suddenly recovered, and York's rivals returned to power, York and his Neville allies took to arms. Henry VI was captured at the bloody battle of St Albans, and York formed a second protectorate.[11]

Throughout this time Cecily, duchess of York was a constant companion of her husband. If their child-marriage at first meant very little, and indeed it was without issue for fifteen years, from the late 1430s the couple were, by the standards of the time, inseparable. Their first boy was born in 1441, and named Henry for the king. Thenceforward the birth-places of her numerous children reflect the duties of the father and the dutifulness of the mother: Edward and Edmund were born at Rouen in 1442 and 1443; George was born at Dublin in 1449; most of the youngest, including Richard, at Fotheringhay. How far the duchess's own connections fed into the politics of the time is hard to say. Her mother, of course, was a Beaufort, which perhaps helped York in his early dealings with this branch of the house of Lancaster. More significantly, as a Neville, she probably assisted in the development of the crucial alliance between

North German sallet of about 1480.

York and her brother, Richard Neville, earl of Salisbury, and his son, the earl of Warwick. Nevertheless, given the inter-relatedness of the English nobility at this time, it is unreasonable to attach too much significance to such ties. At the battle of St Albans, even with her husband, brother and nephew as comrades-in-arms, the duchess of York would have had some mixed feelings, as among their opponents, indeed among the slain, were a nephew and cousins.

For a time after 1455 England enjoyed an uneasy peace, but in reality divisions were hardening. A determined court party was reassembling, composed of many young lords whose fathers and brothers had been butchered at St Albans. It was led by Margaret of Anjou, Henry VI's queen, who would henceforward fight tooth and nail for the succession of her son, Edward, born in 1453. Despite attempts at pacification, the rival groups of noblemen took to arms in 1459, and after failing to hold his forces together at Ludlow the duke of York was forced to flee the realm, leaving his wife with the younger children to the mercy of his enemies. At this stage, if not earlier, she showed her mettle, bravely confronting the Lancastrian forces in the market-square. She was then forced to witness the attainder of her husband and brother at Coventry, and suffered the indignity of being committed to the custody of her sister, the duchess of Buckingham. Nevertheless the tables were soon turned. A group of Yorkist lords recaptured Henry at the battle of Northampton, and when York returned in triumph from Ireland she rushed in a carriage covered with blue velvet to meet him at Hereford.[12]

In 1460 Richard of York clearly aimed for the crown. From his landing at Chester to his arrival at London, he made more and more explicit his claims, assuming the Mortimer quarterings in his standard and acting like a king. What is significant, however, is that at this stage his Neville allies were unwilling to support his higher ambitions. There was no deposition of Henry VI, and no acclamation of Richard. For the moment all that was agreed upon was that York should have the succession in preference to the prince of Wales, who was believed in some quarters not to be Henry's son. The battle of Wakefield later in the year, when the duke of York and the earl of Salisbury were slain, however, dramatically changed the situation. With their backs against the wall, the sons of the two senior Yorkists went for broke. Edward, earl of March, York's eldest surviving son, was raised to the throne by a small coterie of noblemen led by Richard Neville, earl of Warwick. Soon after his makeshift coronation, Edward IV convincingly vindicated his title on Palm Sunday 1461, when he annihilated the main Lancastrian army at Towton.

* * *

For the dowager duchess of York the moment of triumph was bittersweet. The civil strife had cost her dear: her husband, a son and a brother, as well as numerous nephews and cousins. Compounding her sense of personal loss was her thwarted ambition. There is no doubt that she felt cheated of a crown. She would always regard her husband as an uncrowned king, and herself as the wife and mother of kings. There was no immediate prospect, however, of a life of honour and ease. Still in her widow's weeds, she buckled down at the beginning of 1461 to the task of supporting her inexperienced son establish himself on the throne, and played a vital role in securing the support of London for the Yorkist regime. Doubtless she was best placed to anticipate the bitter rearguard action that Queen Margaret and others would fight on behalf, not of the befuddled Henry, but of Prince Edward. What she could not have imagined, unless she could look coolly and dispassionately into the hearts of her three sons, was the poisonous discord that would prove so lethal to the house of York.

It was certainly not long before Edward IV proved a disappointment to her. Even as he was beginning to prove himself a statesman and a soldier, the headstrong young king became besotted with Elizabeth Woodville, the young widow of Sir John Grey, a Lancastrian knight. There were many problems with the match, but the most important was that it squandered a major political asset, the king's marriageability, in return for a major political liability, a tribe of stepsons and brothers-in-law expecting advancement. The duchess of York angrily dressed down the king, apparently threatening to declare before a public tribunal that he was not her husband's son.[13] Edward's younger brothers, George, duke of Clarence and Richard, duke of Gloucester, were also probably encouraged to show their disapproval. More politically significant, of course, the marriage played a crucial role in the breakdown of relations between the king and the Nevilles. Warwick now sought an understanding with the king's brother, and in the teeth of royal opposition Clarence married Warwick's daughter in 1469. A rebel army led by the pseudonymous 'Robin of Redesdale' and made up largely of Warwick's northern connection, achieved spectacular results, and defeated forces assembled in the king's name at Edgecote near Banbury. For a time Edward was a prisoner of the Neville faction, but in 1470 managed to regain, at least temporarily, control of government. Escaping to France, however, Warwick and Clarence came to terms with Queen Margaret, and by the end of the year their unholy alliance had in turn forced Edward into exile. It is hard to see what advantage Clarence saw in the 'readeption' of Henry VI, or the crucial marriage alliance between Edward, the Lancastrian prince of Wales and Warwick's second daughter. The agreement that in default of the house of Lancaster the succession would be vested in Clarence and his heirs left him no better placed than with his brother on the throne.[14]

The new Lancastrian regime was surprisingly well-supported, but it was made up of a body of men whose conflicting interests made common action difficult. Showing the sort of boldness and energy which had won him the throne ten years earlier, Edward IV returned and out-manoeuvred his opponents politically and militarily. If the duchess of York had previously encouraged the alliance between Clarence and the Nevilles, she now played a crucial role, along with her daughter, Margaret, duchess of Burgundy, in healing the rift between her sons. By the end of 1471 Edward IV had defeated and slain Warwick at Barnet, and routed the Lancastrians at Tewkesbury. Shortly afterwards it was announced that Henry VI had died in the Tower of London, and since Prince Edward and the duke of Somerset had been killed in battle, it seemed that the Lancastrian cause was doomed. Of the issue of John of Gaunt, only young Henry Tudor, the son of Margaret Beaufort, remained a nominal threat, and of the great magnates, only the earl of Oxford refused to deal with the Yorkist regime.

The solidarity of the house of York at the end of 1471 was not to last. Edward IV had learned somewhat from his earlier mistakes; but his indulgence towards his wife's relations, most notably her brother Anthony Woodville, earl Rivers, and her son, Thomas Grey, marquis of Dorset, was widely resented, not least by the king's brothers. George, duke of Clarence, who had deserted Warwick in the nick of time, continued to brood and scheme. A satisfactory consolation prize could have been the lion's share of the Kingmaker's estates, but the Neville patrimony was set aside for his brother, Richard, duke of Gloucester, who sought to secure and extend his claims through his marriage to Warwick's other daughter, the widow of the Lancastrian prince of Wales. In truth Richard was one of the few men to come out of the upheavals of 1470–1 with any sort of credit, and in the following years emerged as the leader of the Neville affinity and the king's trusted lieutenant in the north. Clarence had no such territorial sphere of influence: even his lieutenancy of Ireland proved an empty honour, when the king forbade him from exercising the office in person. Future prospects looked even bleaker. Edward IV now had sons to succeed him, which not only limited his prospects of inheriting the crown, but also seemed to assure him of the unending enmity of the Woodvilles.[15]

Given this political climate, the birth of a son in 1474 could not help but remind Clarence of his own failure. The king raised the boy from the font, and gave him the name Edward, but the brothers probably only made a show of affability. The re-interment of Richard, duke of York, at Fotheringhay in 1476 was the last public show of family solidarity. The death of the duchess of Clarence in child-birth at the end of the year revealed the true state of affairs. Still in his twenties, Clarence was offered two attractive matches, one to the heiress of the duke of Burgundy and one to the sister of the king of Scotland, but the king prohibited both of them. In 1477 he was committed to the Tower of London. The charges of treason made against Clarence early in the following year appear somewhat contrived. The king and Gloucester seem to have later acknowledged that the proceedings against him were not wholly just. Doubtless the malice of the Woodvilles was crucial in securing his destruction. The actual responsibility for his execution, whether or not in a butt of malmsey, is impossible to establish.[16]

In all likelihood, though, the charges against Clarence bear some relation to the drift of his thinking, if not in 1477 then in his earlier intrigues. One important allegation was that he had publicly declared that Edward IV was a bastard, 'and not begotten to reign upon us'. It is not hard to see what might incline Clarence to take up the tale that Edward was the son not of Richard of York but of a common soldier at Rouen, and in fact he and Warwick probably helped to give the story currency in 1469. It also seems probable, though for understandable reasons it is not on record, that Clarence was taking an unhealthy interest in the status of the king's marriage. It is certainly hard to credit that Clarence should have been so exclusively concerned with the issue of his brother's legitimacy as not to probe at all the possible irregularities of his marriage. Five years later, of course, his younger brother set great store on the 'fact' that Edward was betrothed to another woman in 1464 and that his 'marriage' to Elizabeth Woodville was therefore uncanonical. The man allegedly responsible for breaking the story then was Robert Stillington, bishop of Bath and Wells, which must increase the likelihood that it had some currency in Clarence's circle, with its close connections with the chapter-house at Wells. Another charge against Clarence, which in the light of subsequent events have an odd resonance, is that he was plotting to send his infant son, Edward, later earl of Warwick, overseas for safety. Given his own fears of arrest and execution, such a plan seems perfectly probable. What is particularly striking is that he had in mind sending him either to Flanders or to Ireland, and that he was arranging to find another infant of like age to take his place.[17]

It would be interesting to know what the duchess of York made of this whole affair. It is possible that she had long had to endure speculation regarding the paternity of Edward IV. Her own good looks and vivaciousness, and perhaps some indiscreet behaviour, could have encouraged this sort of gossip about the 'rose of Raby'. By all accounts Edward did not resemble the duke of York in appearance, and his conception and birth in Rouen provided further scope for malicious innuendo. If in her row with Edward over his marriage, she angrily threatened to deny that he was York's son, she could herself have fuelled this sort of allegation. Still, it must have been most distressing to her for the slanders to be publicised in this fashion by her own flesh and blood. Apparently she bore it stoically. At the time of Clarence's trial, she joined with other family members to celebrate the marriage of the king's four-year-old son, a second Richard, duke of York. Two years later she stood godmother to the king's youngest daughter, naming her Bridget in honour of a favourite saint.[18] Despite the presence of so many of the queen's kinsfolk at the christening, she could perhaps still take some delight in playing the matriarch. She was now surrounded by a large brood of grandsons; Edward, prince of Wales, Richard, duke of York; Clarence's son, Edward, earl of Warwick; Gloucester's son, Edward, earl of Salisbury. Possibly she took most pleasure in the rather older sons of her daughter, the duchess of Suffolk: there was John de la Pole, earl of Lincoln, now on the verge of manhood, and Edward de la Pole, a pious young scholar recently enrolled at Oxford.

For ever longer periods, though, the ageing duchess of York retired from public life. The court of Edward IV in his last years was no place for the increasingly pious and fastidious duchess of York. In 1480 she enrolled herself as a sister of the Benedictine order, and though for a while she continued to make occasional excursions from Berkhamstead she thenceforward committed herself to a life of regular religious observances. In the spring of 1483 the king was dead, leaving his sons and daughters in the careless hands of his wife and her kinsmen, and leaving the government of the realm dangerously prey to factional struggle. In the following months Baynard's castle, her London home, was the headquarters of Richard, duke of Gloucester, protector of the realm and her sole surviving son. It is possible that she encouraged him in his ambitions, even though it meant reviving the old slanders. Fortunately, in his contest with the dowager queen and her party, Gloucester had less reason than Clarence to focus on Edward's legitimacy. The story of his brother's pre-contract offered him a sharper instrument with which to challenge the title of Edward V and his siblings. Like many other people at the time, the duchess of York might well have seen Richard's *coup d'état* as the least unfortunate of a number of possible outcomes to the troubles of the time. Perhaps she relished the vicarious realisation of the dream so cruelly thwarted in 1460: a third king Richard and a Neville queen.[19]

*   *   *

There is no evidence that the duchess of York ever came to the view that Richard III was a tyrant and a monster. Even after the rumours had spread abroad that Edward IV's sons had been murdered in the Tower of London, her relations with Richard seem to have remained cordial. She visited him at Cambridge in March 1484, and a letter written by him to her in June does not suggest any coldness between them. Her increasing withdrawal from public life in these years was doubtless dictated by age and piety, but also perhaps reflected a growing distaste for news from the world. The news of the death of Edward of Middleham, Richard's only son, was a tragedy in which she perforce shared. After a life-time of such scandal, she would have resolutely refused to entertain rumours that Richard had poisoned his wife in order to marry his niece. In all too short a time, however, all the branches and off-shoots of her family seemed to be either perilously exposed or withering and dying. A small group of survivors, including Edward's daughters and Clarence's son, were kept in close confinement at Sheriff Hutton castle, likened by P.M. Kendall to 'a stone chalice' holding the remaining blood of the house of York.[20] She can scarcely have given credence to the report that the Lancastrian pretender, Henry Tudor, was planning an invasion of England. The tidings from Bosworth, the defeat and death of her last son, Richard, defied belief.

The proud old lady was to live another ten years after 1485 in her quiet retreat at Berkhamstead. Her daily routine in this decade can be reconstructed in some detail, because some time shortly after the accession of Henry VII she caused to be drawn up a schedule of devotions and pious observances. The harmony and tranquillity of her closing years, of course, seem to stand in sharp contrast to the fury and bombast of her life as the duchess of York and the mother of kings, though, just as with other discordant images in fifteenth century England, it is important to see them as part of a single, albeit richly textured picture. She rose at daybreak to recite matins with her chaplain, and then to have a low mass celebrated in her chamber. After breakfast she attended services with her household in the chapel, and began a round of devotions and pious works which lasted until evensong, which included listening to saints' lives and other edifying works over dinner, receiving suitors and dispensing charity in the early afternoon, and private reading from mystical and contemplative works after her light supper. Sometimes Cecily, 'late wife unto Richard, rightful king of England', would perhaps just gaze at the tapestries hanging on the wall, depicting the Passion, the lives of St John the Baptist, St George and St Mary Magdalene, and, less ruefully and more resignedly with the passing of years, the Wheel of Fortune.[21]

3 The Tudor Interlude

The news from Bosworth was wondrous and awesome. An anointed king of England, leading most of the peerage and the nation in arms, had been defeated by a largely unknown and untried adventurer, whose mongrel army was predominantly Welsh and French. As at least one historically minded commentator observed, England had not seen such a remarkable event since 1066. As the news swept across the countryside, it was received with mixed feelings in most quarters. Of course, there were people and indeed communities whose fortunes were so decisively effected by the result of the battle that their reactions were wholly joyful or dolorous. At Westminster and elsewhere the political enemies of the Ricardian regime issued forth to celebrate the Tudor triumph, while at York the city-fathers received the news of their royal patron's death with great heaviness of heart and felt that they could not guarantee the safety of the king's messenger in the streets.[1] For the majority of the population there was sufficient ill-will towards Richard III to give cause to rejoice in his fall, but insufficient commitment to Henry Tudor to applaud unreservedly the turn of events. To the more thoughtful, it was a dangerous upset, confirming the giddiness of the age. The Wheel of Fortune was not simply rotating; it was lurching with an unwonted violence and caprice.

People had cause to fear what was hard to understand. The incomprehensibility of the upset at Bosworth invited anxious speculation. A common view was that God had made his judgement on Richard III, a ruler whom many, perhaps including himself, had felt marked down for divine retribution. Naturally, partisans of Henry Tudor sought to encourage this sort of thinking and, more importantly, to establish its corollary that God had positively endorsed the title of the new monarch. In the long term, especially when developed as part of a broader Tudor view of English history, this providential version of events was to prove seductive and comforting to many people. In the immediate aftermath of the battle and in the early years of Henry VII's reign, however, it carried less conviction. It was hard indeed to see justice and honour, let alone the workings of providence, in the shady manouevres that gave Henry the battle, and the unscrupulous political horse-trading which helped establish his regime. In a realm awash with tales of double-dealing, cynical opportunism and treachery, it was hard not to be cynical. The debut of Henry Tudor on the national stage looked less like the happy resolution of the main drama, the inauguration of a

Elizabeth of York, (died 1503).

new era of peace and prosperity, than a hastily contrived interlude, marking time for a further escalation of tension and uncertainty.

*   *   *

The progress of Henry Tudor from victor in the field to duly constituted monarch is customarily presented as a smooth and natural transition, punctuated only by episodes of celebration and pageantry. After refreshing himself and his following at Leicester, he moved in stately manner to London, where he was joyfully received by the city fathers and the populace in general. After establishing a new government, and securing the orderly transfer of power, he proceeded to the summoning of the estates of the realm and the staging of his coronation. His title to the throne having been ratified by parliament, he then gave his mind to the securing of the dynasty, and the reconciliation of the nation, and set in train the necessary formalities and dispensation for his marriage to Elizabeth of York. However, even if there were no other evidence of major hurdles confronting the fledgling Tudor regime, the length of time involved in the transition indicates a rather rougher ride than is commonly allowed. A fortnight separated his victory at Bosworth and his entry into his capital, and another three weeks passed before the machinery of government began to crank into action. Another month passed before his coronation, and the parliamentary ratification of his title. It was early December when, prior to their dispersal and themselves perhaps anxious regarding the delay, the commons petitioned the king to carry out his promise to marry Elizabeth of York. A fortnight into the new year, a little short of six months of his first landing in England, the long awaited union of the houses of Lancaster and York finally took place.

In the first three months there were clearly many obstacles in the path of settlement.[2] Much time was needed to probe and ponder, interrogate and interview, punish, conciliate or reward, overcome obstacles, make deals, explore possibilities, and plan for the future. Even in the midst of his celebrations, King Henry knew all too well that he had won his victory very largely by default, and that his defeat of Richard III and his battlefield coronation were really only the first stages in the winning of the kingdom. The leader, or perhaps even only the figurehead of a narrow faction, he had first to forge a settlement with the rest of the political establishment. The host assembled by King Richard was far more broadly representative of the political nation than has sometimes been supposed, but since a good number of lords and gentry fought either half-heartedly or not at all, there was a great deal of scope for reconciliation. It is instructive that most of the men marked down for attainder, notably Richard himself, the duke of Norfolk and Lord Ferrers of Chartley, were already dead. The earl of Northumberland, who betrayed the king but gave no assistance to his rival, was committed to prison for a time, apparently because his aim was to secure the succession of Clarence's son. Lord Stanley, on the other hand, who offered Henry Tudor little more than indirect assistance and moral support, was heavily rewarded, being created earl of Derby. Generally speaking, it seems that the new king and his counsellors were all too willing to pardon men who excused themselves on the grounds of obedience and fear, swore loyalty to the new regime, and entered into bonds for their good behaviour. Most lords and county notables, including prominent Ricardians like the earl of Lincoln, Lords Scrope of Bolton, Fitzhugh and Scrope of Masham, presumably came to terms with the new dispensation in this fashion, either in the immediate aftermath of the battle or in the week or so afterwards.

In this fashion progress was made in converting military success into political advantage. It is hard to know, however, how far Henry Tudor and his party were in a position to dictate terms. The slaughter of Richard III and his more committed retainers could not be more than the first step to eradicating Ricardian loyalism in the realm. A number of close friends of the late king, most notably Viscount Lovell, had escaped from the field, and could be expected to organise opposition to the regime. The north was an obvious focus of concern. It was where Richard III had been most popular, and there was a grave danger of intervention from Scotland. With no reliable agents in the region at this stage, Henry Tudor was forced to show forbearance to the northerners who promised to mend their ways. To underline further the need for caution, even disenchantment with the old king did not necessarily lead to loyalty to the new order. According to the *Crowland Chronicle*, rumours that Richard had poisoned Queen Anne in order to marry Elizabeth of York alienated many of his northern retainers, whose traditional loyalties were to the house of Neville. In the increasingly uncertain political climate of 1485, many supporters of the Ricardian regime must have given thought to the succession, and like Northumberland looked to Clarence's son, the earl of Warwick. Given the role of defection and betrayal in the defeat of Richard III, the battle of Bosworth provided only a doubtful mandate to his rival.

The claim of Henry Tudor to the English throne cannot have seemed impressive even to his well-wishers. The attachment to the royal family which most fostered his self-awareness as a prince, namely his kinship with Henry VI, in actuality gave him no claim to the throne at all. His father, Edmund Tudor, was indeed the half-brother of the saintly king, but only through the *mésalliance* of Henry V's widow with a Welsh courtier. More important was the descent of his mother, Margaret Beaufort, from John of Gaunt, duke of Lancaster. There were problems, however, in using this line to provide a title to the crown. The first Beauforts were illegitimate, and though subsequently legitimised by their father's marriage to Catherine Swynford, they were specifically debarred from the royal succession. The Lancastrian title, after all, was based initially on descent through John of Gaunt's first wife from Edmund 'Crouchback'. Even if the bar on their eligibility were lifted, there could only be a claim if descent through a female were allowed, in which case the house of York had stronger claims. In so far as there was increasing acceptance of the idea that the crown could descend through a female, of course, it added immensely to the significance of Henry's promise to marry Elizabeth of York. Between them, the two could claim to be the heirs-general of both Lancaster and York, and the next of kin of both Henry VI and Edward IV.

Lacking any single compelling title to the throne, Henry Tudor at least had a number of claims that cumulatively looked impressive. However inglorious in practice, the victory at Bosworth enabled him to establish himself militarily, not only over the Ricardian loyalists, but also over many lords who probably supported other candidates for the crown. Once he left Leicester for London, he could present himself as the conquering hero and God's champion against tyranny. His stately progress to the capital gave many people the opportunity to accustom themselves to the idea of their new prince. In the circumstances it was perhaps deemed politic to gloss over points of genealogical detail and rules of inheritance, and even perhaps to play down the rhetoric of Lancastrian legitimism. In southern England, indeed, his assumption of power looked more like a Yorkist restoration. Aside from the earl of Oxford, most of the English lords and knights in his company had been prominent supporters of Edward IV, who had fled into exile after the failure of the rebellion of 1483. Even more with the government officials, lawyers and churchmen, it was necessary to stress the legitimacy of the Yorkist monarchy prior to the usurpation of Richard III.

Obviously a crucial element in the re-establishment of stability was the projected marriage to Elizabeth of York. This match had been planned as far back as autumn 1483, when it was the condition on which the pretender won the support of the many lords and gentry, who, though supporters of the Yorkist monarchy, turned against Richard. Earlier in 1485 there had been a great deal of consternation among the exiles when the rumour spread abroad that Richard himself was seeking to marry his niece. After the triumph at Bosworth a first priority had been to secure the person of the princess. To this end, Sir Robert Willoughby was despatched to escort Elizabeth of York from Sheriff Hutton castle to London. Almost certainly, in the deliberations at Leicester and later in the capital, there were many counsellors who urged the necessity of an early wedding. Over the next few months Henry seems to have preferred a policy of procrastination. By early December the lords and commons in parliament were sufficiently anxious to petition the king to proceed without delay. The wedding was finally celebrated in the new year, on 18 January. Even then the queen's coronation did not take place until over two years after the king's own coronation.

It is not hard to find explanations for this reluctance to proceed immediately with the marriage. As the young couple had never met, it was fitting for them to get to know each other. Then, since both Henry and Elizabeth were descendants of John of Gaunt, and thus within the prohibited degrees of kinship, a dispensation for their marriage was required. While it seems that the wedding followed immediately on the king's being advised that an authorisation from Rome was forthcoming, the suspicion must be that this side of the proceedings provided welcome opportunities for delay. Although there were grave dangers in entirely repudiating the match, there were important advantages to be gained by the new king in deferring it for as long as he decently could. Through this expedient, he could win support from people whose primary loyalty was to the house of York, while making it clear that his title to the throne did not derive from his marriage to the daughter of Edward IV. To his mind, it was vital that he should be crowned alone, and to have parliament vest the crown solely in him and his heirs, by whatever wife. By the time that the lords and commons found the courage to petition him to proceed with the marriage, it was a plea to which he was probably happy to accede.

The concerns of Henry VII and his counsellors are, of course, hard to establish, when so many of the factors in the equation were highly sensitive and naturally went unrecorded. Whatever the fates of the princes in the Tower of London, it must be presumed that the new regime learned somewhat more on their arrival in London than historians know. On balance, it seems extremely improbable that they were found alive, and most unlikely that their bodies were discovered. For a number of reasons the government would have been disinclined to set up a public investigation. With firsthand experience of how low the reputation of England had sunk, the new king was reluctant to provide further titillation for European observers by probing too far into the details of a murder–disappearance, whose secrets could now be claimed to have died with the defeated tyrant.[3] If the corpses were discovered, an enquiry into the circumstances of their death could well have opened up new wounds in the body politic. On the other hand, an admission that the bodies could not be found could feed speculation that they were still alive. This latter possibility bore directly on the king's attitude to the marriage, since the survival of one of the princes would undermine any title people wished to attribute to Elizabeth of York. As if this were not enough, there were other allegations dating from the old reign, which would have proved even more sensitive politically and personally. Henry would have wanted to know the truth regarding the match that was mooted between Richard III and Elizabeth. At one stage the dowager queen and the marquis of Dorset had abetted the scheme, and one tradition suggests that the young princess herself was not as hostile to her uncle's advances as was later claimed. There were even the rumours, current in parts of the French-speaking world, that Richard had actually debauched the girl and borne a child on her.[4] Presumably Elizabeth was able to prove herself beyond reproach, but the insinuations and rumours must initially have cooled the ardour of the naturally circumspect Henry Tudor.

*   *   *

After his triumphal entry into London, the king spent a full six months in the neighbourhood of the capital, and though in this time a great deal had been achieved in terms of the establishment of the new order it seems that uncertainty, if not straight-out disaffection, prevailed in many parts of the country. It is instructive that one of Henry's first measures had been to send home with a general pardon almost all the men who had stood against him at Bosworth, to order the immediate cessation of hostilities and to stifle old and new animosities. With the restoration of order and stability as his first priority, he appointed as sheriffs quite a number of old Ricardian retainers. Over the course of the autumn his coronation and first parliament gave him further opportunities to establish working relations with many prominent knights and gentlemen from outlying counties. Yet the confidence of the nation was not to be easily won while the king remained in his palaces around Westminster and while so few magnates were able to give leadership to their regions. It was shortly before and during the king's first provincial tour that the earl of Northumberland was released to help win confidence for the regime in the north, and the earl of Surrey was pardoned to help allay anxieties in East Anglia. It was around this time as well that the duke of Bedford, the earl of Derby and other grandees were at least able to detach themselves from court to attend to affairs in their respective spheres of influence.

The condition of England in the aftermath of Bosworth is hard to assess. The testimony of Robert Throckmorton, appointed sheriff of Warwick and Leicester in the aftermath of the battle of Bosworth, is perhaps instructive. According to his petition to be pardoned arrears on his accounts, he claimed that, during his month or so in office, there was 'such rebellion and trouble' in the realm, and the king's authority so poorly established that he was unable to obtain any revenues.[5] It is also the case that, at least until the middle of October, there was widespread unrest in the north. There were overtones of popular revolt, as rabble-rousers adopted pseudonyms like 'Robin of Redesdale', 'Jack Straw' and 'Master Mend-all', and even the threat of support for a rebellion from Scotland.[6] While Henry VII was spared an early test of his authority, and conditions in most parts of lowland England eased during the autumn, the government faced more determined and protracted opposition in remote areas. Ricardian loyalists continued to defy the Tudor regime from bases in the Pennines. A major centre of resistance was Hornby castle in north Lancashire, which Sir James Harrington and his friends held not only against the king but also, perhaps more pertinently, against the Stanleys, who had long contested ownership with the Harringtons. Private quarrels also helped to entrench Ricardian loyalism in the West Country, where Sir Henry Bodrugan knew that there would be little mercy for him from former rivals who had returned with Henry Tudor.[7] If the extremities of the kingdom of England were not secure, the king's overseas possessions were dangerously exposed. The lordship of Ireland was more or less outside royal control. The earl of Kildare, who had prospered so mightily under the house of York, was not eager to co-operate with the new regime, especially since the earl of Ormond, his old rival, was honoured at the Tudor court. For some time the Dublin mint issued coins without the king's name. In the Channel Islands and the march of Calais, as well, there were many soldiers and administrators, whose careers had flourished under the Yorkists, and whose commitment to the new regime was correspondingly suspect. To add to these difficulties, rumours of Henry's death, presumably from the 'sweating sickness', spread to the English garrison towns in the late autumn, feeding speculation as to the succession.[8]

The great problem for the malcontents was how to forge a single movement out of such a heterogeneous and geographically dispersed group of people. The new king had certainly hobbled the opposition by securing the persons of the late king's nephews. The earl of Warwick, who despite his youth and a suspicion of simplemindedness, had the best claims to the crown, had been put into safe custody in the Tower of London. The earl of Lincoln, a more worthy candidate and possibly the late king's chosen heir, had made his submission soon after Bosworth, but probably was kept for some time under close surveillance. Indeed in the first reports of Henry's victory, Lincoln was actually listed among the slain, perhaps as a ruse to prevent his becoming a rallying-point. Reports of the death of Viscount Lovell, the only other Ricardian with real leadership

Garter stall plate of Francis, Lord Lovell.

possiblities, were likewise subject to misinformation. Though he remained obstinately in sanctuary, there was hope at court that his submission was only a matter of time. Since all the other peers were in custody or had otherwise come to terms with the king, there was no one of stature to canalise the widespread but ill-focused disquiet concerning the change of dynasty. Though not without a capacity for mischief in their own districts, diehards like Sir James Harrington and Sir Henry Bodrugan were as likely to alienate as to attract the middle ground.

Although his reliable friends appeared few and his potential enemies legion, Henry VII won valuable breathing space by holding together his own party, courting the uncommitted, and undermining his opponents by co-opting or incarcerating their leaders. Yet it was scarcely conceivable that Henry Tudor's remarkable seizure of the throne would go uncontested, and throughout the first six months of his reign a major rising was widely expected. According to a letter written from the capital to Sir Robert Plumpton on 13 December 1485, there was speculation in London of another upheaval, involving northerners, Welshmen or even members of the royal household. The correspondent also noted 'much running among the lords, but no man knows what it is; it is said it is not well amongst them'.[10] Whether the lords, knights and burgesses returned to their communities on the prorogation of parliament any more positive and optimistic than when they had first been elected in the aftermath of Bosworth, is thus open to question. Perhaps the keynote over Christmas was cautious hope, as people right across the realm waited anxiously to see what the new year would bring. To counteract the anxious speculation promoted by the circulation of 'prophecies', most of which seem to have run against the king, the king allegedly sought to make prophesying a felony, and probably to down on the import of horoscopes for the new year. In Ireland, it would seem, particularly dire prognostications were current regarding the seventh King Henry.[11]

* * *

Notwithstanding the prophecies, the new year started full of promise. Over the Christmas season the king had presided over a court better attended and more splendid than could have been anticipated. More importantly, the long hoped for wedding between Henry Tudor and Elizabeth of York, firmly promised in December, at last took place. With a dispensation granted by the recently arrived papal legate, Giacomo Pasarella, bishop of Imola, the couple were married on 18 January. It is strange that no account of the ceremony survives. Bernard André claimed that there were festivities, and a grand tournament had been mooted, but it might have been a relatively low key affair.[12] Still, the government would have sought to make as much political capital as possible from its formal union of the houses of Lancaster and York. A special emissary called George Fame was sent with the news to Dublin, where on 2 February the earl of Kildare arranged for a mass for the royal couple.[13] To add to the auspiciousness of the occasion, it seems that the queen conceived on her wedding night, or shortly thereafter: her first child being born almost exactly nine months later. The Tudor regime was beginning to put down roots. The final return to England of the well-respected

John Morton, bishop of Ely, was another promising sign, and his appointment as chancellor in March put his vast experience as a statesman at the disposal of the fledgling regime.

With the coming of spring, it was time for King Henry to make his presence felt in the provinces. Cutting a fine figure as a horseman, and leading a distinguished company, he rode to Waltham Holy Cross on 9 March, and then on to Cambridge, where he was honorably received by both town and gown. His plan was to perform his Easter devotions in the great minster at Lincoln, and he spent most of the week in the round of services led by Bishop John Russell, former chancellor of England. On Maundy Thursday he washed the feet of twenty-nine poor men, one for each year of his age, and on Good Friday dispensed great sums in alms to paupers, prisoners, lepers and the like. In addition to his piety in attending high mass and evensong daily, his magnanimity in hearing divine service in the minster rather than in a private chapel was greatly commended. Presumably the public appearances and receptions at Lincoln and elsewhere were carefully stage-managed. While most people probably received the king with genuine joy, and most communities naturally sought to arrange receptions designed to flatter their new prince, the new regime apparently left little to chance. From what is known of the themes of the speeches, tableaux and so on presented by various towns, it is hard not to suspect the workings of a fairly efficient public relations machine. Perhaps writers in the king's service liaised with local hacks: after all it was Bernard André, the court poet, who had welcomed his master into London after Bosworth. In various permutations the same elements reappear: the blessed union of the roses, the special relationship between the saintly Henry VI and his nephew, and, increasingly, papal support of the new order.[14]

Nevertheless the royal progress was no mere public-relations exercise. According to a letter dispatched from London in February, the king intended to go 'northward hastily after the parliament' and to 'to do execution quickly there on such as have offended against him'. His uncle, the duke of Bedford, was setting out for Wales, presumably with similar intentions. There is no doubt, that when the king took to the road, he did so at the head of a sizeable retinue of lords and gentlemen. To that date, however, there was apparently no suspicion of a major conspiracy. Around this time Henry was warned that Lovell was plotting to break sanctuary and lead a revolt. He refused to believe it, preferring to suspect his informant, Hugh Conway, of seeking his own advantage by tale-telling.[15] While at Lincoln, however, the information was proved accurate, and later intelligence was even more troubling. After the Easter festivities the king led his company rapidly eastwards along Fosse Way, by-passing Newark, where there was an outbreak of plague or 'sweating sickness'.[16] His destination was the great citadel on the Trent, where the Yorkist kings had so often kept watch over the heart of the kingdom.

Henry Tudor was well received at Nottingham. The mayor and his colleagues dressed in scarlet gowns rode out to meet him south of Trent bridge, and the clergy and people lined the road to greet him as he processed through the town. At the castle the king would have been comfortable physically if not mentally in the chambers recently refurbished by Richard III. Like his predecessor, he could see that it was the perfect place for assembling men and receiving intelligence. Given the unrest in the north, the strategic significance of Nottingham was immense: to prevent a general rising it would be crucial to hold the Trent line. In fact, as he was probably already discovering, the conspiracy with which he had to deal had two centres, equidistant from the town. To the south the Stafford brothers were aiming to raise the west midlands, while to the north Lovell was planning a general insurrection which probably aimed to seize York and capture the king.[17] While he knew it was hazardous to leave even a small fire smouldering behind him, Henry rightly judged that there was greater chance of a more widespread and dangerous conflagration in the north.

The king led his retinue north through Sherwood Forest. He was not too well-attended. While the earl of Derby was given leave to order his affairs in the northwest, however, he hoped that he would soon be joined by the earl of Oxford and other lords, whom he had summoned on first learning of the disturbances. At Barnsdale, near Robin Hood's stone, he was met on the road by the earl of Northumberland and an impressive company of Yorkshire knights, many of whom, like Sir Thomas Mauleverer, Sir Robert Plumpton, Sir William Gascoigne, Sir Robert Ughtred and Sir Martin of the Sea, had reputedly fought for Richard III at Bosworth.[18] The king and his company then proceeded to Doncaster. It was perhaps at this point, though it could have been earlier, that Henry learned that rebellion had broken out around Middleham, the heart of the old Neville and Ricardian connection in Yorkshire. Lovell was clearly involved, but apparently, too, there was a local leader with the ominous name of 'Robin of Redesdale'. It was thus probably from Doncaster that the king sent into the troubled area most of the armed men in his retinue, including Sir Richard Edgecombe, controller of the household, and Sir William Tyler, later used as a trouble-shooter in the district. The gamble paid off handsomely, when a show of force and promises of pardons led to the dispersal of the rebels. The king, who had moved up to Pontefract, now made a triumphal progress into York. By this time he had been joined by a whole host of peers, including, in addition to the earl of Oxford, the earls of Lincoln, Shrewsbury, Rivers and Wiltshire, and such northern barons as Lords Scrope of Bolton, Fitzhugh, Scrope of Masham and Clifford.

Lovell's rising, however, had a sting in its tail. While the herald's report implies that the rebels were dispersed before the king left Pontefract, Polydore Vergil places the whole episode after his arrival in York. The eye-witness testimony clearly has to be preferred, and if the later writer simply mistook the town, naming York rather than Doncaster or perhaps even Nottingham, the two accounts would complement each other very well. Nonetheless there is some independent evidence of trouble during the king's time at York, which the herald, who left the city after St George's day, perhaps did not know about, and which would account for Vergil's confusion. The *Crowland Chronicle* makes mention of a plot to kill King Henry at York. It was later alleged, as well, that while in the city with the court, the earl of Lincoln entertained men from Middleham in his lodgings, and even considered going over the walls to join 'Robin of Redesdale'.[19]

The mayor and aldermen of York, at least, resisted overtures from the rebels. Despite their grief at Richard III's death, the city fathers were not the stuff of martyrs. Their prime concern was the defence of their corporate privileges and interests, and at this stage at least their goal was to ingratiate themselves with the new order. As early as the middle of March the city began to make plans for the royal visit, and presumably preparations for the reception proceeded uninterrupted by the commotion in Wensleydale. On 20 April the king was met by the mayor and aldermen outside the city, and escorted through the gates, where he was welcomed by the cathedral clergy and citizens. People in the crowd shouted 'King Henry, King Henry! Our lord preserve that sweet and well favoured face!' Cheered and showered with confetti, the cavalcade moved through the streets, pausing at set points to listen to speeches and look at tableaux. A succession of pageants were staged in which Ebranc of Britain, the mythical founder of York, delivered the city to Henry VII; Solomon and David, the Old Testament kings, accepted him as their peer; and the Virgin Mary commended the people of York to him. However sceptical of the loyalty of York, the king in his turn accorded the city the honour due to a second capital, making his devotions at the Minster, staging a crown-wearing in the archiepiscopal hall, and holding a chapter of the Order of the Garter on St George's day. The Garter feast, in particular, afforded a valuable opportunity for the king to present a show of solidarity among the magnates of the realm, with a prominent Ricardian like Lord Scrope of Bolton sitting alongside a returned exile like Sir John Cheney.[20]

After little more than a week in the northern capital King Henry retraced his path southwards. At Nottingham castle on 3 May he appointed commissioners, including the duke of Bedford, the earls of Lincoln, Oxford and Derby, to enquire into treasons, felonies and conspiracies in Warwickshire and Worcestershire. By this stage the rebellion engineered by Humphrey Stafford and his brother was already faltering. As the king's forces moved on Birmingham, a major trouble-spot, resistance melted away. While indictments of suspected rebels were prepared, a great number of local activists sued for pardons. Even before the king reached Worcester, perhaps on 11 May, the ringleaders fled into sanctuary at Culham, from whence in defiance of the privileges of the church they were dragged by John Savage and forty men-at-arms to answer charges of treason. After lengthy judicial deliberation, focusing wholly on the issue of sanctuary, Humphrey Stafford was condemned to a traitor's death, and hung, drawn and quartered at Tyburn.[21]

Apprehensive but eager to please, the mayor and commonalty of Worcester received the king with nervous sycophancy. Their complicity in the rebellion, it was soon conceded, was limited only to their failure to post adequate guards at the gate. There were other institutions and individuals seeking to exonerate themselves, claiming, for example, that Stafford had claimed that he had a royal pardon. The king and his counsel were inclined to be generous in such cases, but there were aspects of the affair which must have been worrying. There was evidence of national organisation, with apparently co-ordinated movements in Yorkshire, the west midlands and London, where a small-scale, but decidedly seditious riot had erupted. A likely linkman was the old Neville retainer, who sued for a pardon as Thomas Otter of Middleham, Yorkshire, alias of Barkswell, Warwickshire. Apparently the rebels in the west midlands were told that the king had been captured at York by their allies. Predictably enough, given the associations of both districts with Warwick the Kingmaker, the investigations revealed that large crowds in Birmingham and elsewhere had rallied to the call, 'A Warwick, a Warwick!'. Even more disturbingly, the rebels had been inspired by reports that Edward Plantagenet, the young earl of Warwick, was at liberty in the Channel Islands, that he had made his way to join Lovell in the north, and that he would presently enter into his royal inheritance.[22]

The king completed his summer progress in a more relaxed mood, and was well-received in Bristol and other centres. Returning at last to his palace at Sheen, he might well have felt satisfied that he had drawn the teeth of the opposition. Despite its ominous overtones and its general capacity for mischief, the rising had clearly gone off half-cock. Rather than unravelling the ramshackle political structure Henry Tudor had erected, it had helped solidify it. The whole episode had certainly tested and proved the mettle of the military arm of the household. Sir William Tyler, controller of the king's works, seems to have particularly distinguished himself. Over the summer he was granted the keepership of the king's jewels, and then sent back north with a special commission to receive back into the king's grace all rebels willing to make peace.[23] Of course, King Henry knew that he was fortunate in that prominent Yorkists like the earl of Lincoln and Lord Scrope of Bolton were in his entourage when the conspiracies came to light. On the other hand, his gamble of setting at liberty the earl of Northumberland paid off handsomely. Though it was alleged that in 1485 he had hoped to raise Warwick to the throne, his loyalty in April 1486 probably saved the king's life, and his clear commitment to the regime boded well for the pacification of the north. To cap it all, it was discovered that he had arrested 'Robin of Redesdale', and on 13 June the council wrote that 'he be escorted by Northumberland's' men as far as Pontefract or Nottingham, where royal agents would receive him.[24] It is not known who he was, or what was his fate.

Around the same time, the king and his counsellors had reason to congratulate themselves on a diplomatic masterstroke which added substantially to the ideological armoury of the Tudor regime. Shortly after his marriage, he had sent Christopher Urswick to Rome to explain its importance in healing the wounds of civil strife and to request a bull confirming its validity. Allegedly of his own volition, but undoubtedly at the prompting of the king and his agent, Pope Innocent VIII was even more accommodating. In the letter sealed on 23 March, but reaching England at least six weeks later, he affirmed the validity of the king's title as well as the marriage, and threatened with excommunication all who impugned the royal title. The bull was in the king's hands by the time he reached Worcester, and it was proclaimed after a sermon on the same theme at Worcester cathedral on Whitsunday. Thenceforward it was a crucial propaganda weapon. At the council meeting on 13 June the bishop of Lincoln was asked to prepare an English translation, and to have his clerks make transcripts. Doubtless instructions were immediately given for its contents to be declared from pulpits across the realm. To facilitate its dissemination, it was set in type, the first use of the printing press in England for propagandist purposes.[25]

*   *   *

As the anniversary of his accession approached, Henry Tudor could allow himself a touch of complacency. His wife was now approaching her term, and her safe delivery of a son and heir would cap off his remarkable transformation from penniless exile to puissant prince. A statute of the realm and a papal bull notwithstanding, he must have recognised that only a son by Elizabeth of York could win acceptance for his dynasty. For all his initial success, there was a real danger that, without an heir of the blood of both Lancaster and York, his reign would go down in history as a strange and shabby interlude. Tempting fate in his greed for symbolism, the king arranged for the queen to give birth at Winchester, the ancient British capital, and when she was delivered of a son he had him named Arthur. His christening provided an unique opportunity for a display of unity and optimism. Most of the leading noblemen were in attendance, including the earl of Lincoln, the queen's cousin and the senior male representative of the house of York. Of course, it was also an occasion for the ladies. Rather strangely, though she seems to have advised on the protocol, the king's mother was not in attendance. On this occasion, pride of place went to the queen's mother, Elizabeth Woodville. As godmother as well as grandmother, though in other respects not a little incongruously, she was probably the first to utter publically the magical name of Arthur, and to present the baby prince to the congregation as the symbol of a reunited and resurgent nation.[26]

areas of England and the continent, most especially Liège and the French-speaking Netherlands, where the cult was popular. Although the custom was still far from common, a third possibility is that the name was derived from a surname, presumably the maternal grandfather's, in which case it would be persons with this family name, in all its variant spellings, that would repay investigation.[12] One tempting line of speculation would lead to Elizabeth, daughter of John Lambert of London, better known to history as 'Jane Shore', mistress of Edward IV. It was not just the name Lambert, however, that would have made the impostor stand out in a ruck. Curiously enough, the surname 'Simnel' was even less common. Among the thousands of testators in the prerogative court of Canterbury in the fifteenth and sixteenth centuries there are no Simnel's, and the only person with this surname thus far traced is Richard Simnel, possibly Lambert's son, who was a canon of St Osith's, Essex, in Henry VIII's reign.[13] Of course, there is the possibility that it is a foreign name, though its spelling differs from the more obvious French and German homologues. In any case the word 'simnel', meaning light grain, had already passed from Norman-French into English, and it seems more probable that the surname was a nickname derived from the 'simnel cake' eaten at Lent. Overall, the name has the lighthearted mellifluousness appropriate to a pantomine character.

The suspicion must be that the whole name was an invention. Its early use by Henry VII is not in itself good evidence as to its authenticity. It is true that the lad was known for the rest of his life by the name, but that can be explained by the boy's ignorance of his true identity, or by the political sensitivity of his true name, or simply by the king's desire to maintain consistency in the identification. Assuming the name to be a pseudonym, it could also have been the invention of the conspirators. Prior to presenting himself as the earl of Warwick, it would have made sense for the lad to travel and to be introduced under a name other than his own. Whatever the case, a thorough scrutiny of the early sources does indicate that the name itself is less than trustworthy. Between the parliament of 1487 and the testimony of Polydore Vergil a generation later, the only surviving allusion to the boy's name appears in the herald's report, written within a few years of the battle of Stoke. If the original manuscript, as opposed to Leland's edition, is consulted, however, it becomes apparent that, in an otherwise impressively accurate transcript, Leland deliberately miscopied the crucial clause regarding the pretender's identity, which still distinctly and without any tampering reads 'whose name was indeed John'.[14]

If the anonymous herald, an eye-witness within a year or so of the event, is to be believed, the real name of the impostor was simply John. Generally speaking, heralds were good with names, and his specific phrasing, as well as the general context, suggests that the actual identity of the boy was of great moment. Of course, the report does include some errors, though the mistake with the Christian name of Richard Fox, bishop of Exeter, on the previous page, is wholly unrepresentative of its general standard of accuracy. At the same time it is possible that when first captured the frightened lad offered the name 'John', and only subsequently admitted his true identity. Yet, in both circumstances, it would be reasonable to expect some emendation to have been made, either by the author or an early reader, as in fact was done in the case of Richard Fox.[15]

'Herald's report' of the battle of Stoke, showing Lambert Simnel's real name
(BL Cott. MS. Julius B.XII ff.286–29)

Of course, it is not claimed that Leland himself was part of a cover-up. By the time he copied the manuscript it was common knowledge that the boy was called Lambert, and he was doing no more than putting the herald right.

The sheer oddity of the name 'Lambert Simnel', however, makes it difficult to understand why it would be given to him. If the name originated with the government, its invention might have been whimsical, or circumstantial, or propagandist. Apart from the association of the name 'Simnel' with the approaching Lenten season, its similarity with the names of 'Simonds', the alleged priest–mentor, and for that matter 'Fitzsimons', the archbishop of Dublin, who was currently abetting the enterprise, might be significant. The Christian name might even have been deliberately chosen to associate the boy with Edward IV's most notorious mistress. On balance, however, the name makes most sense as a pseudonym under which the boy travelled and by which he was first introduced. With its pleasing, distinctive and faintly exotic flavour, it could not have been better designed to exude a sense of mystery and promise. Its Walloon associations would have been advantageous if it were planned ever to present him as someone who had been living under an assumed name on the continent, or to hint at some connection with the house of Burgundy. At Liège cathedral the bones of St Lambert lay in a splendid gold reliquary donated by Margaret of York's late husband, Charles the Bold.[16] If the boy in Dublin had been travelling under an assumed name, as was likely, it would have been the pseudonym rather than the real name that the government learned first.

If the name Lambert Simnel is false, then, sad to say, there are grounds for doubting all information provided on the background of the boy. At the time the conspiracy first broke, the government claimed to know that he was the son of one Simnel, organ-maker at the university of Oxford, and later in the year parliament was informed that his father was Thomas Simnel, joiner of Oxford. Since the government doubtless communicated this 'information' to the loyalist town of Waterford, it is not surprising to find in the poem on the affair, written early in 1488, a reference to the pretender as the son of an organ-maker.[17] This frank and explicit tone, however, is missing from most other accounts. In a letter to the pope relating to the affair, the king referred to the impostor as a boy of illegitimate birth, which scarcely tallies with the assurance shown elsewhere on the matter of his paternity. The king's biographer, Bernard André, certainly felt there was no certainty on the lad, referring first of all to a 'certain boy, commonly born, whether the son of a baker or cobbler', and later relating that after his arrest the boy was interrogated and it was discovered that his parents and kinsmen were all commoners in mean occupations 'unworthy to be included in this history'. Polydore Vergil, for once, adds little, referring to Lambert Simnel simply as a boy from Oxford. Francis Bacon, following Bernard André and perhaps mindful of 'simnel cakes', felt sure that the pretender was the son of a baker.[18]

It is hard to know what to believe about Lambert Simnel, or to determine what items of information provided by the government in 1487 and what elements in the tradition developed by Polydore Vergil can be given any credit. There are enough strange, unexplained and tantalising facts and coincidences to launch all kind of theories: the boy crowned in Dublin could have been the earl of

Warwick, a bastard of the house of York, a page from some noble household, a school-boy from Liège, or, for that matter, a foundling or orphan of unknown parentage. The best that can be done is to eliminate what seems least probable. From what happened after his arrest in 1487, it is difficult to credit that the pretender was Warwick or any other Yorkist prince, and it seems most unlikely that he was a royal bastard or had any close association with the royal family. Apart from his name there is no hint that he was other than English, and if his name were indeed John, a European provenance would be most improbable. Assuming him to have been of mean parentage, and to have required extensive training for the part, the association with a tradesman of Oxford has an inherent plausibility. With its large floating population of young people, and its numerous 'fringe' schools, Oxford was the easiest place for a boy to shed his original identity, and undergo, unremarked, the sort of extensive tuition required for the impersonation of a prince. At the same time the government, in its own investigation of the conspiracy, can be seen to have suspected an Oxford connection.

From 1487 onwards there was certainly a person living on the fringes of court under the name of Lambert Simnel. In all likelihood his real name was John, but if that were the case it seems beyond hope that further elucidation of his identity and background will be possible. For this reason, at least, it is tempting to cling to the name under which he is known to history. Perhaps, after all, it is not too preposterous. A monk called Lambert Fossedyke became abbot of Crowland without too many titters. If the early statements from the government regarding his affiliation and provenance are substantially correct, there is also the chance that at some stage some reference will be found to a family of this name in Oxford. It can at least be documented that 'simnel cakes' were sold in the town. Since Thomas Simnel was alleged to be an organ-maker or joiner employed by the unversity, he might yet appear in unpublished college accounts. There was certainly plenty of work in his line at Oxford. In 1481 the organ in the recently completed chapel of Magdalen College was repaired, and in 1486 an expensive new one installed.[19] Quite possibly Simnel was an itinerant craftsman, attracted to Oxford by employment opportunities, and his origins lay elsewhere. Perhaps his family was of foreign extraction, hailing originally from the Netherlands, where the best organs were built and where St Lambert was especially venerated.

*　　*　　*

For whatever reasons and with whatever justification, Henry VII claimed to know the identity of the boy at Dublin. What the government either never knew or was never willing to divulge was a satisfactory account of the conspiracy. The lack of any official guidance on the origins and ramifications of the affair is most frustrating, not least because it would help set firm bounds to speculation on the identity of the pretender and other matters. The confession of William Simonds, priest, provides information of a sort, but it is a wholly inadequate support for what became, in the hands of Polydore Vergil, the standard line that the plot was engineered by a single, ambitious priest. Since William Simonds confessed to taking the boy to Ireland, he is probably identical with the priest whom Vergil named Richard Simonds and regarded as the mastermind behind the

Medieval chapel of Magdalen College, Oxford, possibly connected with Lambert Simnel.

conspiracy. Of course, there is the additional discrepancy that William was in custody in February 1487, while Richard was only taken prisoner after the failure of the rising. It is feasible that there were two clerical accomplices, presumably brothers, called Simonds. Yet it is odd, to say the least, that if Henry had one of the ringleaders in his hands he did not discover more than he did about the plot. The suspicion must be that William Simonds was not as important a conspirator as the government wished people to think. In any case no one could have believed that it was all the mad scheme of an ambitious priest. Even the preliminary enterprise of training and transporting the lad presumably required the encouragement of people close to the house of York, and the backing and financial support of people of wealth and standing.

It is extremely difficult to define and bring into focus the conspiracy which coalesced around the boy in Dublin. The king himself almost certainly faced a similar problem. From the beginning of his reign, there were constant plots and rumours of plots, most of which could have used the services of an impostor. After the failure of the Tudor regime to disclose the details of the death of Edward IV's sons, there had inevitably been speculation as to their survival. It might well be that a number of interested parties put their minds to the task of impersonating one of the princes. At the same time there was continous intrigue centring on the person of the earl of Warwick. He was the hope of most Yorkists in 1485, and rumours of his escape encouraged the rebels in Warwickshire in 1486. The tale at this stage was that Warwick was in the Channel Islands, and it is significant that in the autumn Richard Harleston, the Yorkist captain of Jersey, found it wise to sue for a general pardon.[20] In such circumstances it is very hard to know where one plot ended and another began. If talk of the survival and escape of Yorkist princes were not wholly idle, Lambert Simnel began his career as an impostor earlier than usually imagined, or he was only one of several such pretenders. Obviously the chronology of the Simnel conspiracy is crucial. While it is not explicitly recorded before February 1487, it must then have been at least several months' old. If Simonds' testimony has any credibility, he had by this stage not only established the lad in Dublin but also spent time with Lovell in northern England. Quite probably, too, the government had spent some time secretly interrogating him before staging his confession. It seems probable, therefore, that it was this particular conspiracy that was sparking speculation about Warwick's future among Londoners in November 1486, and that prompted Henry to send out summonses in December for the great council which met in February.[21] The presence of 'Warwick' in Ireland before the end of the year seems also to be attested by the Flemish chronicler, Adrien de But. Whether the affair dated back to the summer of 1486 is more doubtful, but remains a possibility, given the rumours regarding Warwick and the activities of Lovell and Harleston.

Undoubtedly, Henry saw the lad in Dublin as part of a whole tissue of uncertainties and dangers. If the priest brought before convocation were a major conspirator, the government was extremely fortunate, but it is more probable that he was a minor figure or even a government stooge. It is clear that the king did not know the full ramifications of the conspiracy, and could not have been satisfied or reassured by Simonds' recorded disclosures, which were in any case designed for public consumption. The assumption that the pretence and the plot could not have made such progress without powerful backing was perhaps strengthened by the report of a special envoy to Dublin, who testified to the cleverness of the impersonation. The finger of suspicion pointed in some obvious but also some unexpected directions. It was hard not to believe that Lovell and other die-hard Ricardians were involved, and Simonds was presumably able to document the connection between the movement in Ireland and the group holding out in Furness fells. The government would have been wise to keep a watch on comings-and-goings at Minster Lovell, not far from Oxford, and, for that matter, Abingdon abbey, with which Lovell had connections. Yet King Henry apparently believed that there were more subtle and potent forces at work than a few renegade lords and knights. In the fullness of time the commitment of the earl of Lincoln and the duchess of Burgundy would be revealed, but even the proven involvement of two senior members of the house of York seems not to have settled the king's mind as to the conspiracy. Needless to say, there is little chance at this distance in time of shedding new light on mysteries that Henry Tudor found obscure. To come as close as is possible to the heart of the affair, the best strategy remains to follow what seem to have been the lines of his thought.

The most startling decision taken at the council meeting which followed the public disclosure of the plot in February was to deprive the dowager queen of her estates and to confine her to a nunnery. Since her son, the marquis of Dorset, was soon afterwards committed to the Tower of London, it appears as if the king suspected some involvement in the conspiracy.[22] Relations between the king and his mother-in-law were probably not of the best, even if on occasion, as at the baptism of Prince Arthur, she had been honoured at court. Her rapprochement with Richard III, which came so close to destroying the Tudor cause, doubtless still rankled. Still, it is hard to credit Elizabeth Woodville's involvement in a plot on behalf of the alleged son of the duke of Clarence against her son-in-law, daughter and grandson. It is no easier to imagine what role her son, the marquis of Dorset, could have played, or been thought to have played in the conspiracy. In his assessment of the business, Bacon merely pointed to the flightiness and inconstancy of the woman. She was indeed an inveterate intriguer, capable in her vanity and fecklessness of some remarkable shifts and turns, and Dorset was cut from the same cloth. At the same time there might have been a substantial grievance in the king's apparent reluctance to proceed with the coronation of her daughter, and other signs of coolness to herself and her family. What seems very possible is that the dowager queen had given countenance to some scheme centred on an impersonation of one of her sons. Vergil claimed that the man who coached Lambert Simnel intended at first to pass him off as one of the princes who had disappeared in the Tower of London, and he might not have been the only person with this idea at the time. Between 1485 and 1487 Sir Edward Brampton, godson of Edward IV and a notable Yorkist, went into exile in the Netherlands, and took into his service a boy called Perkin Warbeck, who several years later appeared in Ireland claiming to be Prince Richard.[23] If assistance or even countenance had been given to activity of this sort, as well it might, it would explain the king's resolution to deprive her of her independence and break up her household.

If a royal puppet-master for the impostor were assumed, it seems rather strange that suspicion did not immediately fall on John de la Pole, earl of Lincoln. Richard III's nephew and intended heir, he was the natural leader of the Yorkist cause. It is certainly the case that soon after the meeting at Sheen he slipped out of the country to join the king's enemies, and one modern scholar at least makes the assumption that he was behind the affair from the outset. With their principal seat at Ewelme in Oxfordshire, Lincoln's father, the duke of Suffolk, and his brothers, including Edward de la Pole, an Oxford don, were well-placed to engineer the charade. Yet the king had good reason for not reading the evidence in this way. Suffolk and his sons had made their peace with the regime, and indeed all the family save Lincoln remained loyal throughout 1487.[24] Lincoln himself had appeared to commit himself to the new regime, and had sat in judgement on the rebels the previous year. Since his attendance at court was fairly continuous, it was likewise hard to see how he could have had the time to organise so complex an enterprise. At the same time it is hard to credit that Lincoln would have initiated a plot to raise the earl of Warwick to the throne. The sudden defection of Lincoln after the disclosure of the affair seems to have surprised everyone, not least because he above all knew that the boy in Dublin was an impostor. It later transpired that Lincoln had given encouragement to the rebels in 1486, and that he had raised funds for a conspiracy over the Christmas season.[25] It is not impossible that he instigated the whole enterprise, though most of the evidence reads as if he joined and then perhaps tried to redirect an existing movement.

Margaret of York, Duchess of Burgundy, (died 1503).

By 1487 Henry VII had no illusions about Margaret of York, the dowager duchess of Burgundy. Throughout his early years he was dogged by her enmity, and when Tudor propagandists hailed him as a new Aeneas they naturally cast her in the role of Juno. With no children of her own, Margaret took a fierce, though selective, interest in her nephews and nieces in England. In vain the king sought to commend himself to her as the husband of the eldest daughter, and the avenger of the murdered sons of Edward IV. George, duke of Clarence, was perhaps her favourite brother, and his orphaned son might well have had a special place in her heart. From 1485, it would seem, her court was the centre of Yorkist intrigue, and in all likelihood her backing was sought for all sorts of schemes, probably including impostures. Of course, Polydore Vergil alleged that it was the Irish lords who, after convincing themselves of the boy's credentials, took the initiative in inviting her to join the enterprise, but given the speed with which ships and men were assembled in March 1487 it would seem that her commitment to an invasion dated back into the previous year. It certainly appears as if she were in a position to give the assurances that Lincoln might have needed to commit himself irrevocably. At the same time there are hints that Lambert Simnel, if not himself of Walloon stock, passed through the Netherlands at some stage. In a letter of 1493 Henry claimed that the duchess of Burgundy had sent the 'feigned boy' against him, which perhaps means more than the financial and military assistance she provided.[26] On the other hand, it does seem unlikely that she originally devised the scheme, and since she had not seen her nephew since infancy she had little to offer to a plot involving his impersonation. Since the affair seemed in origin home-grown, the king was inclined to look elsewhere for his arch-conspirator.

Robert Stillington, bishop of Bath and Wells, was cast perfectly for the rôle. As a doctor of civil law and a veteran of the royal administration, he was a clerk of outstanding intellect and application, but in 1485 he was a man dangerously compromised, morally and politically.[27] It was not that he was a worldly prelate, who had sired children and amassed great wealth to support them. It was no particular liability, either, that he had made his way through service to the house of York. His problem with the Tudor regime was his alleged role in 1483 in questioning the validity of Edward IV's marriage with Elizabeth Woodville, and preparing the case for the bastardisation of their issue, including not only Edward V but also Elizabeth of York. What is especially intriguing in the light of the conspiracy of 1487, however, is the probability that the allegations had been aired ten years earlier in the circle of the duke of Clarence. Stillington was thus not only too closely identified with the Ricardian regime to be trusted, but also a natural advocate of the cause of the earl of Warwick. It is small wonder that, immediately after his victory at Bosworth, Henry Tudor ordered his arrest, and the bishop, 'sore crazed' by his troubles, was soon in safe keeping in York. Though stripped of some of his honours, he acquired a royal pardon on account of 'his great age, long infirmity and feebleness', but in semi-retirement he could well have given himself over to intrigue. Given his association with the house of York, and possibly with the earl of Warwick, he was well-placed to mastermind an impersonation. To add to the circumstantial evidence, Stillington had taken up residence at Oxford, and it was from the university that he was summoned in

February to answer charges regarding certain 'damnable conjurations and conspiracies'. Despite the king's orders and the entreaties of the dons, he remained under the protection of the university throughout March. With assurances of safe-conduct, he was finally escorted to Windsor castle, where he was no doubt subjected to intensive interrogation. What he revealed then is not known, but no formal charges seem to have been laid against him. For the remainder of his life, however, he seems to have continued more or less under house-arrest, playing little or no part in the affairs of his diocese or public life generally.

* * *

By this stage Henry VII was daily bombarded with intelligence which increasingly had more to do with the actual working-out of the conspiracy than with its original blueprint. He perhaps gained some useful information from Edward Hextall of Dover, who in March confessed to treason on 'many strange points', which at first the king had refused to credit.[28] The problem was that the movement was developing a momentum of its own, which perhaps rendered some of the information obsolete. In so far as Elizabeth Woodville had involved herself in the intrigue, for example, she must soon have let it slip from her hands, though it did not prevent the king from stripping of her estates or allowing Dorset, who had been Warwick's guardian for a time, his liberty. Once in the king's hands, Stillington, too, might conceivably have been able and willing to divulge early details of a conspiracy centring on Warwick and his impersonation. More pertinently to the matter at hand, reports from agents in Ireland and the Netherlands could have thrown more light on the impostor and his backers, and certainly confirmed the treasonable activities of a whole range of renegade Yorkist lords. News of the assembly of ships, men and equipment in Holland and Brabant indicated the involvement of the duchess of Burgundy and provided hard information by which to assess the scale and possible location of the threat.

Yet a great deal of this intelligence probably confused rather than clarified an understanding of the conspiracy. It was impossible to obtain a clear view of a movement, which itself perhaps had little unity, but was a coalescence of a number, though by no means all of the strands of Yorkist disaffection and hope. There is a real possibility, for example, that in the spring of 1487 there was an alternative scheme, based on the impersonation of one of Edward IV's sons, which vied for the backing of the dowager duchess of Burgundy. It would certainly explain the curious coincidence that in 1487 Sir Edward Brampton, apparently breaking with his Yorkist colleagues, left the Netherlands for his native Portugal, taking with him as a servant the future impostor, Perkin Warbeck. At the same time the revelation of the treason of the earl of Lincoln was hard to fit into the pattern. The more that was discovered the less straightforward it sounded. Among the reports forwarded to the king in April was the tale of James Tait, who divulged to authorities at York conversations he had had with agents of the earl of Lincoln. He had met them on Lady Day at Doncaster, and won their confidence by recognising the 'white hoby' belonging to Lincoln and asking after him. Apparently they had come from London disguised as merchants, with saddle-bags full of gold and silver, seeking to make contact with Lincoln's friends in Yorkshire. Points on their itinerary included Hull, the ancestral home of the de la Poles, and York, where they planned to meet the prior of Tynemouth at the sign of the Boar. Contract was also planned with Sir Thomas Mauleverer of Allerton Mauleverer, but the earl of Northumberland was to be ignored: 'he doth but little for us, therefore we set little by him'. There was a great deal of loose talk. It was promised that 'John of Lincoln shall give them all a breakfast that oweth him no love nor favour'.[29] What is odd, however, is that there was no talk about Lincoln's aims or the pseudo-Warwick. Until early May, when it became apparent that Lincoln and the forces assembled in the Netherlands were heading for Ireland, it was not clear that the main challenge to the Tudor regime involved the boy in Dublin at all. Even after the coronation of the impostor as Edward VI, it must have been suspected that a successful rebellion would see Lincoln make his own bid for the crown.

Seal of John de la Pole, Earl of Lincoln.

5 The Gathering Storm

In the spring of 1487 storm clouds gathered menacingly around the ship of state. The margins of the realm were most threatened, with ominous rumblings from Dover and Calais to Hull and Tynemouth, as well as from Cornwall and the Channel Islands to Cumbria and Ireland. In truth there were few districts that did not feel the mounting tension from March onwards. In some quarters it was doubtless thought that the gathering storm, however fierce, would at least finally clear the air and purge the body politic of its impurities. With hindsight it is too easy to dismiss legitimist sentiment as a force in fifteenth-century politics, but it could still have been widely felt that the natural order had been violated by the usurpation of Henry Tudor. It is instructive that the men of Waterford, who set themselves against most of Anglo-Ireland in their loyalty to Henry VII, justified their allegiance solely on the grounds of his wife's claim to the throne.[1] What was clear in England by this stage, of course, was that the king wholly repudiated this view of his title, and, to make matters worse, appeared to be in no hurry to accord his wife the honour of a coronation. In such circumstances the challenge mounted by leading members of the house of York looked especially potent. Its public aim was to raise to the throne the last surviving male of the house of Plantagenet, Edward, earl of Warwick. His title to the throne was hard to refute. The rights of Elizabeth of York had been overridden by Henry himself, as had objections stemming from previous attainders. On the basis of a compact made between Henry VI and Clarence, the pseudo-Warwick could even present himself as the heir of the house of Lancaster. Moreover the movement was now led by the earl of Lincoln, nephew of the Yorkist kings, experienced in government, and respected for the soundness of his judgement. Finally it had the active support of the well-loved Margaret of York, duchess of Burgundy. In so far as the new king would be established from foreign bases and through foreign arms, it would not be, as with the invasion of Henry Tudor, through the machinations of England's traditional French enemies, but through the solicitude of old allies and an English princess.

The mood of England at this time, the degree of commitment to the Tudor regime and the extent of good will towards the Yorkist challenge, is obviously hard to gauge. In any case what counted in the short term was the ability of the government to secure the commitment, however reluctant, of the leading magnates and county notables, and the corresponding capacity of its opponents to win sufficient support at least to persuade the politically uncommitted of the wisdom of staying at home. Needless to say, the die was cast for quite a number of people, not least lords like the duke of Bedford and the earl of Oxford who were so prominent in the new dispensation. On the other side, the earl of Warwick, vicariously, and the earl of Lincoln, after great deliberation, had now joined Lovell and other Ricardians in open rebellion. Yet there were many prominent lords whose stance could not be taken for granted, and how the gentry in the different regions would shift themselves depended on many factors. With his father, the duke of Suffolk, still in possession of the family estates, Lincoln did not have a strong territorial base, though he had the makings of a following in various parts of eastern England. The name of Warwick, combining Yorkist legitimism with the old Neville interest, on the other hand, was an extremely potent force in many parts of the country, from London and Calais to the Welsh borderlands and the Scottish marches. Longstanding loyalties to dispossessed noble families, coupled with resentment against the 'new' men of the Tudor regime, threatened to prove dangerous for the government in other districts as well. The earl of Northumberland was indispensable in the north. Briefly at Sheen for discussions with the king early in March, he was immediately sent back north with a new commission as warden of the marches and promises of financial reward.[2] The king's reluctance to reinstate Thomas Howard, earl of Surrey, however, generated a measure of ill feeling among sections of the gentry of East Anglia.

*   *   *

Even after the revelation of the imposture and the flight of Lincoln, there still seems to have been a relaxed atmosphere at the court at Sheen by the beginning of Lent. In the king's projected itinerary through East Anglia, it was still possible on 7 March to look forward to some courtly dalliance. As William Paston informed his brother, the king planned to see for himself proof of the earl of Oxford's 'great boast of the fair and good gentlewomen of the country', and the courtiers looked forward to drinking Norwich as dry as they had left York the previous Easter.[3] Nonetheless, it is instructive that, as the rumblings of invasion and insurrection grew louder, the king should embark on a tour of East Anglia, taking with him a sizeable retinue, predominantly composed of gentlemen from Lancashire.[4] After all, the earl of Lincoln had made his escape through the district, and the marquis of Dorset, who was taken into confinement at Bury St Edmunds, had also been active in the region. A movement against the Tudor regime could be expected to find support among the tenantry of the de la Poles, who were great landowners in Suffolk, as well as among the old Howard affinity. Yet the king was not without his friends in the region. In appointing commissioners of array at this time, he put the duke of Suffolk, Lincoln's father, at the top of the list, indicating that he was still working, in name at least, for the regime. The king's real lieutenant in East Anglia, however, was the earl of Oxford. Since the battle of Bosworth, he had not only recovered his ancestral lands in the region, but had also moved rapidly into the vacuum left by the fall of the Howards. By 1487 he was well-regarded for his magnanimity and even-handed 'good lordship', which had contributed powerfully towards the stabilisation of what were traditionally volatile county societies. From his account books it is clear that he had his tabs on the military resources of the region, and could be depended upon to mobilise them for the king. As it happened, when the summons came, there was a little confusion and hesitation in some quarters of Norfolk, but Sir Edmund Bedingfield spoke for many gentlemen when he declared that he would follow Oxford in preference to anyone other than the king himself.[5]

What was most feared, of course, was that a beach-head might be established for a seaborne invasion from the Netherlands. By the beginning of April the king had apparently received reports of a fleet being assembled along the coast of Holland and Brabant. The commissions of array appointed on 7 April included a special injunction to repair and guard 'the beacons on the sea-coast, for forewarning the people of that country of the advent of the king's enemies'. At Harwich a number of vessels were assembled and victualled for the king's service. Presumably Henry had occasion to regret the neglect into which Edward IV's ships had been allowed to fall. On Easter Sunday, he found time among his devotions to authorise regular payment from the exchequer for the large new ship being built in Kent under the oversight of Sir Richard Guildford.[6]

King Henry celebrated Easter in the cathedral city of Norwich. He arrived there on Tuesday 10 april, and on Maundy Thursday gave the customary alms. He was present in the cathedral for the major services on Easter Sunday, 15 April. On Monday he made a pilgrimage to the popular shrine at Walsingham. Then, with the end of the holiday season, his pace changed abruptly. After a night at Walsingham he made his way to Thetford, then Cambridge, where he remained two nights. Another two full days of riding, punctuated by a meal at Huntingdon and a rest at Northampton, brought him to Coventry by nightfall on 22 April. This sudden move to the midlands requires explanation. Presumably the king had eased his mind as to the stability of East Anglia, and was satisfied with its preparedness for defence against an invading force. He might well have had some intelligence concerning the intentions of the rebel fleet, though he could scarcely have yet received certain information that it was heading for the English Channel. The letter he wrote to the city of York from Huntingdon certainly gives the impression that an invasion along the east coast was still a strong possibility.[7]

The selection of Coventry and nearby Kenilworth as his new operational headquarters, of course, made a great deal of sense. Even if the rebels and their allies in the Low Countries made a landing on the east coast, there was still the possibility of a second invasion from Dublin. It was essential to occupy some central position to co-ordinate the mobilisation of the nation's man-power and to deploy it where it was most immediately needed. A traditional Lancastrian stronghold, Coventry was, for Henry VII in 1487, what Nottingham had been for Richard III in 1485. Nevertheless there is still something in the speed of his movements that indicates that either he had a report of some specific crisis brewing in the west midlands, which is feasible given the unrest in Warwickshire the previous year, or he was seeking in some general sense to phase his opponents by a fearsome unpredictability of movement. Particularly noteworthy is his failure to observe St George's day with the knights of the Garter at

Windsor, which in an only moderately less tight schedule could have been fitted into his itinerary. Apparently the duke of Suffolk and Lord Maltravers, Lincoln's father and brother-in-law respectively, turned up for the feast, but declined to participate because no funds had been made available. From Kenilworth an embarrassed king tried to redress matters, ordering the treasurer to make funds available for 20 May, when it was hoped the disgruntled lords would attend.[8] Given the solemnity with which the Garter feast was celebrated in 1486 and 1488, the farce of 1487, so potentially corrosive to the creditibility of the regime, is an eloquent testimony to the instability of the times.

*   *   *

As King Henry established himself at Coventry, a major part of the forces with which he would have to contend were experiencing all the discomforts of sailing in the English Channel. Exactly when the fleet left the Netherlands, probably from Middleburg and bases in Brabant, cannot be established. It is inconceivable that they had taken to sea and set their course before the king left East Anglia in the middle of April, as even at the end of the month he still thought it possible that the threat would be to eastern England. By 4 May, however, he had completely changed his tune, assuring the city of York that it needed no reinforcement because he had 'certain knowledge in sundry wise that our rebels be departed out of Flanders, and gone westwards'.[9] Of course, by this stage the rebel fleet was approaching the city of Dublin, and since the voyage would have taken, in average conditions, between a week and a fortnight, it can be assumed that the fleet was at sea before St George's day. Given the difficulty of finding favourable winds from ports in the Netherlands, of course, it is more than possible that the rebels had put to sea, and then been forced back, perhaps a number of times.[10]

For the Dutch and Flemish sailors the trip was neither novel nor unusually awesome. The cold and brutal seas from the Baltic to the Atlantic were the source of their livelihood, and few of the crew could count the number of voyages that they had made either to the bleak northern seas or to the turbulent ocean that lashed the western rim of the known world. A fair few of the sailors had probably made the trip to Ireland. Irish ports were frequented by ships from the Low Countries. In Waterford a monument stood to a merchant from Bruges who made a fortune from the Flemish–Irish trade in the middle of the fifteenth century.[11] Doubtless the ship's masters and sailors on this occasion hoped to pick up a return cargo of hides or flax to add to the pickings of the voyage. For the moment, as the ships battled down the Channel towards the Atlantic, they could doubtless take secret pleasure in the pallid faces of their passengers, mainly mercenaries from the forests and high valleys of upper Germany and Switzerland. Recruited the previous year by Maximilian, king of the Romans and would-be regent of the Burgundian Netherlands, their role had been as much to bring to heel the rebellious Flemish cities as to drive the French from Flanders. When their wages were not paid, the soldiers had rioted in the streets of Brussels and other towns, further rousing the ire of the Netherlanders. The leader of the soldiers in the flotilla, Martin Schwartz, was the most arrogant

remembered in 1487, the association of his second cousin, heir general and namesake, Richard, duke of York, certainly was. He had proved a capable governor, respectful of its traditions and attentive to its needs. From Ireland in 1460 he had set forth to win his inheritance, only to be slain by the Lancastrians at Wakefield. It was remembered, too, that back in 1449, during his lieutenancy, his wife had given birth in Dublin to a son, who had been christened at St Saviour's, with the heads of the rival houses of Fitzgerald and Butler standing as godfathers. This child was none other than George, duke of Clarence, who prior to his own arrest for treason in 1477 planned to send his infant heir for safe-keeping to Ireland. Now it was this young boy, the son of Clarence, the grandson of York, the true heir of Richard II, that the men of the lordship of Ireland would crown and send to England as Edward VI.

In their support for the house of York, the Anglo-Irish were able to blend sentiment and self-interest. What the magnates and burghers of the lordship required from the English government was a sensitivity to the needs of the colony and a proper respect for its traditions and privileges. If the king or at least a prince of the blood could not take it upon himself to attend personally to affairs in Dublin, such ends were best achieved through delegation to the dominant Anglo-Irish lineages. What were to be most resisted were attempts to foist on the lordship English governors with no stake in the province and to subject the lordship to the crown of England. The Anglo-Irish had been content, for the most part, with arrangements under Yorkist rule, which in many respects pre-dated 1461. In the famous Irish parliament of 1460, presided over by the attainted duke of York, statutes had been passed asserting the independence of the lordship in terms of coinage, judicial immunity and legislation. While such claims were never formally acknowledged by Edward IV, and on occasion he showed himself less than sensitive to Anglo-Irish susceptibilities, the government of Ireland was generally left in local hands, which in practice meant the hands of the great Fitzgerald clan, headed by the earls of Desmond and Ormond. It was they who served as deputies to absentee royal lieutenants, including, significantly the duke of Clarence and the earl of Lincoln, and headed the opposition to active English-born governors like the earl of Worcester and Lord Grey of Codnor. From the late 1470s Garret Mor Fitzgerald, eighth earl of Kildare, had achieved a virtually viceregal eminence: it was he who was elected chief governor by the Irish council after the death of Clarence in 1478, it was he who was confirmed in the deputyship in 1483 by Richard III, and perforce reappointed in 1485 by Henry VII.[21]

With the accession of the Tudors, however, the Kildare ascendancy and Anglo-Irish liberties could be seen to be threatened. Of course, no vigorous experiment in direct rule was on the cards in 1485, but what was clearly anticipated was the revival of the fortunes of the Butlers, earls of Ormond, the Fitzgeralds' old rivals. It was their association with the house of Lancaster, their attainder in 1461, and their defeat in Ireland in 1463, which had so successfully cleared the ground for a broadly-based Fitzgerald supremacy. With his attainder reversed in 1477, the new earl of Ormond had been slowly rehabilitated in the last years of Yorkist rule, but, now with his impeccable Lancastrian credentials and court connections, he could become a potent force in the lordship. Even if he could never quite aspire to match the Great Kildare's pre-eminence, his advancement would necessarily undermine the unwonted unity and solidarity of Anglo-Irish society, which had been fostered by, and in turn provided support for, and helped to justify the Fitzgerald hegemony.

For some time after the battle of Bosworth, the government at Dublin held back from recognising the Tudor regime. Henry VII's appointment of Kildare as deputy of Ireland and his marriage to Elizabeth of York could perhaps have allayed some fears in the Fitzgerald camp, but the arrival of the Yorkist pretender, presumably some time late in 1486, offered an irresistible opportunity to raise the stakes. Though it is impossible to be certain, there are grounds for believing that the boy was actually thought to be the genuine earl of Warwick. His cause was most actively championed by Thomas Fitzgerald, Kildare's brother and chancellor of Ireland. He convened an assembly of peers and prelates who acclaimed the boy as king, and doubtless handled the correspondence with other Yorkist conspirators. The reported appearance of the 'real' Warwick in London was haughtily dismissed as a government-sponsored charade, though it must have raised doubts in the minds of some notables. A letter from his 'brother' archbishop of Canterbury convinced Octavian del Palacio, the Italian-born archbishop of Armagh, that the boy was an impostor, but he seems to have been unwilling or unable to dissuade the archbishop of Dublin and other Irish prelates from persisting with the enterprise. There were other doubters, most notably the genial Nicholas St Lawrence, later Lord Howth, who subsequently made merry at the expense of his credulous peers, and the stout-hearted men of Waterford, who commissioned a poem to chastise the Dubliners for their folly. Of course, their independent stance probably had as much to do with their factional connections as with their perspicacity. Robert, Lord Howth, Nicholas's father, lived in England, and had connections with the house of Butler. The mayor of Waterford was likewise a Butler, and indeed the whole county of Waterford was Butler country. Still, the city of Waterford at least had the courage of its convictions, and openly defied the government in Dublin. Messengers sent to Kildare to remonstrate against the new regime were given short shrift, however, and to the consternation of some of the council were summarily hanged on Hoggen Green.[22]

In the spring of 1487, more than at any other time in his long and tempestuous career, the Great Kildare was the 'uncrowned king' of Ireland. Over the previous years uncertain conditions in England had provided him with an unusually free hand to expand his power-base, not only at the expense of Anglo-Irish rivals and the royal lordship, but also through inspired adventurism among the Gaelic chieftains beyond the Pale. Though the city of Waterford insulted his herald from behind the safety of its walls, most of the colony stood in awe of a lord who could offer them so much. Guardianship of the young 'king' and the arrival of a large force of foreign soldiers added immensely to his power and his arrogance. The coronation of 'Edward VI' in Christchurch cathedral testified splendidly to his protector's puissance and magnanimity. Though the archbishop of Armagh absented himself, the archbishop of Dublin presided, with the bishops of Meath, Kildare and Cloyne, as well as a number of abbots and priors, in attendance. Particularly prominent was the warlike prior of

Kilmainham, James Keating. There was an even more impressive showing of Anglo-Irish lords, including Kildare's father-in-law Sir Roland FitzEustace, Lord Portlester. A parliament was convened around the same time in the name of the new king, whose title now appeared on coins and government instruments. Its business included the attainder of opponents of the new regime, including a gentleman called Thomas Butler, who had fled to England to inform Henry VII of developments in Dublin, and his brother, William Butler, parson of Kilberry, who had abetted the 'treason'.

Despite his kingmaking role, however, Kildare's commitment to the Yorkist restoration in England was perhaps less than total. He was obviously most concerned to consolidate his position in Ireland, and he was understandably reluctant to leave his own power-base with his rivals cowed and contained, but by no means subdued. According to Bacon, there was some debate after the coronation as to whether the whole army should remain in Ireland, to see the new king's authority fully established and, it was hoped, to draw Henry Tudor out of his kingdom.[23] Kildare doubtless saw the gains to be made from a strategy which enabled him to use professional soldiers, with the latest firearms, against rebellious towns and Gaelic chieftains. It was also the case that Henry VII was giving consideration to an invasion of Ireland, which could indeed have been his undoing. Yet there were strong counter-arguments, whose force Kildare must also have recognised. It would be difficult for Ireland to support such a large host for any length of time, and the English king might make no move at all for several months.

Irish warriors of the early 16th century, engraved by Durer.

Within a few days of the coronation of 'Edward VI', the die was cast. Given the speed of embarkation, it must be assumed that Kildare had been mobilising forces for some time. The man-power resources on which he could call were extremely varied.[24] The élite corps of the counties around Dublin, containing most of the leading lords and select retinues, was the Fraternity of Arms, while the standard levies from the area would be English-style billmen and archers. Beyond the Pale there were the formidable galloglasses, Scots mercenaries recently settled in northern Ireland; the lightly armed but highly accomplished Irish horsemen; and finally the kernes, poorly armed footmen. The troops Kildare dispatched were almost certainly a mixed force, but with the poorest type predominating. Judging from the reports of the slaughter of 'naked' Irish footsoldiers, it is probable that the rank-and-file were predominantly Gaelic, recruited from allied clans like the O'Connors. Despite the leadership of Thomas Fitzgerald, the Anglo-Irish contribution cannot have been large, but included, perhaps among other scions of noble families, Edward Og Plunket, the son of Lord Killeen.[25] Since Kildare himself remained in Ireland, there is additional reason to suppose that the cream of the Fitzgerald fighting machine was missing from the expedition. Still, there is no reason to doubt that the invasion was launched with high hopes, and if the Irish compared unfavourably with the Germans in discipline and equipment they compared most favourably in keenness and spirit.

6 The Struggle for the Kingdom

Over Whitsuntide the king kept court at Kenilworth castle. Pleasantly sited in Warwickshire woodland, warm-stoned and commodious, more a palace than a stronghold, Kenilworth could not but have soothed his nerves. Perhaps momentarily in the round of devotions and festivities associated with this major holiday, he could put to the back of his mind the clouds gathering around him which might like a summer storm suddenly turn so violent. He knew that it was his last opportunity for a while to relax in the company of his family. Around 13 May he made arrangements for his wife and mother to join him, though whether his baby son was brought is doubtful.[1] His uncle, Jasper Tudor, duke of Bedford, and his stepfather, Thomas Stanley, earl of Derby, were also apparently at his side. Since quite a number of the courtier-lords had been dispatched to their 'countries' to raise their retinues, the time might have afforded a few precious moments of domestic repose. Presumably most of the government officials and troops that had already answered the royal summons were quartered in nearby Coventry.

Nonetheless the king can scarcely have passed a day without attending to business. Of course, at this stage there was more to be discussed than actually done, save the perennial task of raising money, left very largely to Reginald Bray, who was busy negotiating loans from the city of London and other parties. The dispatch of an army to Ireland was certainly under active consideration until late in May.[2] For the most part, however, the initiative lay with the rebels, and indeed the people of England who might now either be responding to the king's summons to arms or preparing to give succour to his enemies. The business at hand consisted very largely in receiving and interpreting intelligence, identifying possible dangers and designing responses to them, and generally placing obstacles in the path of his rivals and to ensure the smooth mobilisation of his own forces. His agents were ubiquitous, and doubtless messengers rode daily into Kenilworth to be given an immediate hearing. The city of York sent him a man suspected of having information on the conspiracy for further questioning.[3] Supporters in Ireland sent reports, and since he had learnt of the rebels' arrival in Dublin in around a week it seems likely that he was kept abreast of developments at a few days' remove. Probably reports of the gathering of troops, provisions and ships in Dublin prompted him to send Christopher Urswick, his almoner, to Lancashire to check out possible landing-places.[4] By Whitsunday he

Keep of Kenilworth Castle, Warwickshire, where Henry VII stayed, summer 1487.

must have known of the coronation of the pretender and had good reason to expect an imminent invasion.

Information of this sort had to be properly controlled. The realm was awash with rumours. In a writ sent to major population centres on 3 June it was noted that many of the king's subjects 'be disposed daily to hear feigned, contrived, and forged tidings and tales; and the same tidings and tales, neither dreading God nor his highness, utter and tell again as though they were true, to the great hurt of divers of his subjects and to his grievous displeasure'. Such behaviour was to be curtailed, and mayors and bailiffs were enjoined to retrace the steps in the chain of rumour-mongering. All tale-tellers had to produce the source of their stories or to be set in the pillory.[5] Whether this government directive managed to stifle news of the coronation of 'Edward VI' is to be doubted. The report with which diligent local officials had to contend immediately on receipt of the writ was of the invasion of England by the new king, a group of Yorkist lords and an army of German mercenaries and 'wild Irish' footsoldiers.

*   *   *

Foulney Island was an unpromising landfall. Lashed by the sea and wind, it was bleak and incommodious, almost elemental. No trees or even bushes served as a wind-break, and only sea-birds made their homes among the boulders and rough grass. The square pile of Piel castle, weather-scoured and dilapidated, was barely one and a half centuries old, but looked far older. Still, it commanded the entrance to the harbour, and it was a relief to find no ordnance to challenge their approach. Moreover, Foulney did provide a safe, natural haven, which even at low tide was six fathoms deep.[6] It was there that the handful of ships, doubtless driven by a firm southwesterly wind from Dublin, landed on 4 June. It was also here that the oddly assorted army, predominantly German and Gaelic speaking, first trod on English soil. It was there that a ten-year old boy, pale and shaken by his sea-passage if not the giddiness of his undertaking, was first acclaimed in England as Edward VI.

Their beach-head off what is now Cumbria, and what was then 'Lancashire beyond the sands' was predictable. The rebels can have seen little prospect of raising the West Country, could have expected fierce opposition in Wales, and must have been less than hopeful of prising the Stanleys, dominant around the Mersey and Ribble estuaries, from their well-rewarded allegiance to the Tudor dynasty. Fortunately a landing in the far northwest, the only feasible option, made considerable strategic sense. It was even more remote and inaccessible than the Pembrokeshire harbours into which Henry Tudor had sailed two years earlier. At the same time there were allies in the neighbourhood to secure the landing, and there were many others in the region who were loyal to the memory of Warwick the Kingmaker and Richard of Gloucester, who had ruled the region as a palatinate in the 1470s.[7] The Cumbrian coast, moreover, offered more than a secluded beach-head and a favourable reception. It opened up a reasonably secure corridor to York through Wensleydale, the heartland of Ricardian loyalism.

The key man in the first stage of this enterprise was Sir Thomas Broughton, a prominent landowner in this remote corner of Lancashire. He had been a retainer of Richard III since the 1470s, and fought stoutly on his behalf at Bosworth. Escaping from the field after the death of his master, he was one of a number of Ricardian supporters who held out against the government in Furness fells. After the abortive plot in 1486 Broughton Tower provided a temporary refuge for Viscount Lovell, and throughout the following year played a pivotal rôle in the widening network of intrigue centring on Lambert Simnel.[8] If he had not crossed over to Ireland to meet them in Dublin, he was assuredly present at the landing-stage to greet the rebels, and to offer what hospitality his good offices could provide. His brother, John Broughton, and the Huddlestons of Millom, a little further along the coast, were also probably in the welcoming party. Yet the reception cannot have been other than gauche and stilted: language barriers got in the way of communication, and doubtless there were problems of protocol in addressing the prickly earl of Lincoln and the baffled boy-king.

Disappointment was perhaps the order of the day all round. The abbot and convent of Furness, the owners of the harbour and castle, and the lords of much of the surrounding countryside, were probably less than wholehearted in their welcome. This wealthy Cistercian house, which aside from running sheep on the fells ran ships in the Irish trade, was certainly in a position to play more than a token role in the rebellion, but there is no reason to believe that it did more than provide the rebels with food and supplies. Alert to the likelihood of a landfall in the area, the Tudor regime had been careful to bring countervailing pressures to bear, most notably the king's trusted agent, Christopher Urswick, who happened to be the son of a lay-brother at Furness. Among several diplomatic missions to the continent in the first years of Henry VII's reign, Urswick was sent twice to north Lancashire, once late in 1486 to treat with the dissidents at Hornby castle and then again shortly before the invasion to check on possible landing-places. The king likewise enlisted the full weight of papal authority and ecclesiastical influence. On 4 May he wrote to instruct the archbishop of York to have promulgated at Furness and neighbouring Cartmel the papal bulls censuring opponents of his royal title. If all had gone according to the government's plan, the people of the district would have heard from the pulpit, perhaps the very day before the landing of the rebels, the dreadful curse 'by bell, book and candle' being laid on all that make 'new troubles, commotions or stirrings' and who 'help, succour or assist them in word, counsel or deed'.[9]

According to local tradition, the rebels spent their first night in England camped on Swarthmoor near Ulverston, less than ten miles from their landing-place.[10] Disembarkation would have taken some time, and the need to organise assembly-points for recruitment and supply made the going slow at first. From Tuesday 5 June the advance became more rapid, and during the next few days remarkable progress was made. By Friday afternoon the rebel leaders were in Masham, over seventy miles from Furness across difficult countryside. Their route is unclear, and given their speed it is most tempting to assume that they followed the most direct route through Newby Bridge, Kendal and Sedbergh into Wensleydale. There is some reason to suppose, however, that the

Furness Abbey, Lancashire.

rebels might have first headed in a more southerly direction through Cartmel and across the Sands to Carnforth, before veering back up Lonsdale to Sedbergh. This route, though longer, might have been no more arduous than the shorter but less tractable road through and beyond Kendal. The positive evidence for it, however, is limited to the fact that the prior of Cartmel subsequently felt obliged to pay an indemnity of 100 marks to the king, the questionable assumption that Molinet's 'Scanfort' is to be identified as Carnforth, and the rather dubious tradition that the rebels approached Lancaster.[11]

The southerly route could have made strategic sense as well. While the German and Swiss soldiers, many of them mountain-men, would not have found the fells of Furness and Cartmel too daunting, it remains the case that a sizeable army, moving with a baggage-train during the summer, would have sought to keep to the low ground for as long as possible. A decision to move around the jagged coast-line to Cartmel and then across to Carnforth made it possible, as well, to have heavy equipment and bulky supplies transported by water. There could also have been sound military objectives in thrusting southwards. Most obviously, it linked up with Sir James Harrington and his colleagues, who had long defied the Tudor regime from Hornby castle at the gateway to Lonsdale. It would also serve to test the waters in the rest of Lancashire, where there were a number of Ricardian stalwarts like Sir Thomas Pilkington, who certainly joined the rebellion, and the notorious Sir Ralph Ashton, who apparently to the relief of his tenants at Ashton-under-Lyne disappeared around this time.[12] Given their previous record, moreover, it was not wholly inappropriate to probe the loyalty of the Stanleys. In any case this push southwards, at probably little extra cost in terms of time, had the advantage of keeping the king guessing a little longer as to their strategy.

It seems likely that the rebels, therefore, spent the night of 5 June at Cartmel. Sir Robert Harrington, one of the rebels, lived in the locality, and Cartmel priory was very much the family church. The next stage in the move south was a forced march across the Sands to Hest Bank in between Carnforth and Lancaster.[13] It was a common enough thoroughfare, cutting a dozen miles off the route by normal roads. At the right time and with good guides it was not too dangerous, though for strangers to the district, as most of the rebels were, the oratory established on the bankside for the benefit of travellers was scarcely reassuring. In the event the seven mile hike across the mud-flats of the Kent estuary must have been an exhilarating experience, intoxicating in its apparent audacity and natural splendour. From the left side the river Kent flowed gently enough into the bay, but when it was reinforced by the turning tide it would become a savage torrent. Ahead the Lancashire coastline presented a pleasant vista, but further to the right there was again stark evidence of the ferocity of the sea, where the ancient church and tiny fishing-village of Heysham clung desperately to the storm-lashed cliffs.

On reaching firm ground, Lincoln and Schwartz would have needed to set their men immediately in battle array. The major thoroughfare onto which they filed could bring loyalist forces, whether from the south under Lord Strange or from the north under Lord Clifford, rapidly down upon them. If Molinet is read aright, the invading forces met with allies at Carnforth. An important staging-post on the highway, it was a relatively safe as well as an accessible location. Most of the gentry of the district, like the Harringtons and Middletons, were firm opponents of the Tudor regime, and were well-placed to organise from Hornby castle the mobilisation of well-wishers from Lancashire and perhaps even further north. The gathering of all the forces must have been an impressive spectacle, especially with the Germans going through their paces to the sound, novel in England at this stage, of fife and drum. Though it is unlikely that the rebels entered Lancaster, it is possible that supplies were sought in the town. The next goal was Hornby castle, approached perhaps across Swarthdale, where the rebel leaders might have taken their ease on the night of 6 June. Standing sentinel in lower Lonsdale, the castle was admirably placed to protect their rear as the rebels pressed on, doubtless much strung out along the delightful valley of Lune. By nightfall they would have climbed northeastwards and have crossed into Yorkshire near Sedbergh, probably the major assembly-point for Cumbrian recruits like Clement Skelton of Bowness, Alexander Appleby of Carlisle and Nicholas Musgrave of Brackenthwaite. Since Richard Redman, abbot of Shap and bishop of St Asaph, was in some ways implicated in the rising, it might well be that this group of rebels had gathered first at Shap abbey.[14]

Within four days of their landing, Lincoln was leading his men across the Pennine watershed near Baugh Fell, and then down into the lush splendour of Wensleydale. Expectations of support from the men of the valley were high, and were not wholly disappointed. Most of the lords, gentry and yeomen hereabouts were tenants of the lordship of Middleham, who had prospered first in the service of Warwick the Kingmaker and then of his son-in-law Richard III. Under 'Robin of Redesdale' in 1469, the men of the district had ridden southwards to humiliate Edward IV, and, along with other Neville retainers and tenants from Cumberland, had risen again under Henry, Lord Fitzhugh in 1470.[15] More recently, of course, the lordship of Middleham had been the centre of the Lovell plot of 1486. The arrival of 'King Edward' must have been a cause for great rejoicing on the part of the dalesmen, and Middleham castle doubtless echoed again to old Neville battle-cries. The abbey of Jervaulx, which had long enjoyed the protection of the lords of Middleham, also seems to have offered hospitality. Nevertheless Lincoln and his friends did not win the immediate and total commitment for which they had hoped. After the aborted rising of the previous year, the lords and gentry of the region were naturally circumspect. Richard, Lord Fitzhugh, was Lovell's brother-in-law, but his loyalties were by no means clear-cut.[16] Though still a young man, he died later in 1487, so perhaps sickness spared him a difficult decision. It is conceivable, though, that he joined the movement, and later died from wounds. John, Lord Scrope of Bolton, the oldest and most experienced of the local lords, and Thomas, Lord Scrope of Masham, were certainly implicated in the rising, but neither moved with great alacrity.

Nonetheless King Edward and Lincoln were ensconsed at Masham on 8 June, and with them were local squires like Edward Frank of Knighton and Thomas Metcalfe of Nappa. Letters were hurriedly written to potential supporters in Yorkshire and further afield, and agents dispatched to work behind Henry Tudor's lines. Judging from the tone of the letter sent to the mayor and aldermen of York, however, the rebels either did not wish, or were in no position to dictate terms. Claiming that he had come into 'this our realm, not only, by God's grace, to attain our right of the same, but also for the relief and weal of our said realm, you and all our other true subjects, which hath been greatly injured and oppressed' in default of the 'ministration of good rules and justice', the new king, made an appeal for aid and favour, which seemed more designed to arouse sympathy, than to demand obedience.[17]

*   *   *

By this stage Henry VII was on the move, riding out through the gates of Kenilworth castle at the head of a distinguished company of lords and retainers. His intelligence network had worked well. Almost certainly beacon-fires first alerted him to the invasion, but messengers could not have been far behind. Christopher Urswick, who had been inspecting likely anchorages and their defences in Lancashire, was apparently still in the area at the time of the rebels' landing, and rode breakneck to bring authoritative report to his royal master. Certainly on 5 June the king made known his intention to come in a short time to the north 'accompanied with great multitude of his nobility and subjects' for 'the repressing and subduing of the malicious purpose of his great rebels and enemies', and instructed all victuallers in the northern parts to have available at a reasonable price large stocks of bread, ale and other food for man and horse, as they 'intend the weal of his most royal person and of this his realm, and to avoid his great displeasure'.[18] At the same time orders went out for immediate mobilisation at Coventry, and urgent summonses were sent to absent lords to meet him there or perhaps in a week's time at Nottingham.

Even before he left Kenilworth, King Henry and his advisers had made important decisions as to formation and strategy. The duke of Bedford would command the king's battalion, which probably included Welsh veterans of Bosworth like Sir Rhys ap Thomas. The earl of Oxford, the most experienced general, was naturally given command of the 'foreward' or vanguard. Edward Grey, Viscount Lisle, would serve under him, as would a number of younger lords like the earl of Shrewsbury, the earl of Devon and Lord Hastings. The vanguard would have two cavalry 'wings', composed, at first at least, mainly of young gallants from the king's household. The cavalrymen in the right wing, under the command of the queen's uncle, Sir Edward Woodville, Lord Scales, were immediately dispatched north as 'foreriders' to prepare the path for the royal host and to hinder rebel recruitment. Trusting that the Stanleyites under Lord Strange, the earl of Derby's son, would play a similar role west of the Pennines, Lord Scales's cavalrymen were instructed to head into Yorkshire.[19]

In the meantime public order and discipline were to be firmly enforced. On the advice of Archbishop Morton and other counsellors, the king proclaimed a series of regulations, tantamount to declaring martial law. No one, on pain of death, was to rob or despoil the church, or to set hands on the pyx containing the blessed sacrament, or to rob or despoil anyone, or to ravish any nun, married woman, maiden or female servant. More specific to the problems of the hour, no one was to trouble or vex anyone else 'by colour of any offense heretofore done or committed against the royal majesty of the king our said sovereign lord, without his authority and especial commandment', and no one was to take victuals at other than the price set by the clerk of the market or the king's officers. To faciliate mobilisation, no one, under pain of imprisonment, was to take a billet other than that assigned by the king's harbinger, or to harrass in a way persons bringing supplies to the host. Among the troops themselves, quarrelling and fighting at all times, and shouting and horn-blowing after curfew were strictly forbidden. Vagabonds, 'common women' and other camp-followers were to be sent packing, on pain of imprisonment. All the royal forces were strictly enjoined to follow immediately the orders not only of the king but also of the constable, marshal and other officers acting in his name. The members of the royal household were to be especially well-drilled: on successive blasts of the trumpet they were to saddle, bridle and then mount their steeds to wait on the king.[20]

King Henry was wise not to tarry at Coventry. Without doubt the royal entourage had overstayed its welcome in a city which in any case was experiencing a great deal of economic distress and social unrest. For the best part of six weeks the court and many government officials had been quartered in the city and at nearby Kenilworth, and over the preceding week or so dozens of lords and knights with their retinues and levies had been seeking billets in the neighbourhood. Presumably there were some citizens who profited from the increased demand for goods and services, but the majority, whether aldermen required to show their good will through costly hospitality or ordinary townsfolk experiencing congestion, shortages and inflated prices, cannot but have found themselves out of pocket. Then, as the king's regulations reveal, there were all the other problems attendant on the congregation of large numbers of armed men, and of the hustlers, pimps and prostitutes who swarmed around them: the thieving, the fights and the fornication. Coventry would be counting the cost for some time to come.

Strategically it was also time to begin to move north. Even if it were still not certain along which side of the Pennines the rebels were advancing, Leicester would make a more appropriate forward base. After just the one night in Coventry, therefore, he sent the bishop of Winchester to attend his wife and prince, and made provision for their expenses, and then led the main body of his army northwards.[21] The road to Leicester led him within a few miles of Market Bosworth, but whether he took the slight detour needed to take him to the site of his victory less than two years earlier is doubtful. Henry Tudor was not a man to look back. Yet he had good reason at least to pay homage to the dead at the church at Dadlington, and not merely the bold men who had laid down their lives in his cause. His time as king must certainly have inclined him to see more virtue in stance of those of his opponents at Bosworth, who claimed to be doing no more than fighting for their consecrated monarch. As he approached Leicester, it was scarcely possible to hold the dykes against the flood of memories. It was from this town that Richard had sallied forth the morning before the battle, and thither he himself had repaired after his stunning victory. Even now, as Henry led his army across the bridge and through the gates, it was a town haunted by the man he had supplanted. There was the inn in which his rival had spent his last few days as king, there was the bridge over which he rode, there was the inn in which he had lodged, and there was the Greyfriars where his corpse lay mouldering.

Doubtless Leicester put on a brave face as the king and his followers made themselves free of the amenities of the town. Fortunately it was a town which prided itself on its association with the house of Lancaster, an association indeed more deeply rooted and authentic than that claimed by Henry Tudor. Its collegiate church of St Mary was the resting-place of Henry of Grosmont, the first duke of Lancaster, the ancestor of the Lancastrian kings but not of their Beaufort or Tudor kinsmen. It would be interesting to know whether he paused before the tomb on Trinity Sunday to consider the disconcerting fact that the Lancastrian title to the throne in 1399, which was based on Henry IV's descent through his mother, Blanche of Lancaster, necessarily excluded from the succession the issue of John of Gaunt by his subsequent wives. Still, whatever his lineage, Henry Tudor knew how to act as king, and doubtless Trinity Sunday was honoured with a great deal of ceremonial piety. It was also an appropriate time to put into execution his proclamation regarding public order and discipline, and there was a great purge of camp-followers and other unruly elements.[22]

During his time at Leicester the king must have received firm intelligence of the rebels' advance into Yorkshire. He had reason to be alarmed by the speed and resolution of this movement which could trigger a general rising in the north. He now had to wait anxiously to discover how far the contagion of rebellion would spread, and how well lords to whom he had shown favour would repay him. Doubtless it was expected that some of the lords and knights of the Neville and Ricardian connection would stir against him, but what had to be hoped was that the shambling earl of Northumberland would act as a counterpoise and throw his weight decisively behind the Tudor regime. Meanwhile there were other lords who were conspicuous by their absence. Viscount Welles had still not arrived with men from London and the Home Counties.[23] The Stanleys could well be hedging their bets: the earl of Derby was with the king, but Lord Strange, with the immense military resources of Cheshire and Lancashire at his command, could be playing an independent game. Like King Richard in Leicester in August 1485, Henry was beginning to wonder whether he could distinguish between hesitant friends and secret enemies.

*　　*　　*

The city of York was uncertain and divided. Contrary to common assumption, its loyalty to the house of York could by no means be taken for granted. During the civil wars large contingents from York had fought for Henry VI at Wakefield, followed Queen Margaret on her advance on London, and had been slaughtered fighting against the Yorkists at Towton. In all likelihood the civic community was unmoved when Edward IV was driven from the realm in 1470. Certainly, on his return from exile in 1471, the city-gates were held against him until he had humiliatingly affirmed that he had come to recover his patrimony and had no designs on the crown. Even then he was not permitted to remain in the city, and had to march south to confront Warwick the Kingmaker without assistance from this quarter. In so far as the label has any value, York was far less 'Yorkist' than London and several other towns at this time. Nevertheless it does seem that, after this hesitant start, its commitment to the Yorkist monarchy grew in intensity in the 1470s and the early 1480s. Credit for this development must go to Richard III. As the heir to the Nevilles and his brother's trusted lieutenant in the north, he made the region his home and its interests his own. He showed signal favour to York, which through his grace and favour not only received many material gains but briefly enjoyed again a status akin to a second capital.

Understandably, the city of York was at first surly and recalcitrant in its dealings with the Tudor regime. Yet it soon began to adjust to the new order. This process of adjustment was greatly facilitated by the rise to prominence of a new group of aldermen, including Richard York and William Todd, and by the earl of Northumberland's settlement with the king and re-establishment in the north.[24] King Henry's visit to York in April 1486 confirmed both the advantages to be derived from good relations with the crown and the folly of continued resistance. As rumours of invasion and insurrection spread in the spring of 1487, therefore, the mayor and aldermen of York acted with studious loyalty, keeping the government informed of all matters that came to their notice, and taking the initiative in making the city a loyalist stronghold. In response to their appeals for assistance at the end of April, the king wrote to Sir Richard Tunstall and other local knights to move, in the event of an attack, to the defence of York, and also to the constable of Scarborough castle, to send twelve serpentines and supplies of gunpowder. When it became evident that the invasion would not take place on the eastern coastline, the sense of urgency subsided somewhat, but the mayor remained in close communication with the king at Kenilworth. A number of obscure incidents within the city early in May, moreover, suggest that even if the ruling council had reconciled itself to the new regime some of the townsmen at least were less than happy about it. Two tradesmen were reported to the authorities for declaring on separate occasions that the people would not tolerate knights and men-at-arms being brought in to secure the city. Then one night William Welles, a former mayor, was murdered while commanding the watch at Bootham Bar.[25]

For all their foresight and attempts to prepare themselves, the mayor and aldermen must have been startled by the suddenness of the rebels' push into Yorkshire. How far the town walls had been patched up is not known, but certainly the guns had not arrived from Scarborough, since the constable claimed that he had only four, which he could not spare. Fortunately the news of the invasion travelled even faster than the rebels themselves, and the city learned of the landing at Furness within two days. Their source was the earl of Northumberland, though it is not explained how he had heard so soon. Writing from Leconfield on 6 June he declared his intention to resist the rebels, and to come in force to York in four days' time. It is at this point that the speed of the rebels' movement appeared unnerving, because before Northumberland's mobilisation was half complete the new king and his counsellors were writing to York from Masham, only thirty miles away. The city-fathers acted with resolution and efficiency, immediately dispatching copies of the letter to the king, Northumberland and Tunstall, and attending to the safe-keeping of the city. Apparently without waiting for replies, moreover, they wrote to Lincoln and Lovell expressing their determination that 'he whom the said lords called the king, they, nor none of their retinue or company intending to approach this city, should have any entry into the same', and that they would 'withstand them with their bodies and goods, if they would attain so to do'. On the next afternoon, Saturday 9 June, the men deputed to take the letters returned with the news that the rebels were advancing directly southwards through Boroughbridge and would not be approaching York. It was just as well for the city. It was early evening before the Lancastrian diehard, Henry, Lord Clifford, joined the garrison with four hundred men, and not until the next day that Northumberland finally arrived in force.[26]

The earl of Lincoln and his colleagues maintained an alarming momentum. Pausing only briefly in friendly Wensleydale, the rebel host pushed on to join the Great North Road at Boroughbridge on the Saturday, and then advanced south to Bramham Moor, where they camped on Sunday night. Lord Clifford, who had lived under Yorkist rule disguised as a shepherd boy, resolved to strike an early blow for the Lancastrian cause. Sallying forth from York, he established himself at Tadcaster, but in a twilight skirmish with the rebels he was worsted, and losing his baggage-train retreated to the shelter of the city.[27] It was Lincoln's strategy at this stage to keep the main body of his army on the move. In this fashion he could make the running, maintain morale among his troops, and minimise resentment in the countryside through which he passed. He must have realised that his best hope was that his attack, by its very impetus, would skittle the opposition before it could be properly welded together. It was. also imperative for his army to drive a firm wedge between the local loyalists led by Northumberland and the main body of the royal host south of the Trent.

A problem was that there was little time for recruitment. Some well-wishers, unable to mobilise in time to join the main rebel host, presumably never declared themselves. Others perhaps rose in its wake, but settled on some localised or private objective. It is hard to know what to make of the behaviour of the two Lords Scrope, who certainly did not immediately join the rebels in their push southwards. Lincoln's rapid progress across the Pennines had probably found them unprepared, and after the rebel host pressed on from Masham, they would have needed to remain behind to complete the marshalling of men and the organisation of supplies. In terms of overall strategy, moreover, there might have been compensations for what seems like poor co-ordination. It was perhaps proposed that their companies should pin Northumberland and Clifford down in York, and then come in behind the rebels as a rearguard. It is certainly the case that when Northumberland and Clifford set out from York to join King Henry on 12 June, the two Lords Scrope led companies of horsemen to the city, proclaimed King Edward at Bootham Bar, and made an assault on the gates. The mayor of York made a determined defence, but the otherwise unsuccessful attack achieved the object of drawing Northumberland and his 4,000 men back to the city for another vital two days. It was not indeed until noon on Corpus Christi that he felt it opportune to leave. He had certainly not stayed to enjoy the

Bootham Bar, York, besieged by the Lords Scrope in the name of 'Edward VI'.

mystery plays: the mayor and aldermen had wisely postponed them. When he left, according to the York house books, he headed northwards, out-of-danger, not southwards to assist the king.[28]

Where Lincoln and his forces were by this stage is not known. On the morning of 11 June, they were doubtless sorting through the spoils of Clifford's baggage near Tadcaster, but thenceforward there is no firm record of their movements until their arrival, on the eve of the battle, on the banks of the Trent. Perhaps they paused at Bramham Moor to give time for Sir Edmund Hastings and Robert Percy of Scotton to bring in companies from the vale of Pickering and Knaresborough forest. Moving south again, the rebels would have kept as close as possible to the Great North Road, though they would have needed to by-pass centres like Pontefract which were held against them. Probably there was another assembly-point in south Yorkshire for men and provisions. Molinet's 'Scanfort' might not have been Carnforth, but Castleford or a village a few miles outside Doncaster called Stainforth. It is certainly the case that immediately following his notice of the rendezvous at 'Scanfort', the Burgundian chronicler described a clash with Lord Scales and his cavalrymen, who had recently arrived in Doncaster. This incident, again, attests the alarming speed of Lincoln's advance. According to Molinet, the rebels butted the king's 'foreriders' from encampment to encampment for three days, until what was at first an orderly withdrawal became for the cream of the royal cavalry a headlong flight through Sherwood forest to Nottingham. When news of the rout reached York, the city allegedly declared itself for King Edward.[29]

*   *   *

The short week between Trinity Sunday and Corpus Christi brought little joy to Henry Tudor. On Monday morning he left Leicester, still ignorant of the progress the rebels had made in Yorkshire and of the ineffectiveness of the loyalist response. Although he was accompanied by a distinguished company of lords, his own mobilisation of men and resources was far from complete. Regretfully he parted company with Archbishop Morton, his chancellor and most experienced adviser, who could now do no more than commit to his master's service his own company of men-at-arms led by his nephew, Robert Morton. Heading northwards in a sombre mood, King Henry found himself in an increasingly martial ambience. At Loughborough he faced further problems of discipline among his troops, and large numbers of camp-followers were set in the stocks. Crossing into Nottinghamshire on the following day, he doubtless felt that each mile brought him further into hostile country. By nightfall he was at Bunny, where he camped with his troops in a field by the wooded hillside. At day-break on Wednesday 13 June there loomed before him the craggy edifice of Nottingham castle, where King Richard had spent several languid summers, not least in waiting in the months before Bosworth.[30]

It was a beautiful day, apparently 'a royal, and a marvellous fair, and a well-tempered day', but it was a less than happy day for the king. In the first place the advance on Nottingham, only a few miles distant, was not prepared for adequately. King Henry and his men perforce 'wandered here and there a great space of time', because his marshals and harbingers had failed to find adequate lodgings and camping ground. Though his movements and final dispositions are hard to reconstruct, it seems that he advanced beyond Nottingham as far north as Redhill. The herald's report states that after a time the king brought his men 'to a fair long hill', where he set them in battle array, that is with 'a bow and a bill at his back', and then having lodged his vanguard thereabouts he himself returned to lodgings 'a this side Nottingham'. The household accounts actually record a stop at a place called 'Redhill', though oddly for the night of 12 June.[31] The push north of the Trent had much to commend it, not least perhaps to secure for the king the fighting men being raised in Derbyshire and the northwest. More obviously there was the need to give support to the advance party under Lord Scales, who had advanced as far as Doncaster. The crisis came during the night, when the disturbing rumour spread through the royal camp that the king had fled.[32] Apparently rebel agents were responsible for the misinformation, which prompted many levies to take to their heels, but other circumstances, including accurate reports from the north, could have fed the panic. After all the king had pulled back to the south of Nottingham, and retired to undisclosed lodgings.

On 14 June, the feast of Corpus Christi, there was further excitement. King Henry re-appeared and immediately sought to restore confidence in his army. A number of spies and rumour-mongers were given short shrift, and hanged on the ash-tree at the end of Nottingham bridge. After hearing mass in a village church, perhaps at Ruddington, he put his own retinue through its paces. Then Henry again undertook an action almost calculated to disconcert his troops. According to the herald, 'after the trumpets had blown to horse, the king not letting his host to understand his intent rode backwards', that is back in the direction from whence he had come. His unstated purpose was to meet with Lord Strange, who was approaching with a large force from the northwest, and soon after he indeed returned with them, much to the initial fright of his own army, 'all fair embattled'.[33] Perhaps Henry deliberately sought to heighten the drama of the moment as a morale-boosting exercise. On the other hand, this episode, along with the events of the previous night, is an eerie echo of an episode attributed by Polydore Vergil to the Bosworth campaign. Then, too, Henry had disappeared, spending the night in some unnamed gentleman's house, to reappear in the morning with assurances of support from allies.[34] The whole business seems to indicate that the king still felt the need to make doubly sure that he would have at his disposal the Stanleyite forces, which the herald thought were in themselves more than a match for all the king's enemies.

By this stage the royal host had re-grouped west and south of Nottingham, very much in the shadow of the castle. The king's vanguard was tactically withdrawn from its exposed positon on Redhill, and in the afternoon joined with the rest of the army in musters and manoeuvres. Night-fall saw the vast host in a series of encampments around the town, with the king's 'battle' positioned towards Lenton, the earl of Derby's men on the meadows to the left, and the 'foreward' by Nottingham bridge. Despite Henry's efforts to instil discipline and boost morale, there was 'a great scry' during the night and quite a number of desertions. Perhaps the troops had been startled during the night by the precipitate arrival of the 'foreriders' retreating in confusion before the enemy advance. Still, on the following morning, 15 June, the king was allegedly in good spirits, and the speed with which his men put themselves in battle order brought great cheer.[35] Issuing forth from their camps in the shadow of Nottingham castle, the king's army began to move in three great columns, with cavalry wings, in the direction of the morning sun.

King Henry was certainly now in command of a most impressive army. With him were most of the peers most closely associated with the Tudor regime: the duke of Bedford, the earls of Oxford and Derby, Viscount Lisle and Lord Scales. Then there was a group of younger peers: the earls of Shrewsbury, Devon and Wiltshire, Lords Strange, Hastings and Grey of Powis. A large number of the knights and men-at-arms were members of the royal household or an aristocratic retinue. Some were experienced soldiers like Sir John Cheney, Sir James Blount, Sir John Savage and Sir Rhys ap Thomas. Others were young gallants like Anthony Brown, the king's standard-bearer, Charles Somerset, Richard Pole, James Parker, Robert Brandon, Robert Clifford and Edward Norris. Magnates brought from their spheres of influence large companies, drawn in part from their own retinues and in part from their commissions from the crown. The earl of Oxford's influence ensured an impressive turn-out from East Anglia, including Sir Edmund Bedingfield, William Knyvet, George Hopton and John Paston. The king had also recruited extensively among the gentry of the north midlands, with Henry Willoughby, Gervase Clifton, William Pierpont, Edward Stanhope and William Mering joining the king's standard at

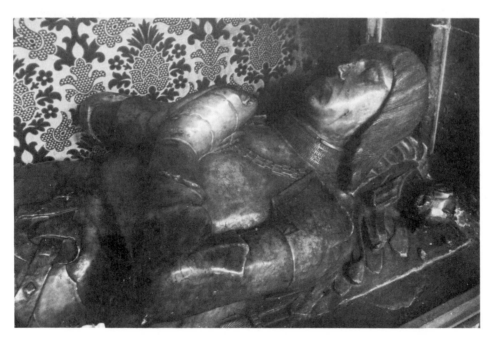

Sir John Savage, (died 1492), Macclesfield, Cheshire.

Nottingham.[36] Naturally, the royal host was largely composed of billmen and archers, some raised privately by nobleman, others raised as levies in the loyal counties of the midlands and the south. The toughest bowmen were among the latest recruits, brought in from the Derbyshire dales by Henry Vernon 'king of the Peak' and from Cheshire and Lancashire by Lord Strange.

The royal host now edged along the south bank of the Trent, presumably attempting on the basis of intelligence received to shadow rebel manoeuvres to the north of the river. Its right wing probably hovered close to Fosse Way, whose strategic importance, anticipated by its Roman builders, was not lost on Henry Tudor. The long, straight road, facilitating communications and allowing the rapid movement of men, was the perfect line from which to command the Trent, especially in the dangerous sector between the fortified crossings at Nottingham and Newark. The two sources disagree as to how far eastwards the king progressed. Polydore Vergil claims that the king proceeded as far as Newark to prevent the rebels having the amenity of the town, and then camped some miles beyond it. The herald, whose eye-witness testimony must be preferred, states that the king spent the night at Radcliffe on Trent, conveniently positioned close to Nottingham and Fosse Way, and directly opposite Lord Lovell's manor of Stoke Bardolph.[37] While it must be supposed that Vergil misunderstood his informants about the king's dispositions before the battle, however, it is reasonable to suppose that, while the king positioned the bulk of his army at Radcliffe, he would have dispatched forces to garrison Newark castle, and perhaps also a cavalry unit to guard against an easterly push into Lincolnshire.

By this stage King Henry could presumably monitor the rebel dispositions quite closely. Perhaps there were suspicious signs of activity in the neighbourhood of Stoke Bardolph, suggesting a crossing there. The king was not short of local intelligence. The lord of the manor of Hoveringham, a few miles further along on the north bank and the site of an important ferry, was none other than the king's stepfather. Yet, with the initiative so completely in the rebels' hands, it was a dangerous moment. Under cover of darkness, the rebels could attempt a breakthrough at any number of points, and steal a march on the royal army in any direction. Throughout the long twilight, the king, his counsellors and his scouts peered through the gathering gloom for the tell-tale signs of camp-fires. It could have been a pleasant night, with the balmy smells of summer and the gentle sounds of the river, but there were few men in the royal host who slept peaceably. During the short hours of darkness, the stillness of the night was broken more than once by cries, alarms and the scurrying of feet. Panic, however short-lived, would ricochet through the camp, as one man waking up in alarm would startle his fellow. For the men to be told they were not under attack was not wholly comforting. Even for the stout-hearted it was hard to sleep to the sound of more of their comrades deserting or, even more disturbing, defecting to the enemy.[38]

*   *   *

To the north of the Trent the earl of Lincoln and his allies probably relaxed somewhat on Corpus Christi. After their success in putting to flight the foreriders of the king's vanguard, their spirits were doubtless high. With north Nottinghamshire cleared of their enemies, they were able to range freely in their search for provisions, perhaps venturing as far as the outskirts of Nottingham. The site of their headquarters at this time is unknown, though a monastery or manor-house in the neighbourhood of Worksop, Mansfield or perhaps even Southwell seems plausible. As for the rank-and-file of the army, it is not too fanciful to imagine them quartered in Sherwood forest, feasting on venison and resting under the greenwood. The English rebels perhaps entertained their comrades with tales of Robin Hood. Richard Harleston, the former governor of Jersey, was a great believer in the longbow, and no doubt sung the praises of English bowmanship.[39] The Irish and Germans had stories to relate of their own heroes, men who fought with axes and crossbows. In the warm sunshine it was hard for the men not to see themselves as part of a great adventure, which would in time be celebrated in song and verse. The name of the redoubtable Martin Schwartz was indeed already finding a place in English folk memory. The refrain of a popular ballad would later run: 'Martin Swart and his men, sodledum, sodledum, Martin Swart and his men, sodledum, bell!'[40]

The day or so around Corpus Christi offered not only a welcome breathing-space for an army which had covered an average of twenty miles a day for over a week, but also provided a crucial, last opportunity to secure reinforcement before the advance into the heartland of England. John, Lord Scrope of Bolton and Thomas, Lord Scrope of Masham had mobilised their retinues by 12 June, when they probed the defences of York, but clearly needed time to catch up with the main rebel forces. At the same time the march south had opened up other potential recruiting-grounds. William Kay, gentleman, rode in from Halifax. The de la Poles still had influence around Hull, their ancestral home, and at least one man from the town, William Hamond, joined the rebellion. South of the Humber, of course, was Lincolnshire, and though the earl of Lincoln only had a few manors in the county he might have hoped that his name would stir some sentiments. To the west of his advance, there was still a chance that some of the lords and gentry of the north midlands and the northwest would ride in, or at least be sufficiently impressed by his showing to resist the summonses of Henry Tudor. Beyond the Trent, there were expectations of support in the whole band of counties running across from East Anglia to Warwickshire.

On the morrow of Corpus Christi, however, it was clear that such hopes were to be disappointed. Judging from the names of the people implicated in the rising, there was no significant mobilisation on the rebels' behalf south of the Humber.[41] Robert Manning of Dunstable and the three Northamptonshire gentlemen called Mallary might well, like Viscount Lovell, have joined the movement prior to the invasion of England. Rather instructively, George Ascough of Nuthall and his brother are the only Nottinghamshire men known to have been involved in the rebellion. While the names of numerous Yorkshire rebels are known, moreover, it is far from certain that they actually took part in the campaign that led to the battle at Stoke. The three lords of the old Middleham connection are cases in point. If Lord Fitzhugh joined the rising, there is no evidence of it, and the documented involvement of the two Lords Scropes is limited to the assault on York. Yet there were certainly quite a number of northerners in the field, and the balance of probability must be that the Scropes, along with other local notables like Sir Thomas Mauleverer, Sir Edmund Hastings, Robert Percy and Thomas Metcalfe, brought in their retinues. Overall, however, it was a disappointing showing. According to an early chronicle, Martin Schwartz felt himself let down by Lincoln and Lovell, who had promised, but failed to deliver substantial support in England.

All that was left was to press on, and to rebuild the momentum which had hitherto proved so successful. A show of boldness could shake loose the flimsy supports holding together the Tudor regime, and might still achieve a Yorkist restoration. On 15 June the rebel forces began to seek the best place to cross the Trent. With time of the essence, and little at all in the way of siege equipment, an assault on Nottingham or even on Newark was judged unwise. Fortunately there were men in the rebel camp who knew the Trent to be fordable in summer, and could find guides as to the safest crossings. In addition to Lovell, with his manor of Stoke Bardolph, there was William Claxton, uncle to Lord Scrope of Masham, whose manor of East Bridgford adjoined the king's camp at Radcliffe.[42] It probably did not take long to settle on Fiskerton, where a northward bend in the river not only offered the best shallows to ford but also perhaps the most secluded point to establish a beach-head. As night fell Lincoln and his troops slowly waded across to the little village of East Stoke.[43]

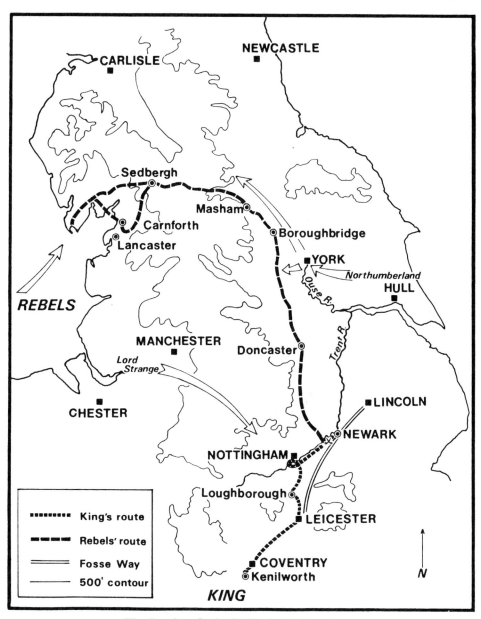

The Road to Stoke Field, 4–16 June 1487

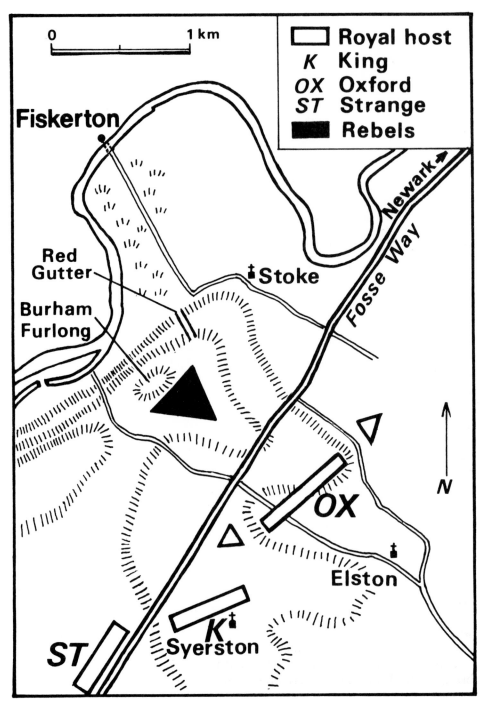

Stoke Field, 16 June 1487

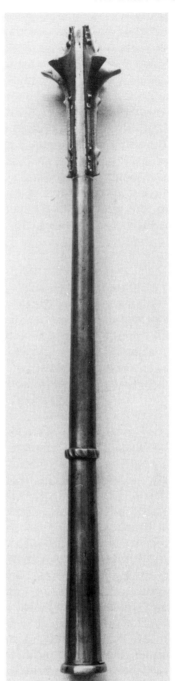

Ballock dagger, North German, 15th century.   *Mace, Italian, late 15th century.*

battalion, and Molinet certainly reports that the rebels fought in a single massed unit.[11] At first the battalion would have been stretched out along the brow of the hill. This position is attested both by André and Vergil, though the latter's implication that the rebels faced northeast towards Newark is clearly wrong.[12] Each segment probably comprised German pikemen, English billmen and Irish foot-soldiers, with small units of arquebusiers, crossbowmen and archers in between. According to Vergil, the more experienced Germans were set in the front line. Mixed companies of heavy cavalry and light horsemen would have been stationed on the wings, ready to relay orders from the commanders who were probably positioned on Burham furlong, and to reinforce the main lines as needed. Lincoln and Schwartz doubtless hoped that at the appropriate time the whole army, to the sound of fife and drum, would file into a wedged-shape phalanx, and with the Germans to the fore would demonstrate on English soil the capacities of a well-drilled infantry formation.

*   *   *

The royal camp around Radcliffe arose at first light on 16 June. Even if there were no definite news of the movements of the rebels, King Henry would have surmised that they had already crossed the Trent. He heard two masses in Radcliffe church. Richard Fox, bishop of Exeter sang the tone. The sprawling and anarchic camp-ground transformed itself rapidly into the shape of a tight and orderly column of men and horses. The trumpets rang out, and the first lines were ready to move. With the vanguard, lodged further to the northeast, already on the road, the king's battalion likewise began its march towards Newark. What path it took is not known. According to the herald, the king and the earl of Oxford drew on the local knowledge of 'five good and true men of the village of Radcliffe, who 'showed where were marshes, and where was the river of Trent, and where were villages of groves for bushments, or straight ways, that the king might conduct his host the better'.[13] While assistance was perhaps required to find the best path from Radcliffe to Fosse Way, this testimony rather implies that the royal host sought to follow the course of the river, at least as far as East Bridgford. It was probably not yet certain where the rebels had made their crossing.

It cannot have been long after dawn, however, that the king's scouts, as they patrolled Fosse Way around Syerston, found the rebels in battle-formation on the ridge beyond. According to the herald's report, the vanguard and probably the main body of the royal army were in place near Stoke by nine o'clock in the morning. There is no clear evidence as to the positions they took up, but it would have made sense for Oxford to lead the vanguard a little way around the escarpment on which Lincoln and the rebels were established. By veering eastwards towards Elston he would open up space for the other battalions of the king's army to be brought into play, deny the enemy army the advantage of fighting with the sun at their backs, and be in a position to cut off its line of retreat to Newark. This reconstruction of the setting of the battle seems to fit with the local traditions and the, albeit limited, archaeological evidence, which point to the fields south of Stoke as the site of the main fighting.

The royal host was immense, comprising perhaps as many as 15,000 men. The order of battle had been long determined.[14] The vanguard under the earl of Oxford, probably some 6,000 strong, included some of the best troops and, if all went well, would bear the brunt of the fighting. It included the retinues of the earl of Shrewsbury, Viscount Lisle and several other lords. In addition, it seems to have been further reinforced by a section of the Stanleyite forces, presumably extra contingents of archers. Protecting its flanks were the cavalry units, also substantially augmented since their first constitution. The right wing, commanded by Lord Scales, was still licking its wounds from its encounter with the rebels north of the Trent. With a great deal more ground to cover, it was substantially larger than the left wing led by Sir John Savage, who had held the same place at Bosworth. The command structure and the morale of the troops alike required some promotions before the battle. Sir Gilbert Talbot, Sir John Cheney and Sir William Stonor were created bannerets, and a number of other worthy gentlemen were knighted, a token of the honours and rewards that would follow a victory.[15]

It is not known how long the front lines stood, grimly seeking to face down their opponents, but each long minute favoured the King Henry, as more of his troops filed into position. In the moments before joining battle, he probably made a speech to his men. Bernard André, his biographer, certainly provides him with a battle-field address, though it is not without anachronism. 'Most trusty lords and most valiant comrades-in-arms, who have experienced with me such great dangers on land and sea', he is alleged to have begun, 'behold again we are assailed against our will in another battle'. He continued by placing the blame for the bloodshed on the 'perfidious' and ungrateful earl of Lincoln and on the 'silly and shameless' duchess of Burgundy, who were unjustly and spitefully in contention with him. He called God to witness that he laboured incessantly for the safety and peace of the realm, and that the Devil himself thwarted his efforts by setting up enemies against him. Nonetheless he promised, presumably without blushing, that 'just heredity will be stronger than their iniquity', and ended, on a strong note, by instructing his men to have faith that 'God Himself, who made us victors in the previous battle, will allow us now to triumph over our enemies', and incited them to attack fearlessly, 'for God is our helper'.[16]

*   *   *

There was no stirring speech from King Edward VI to give heart to the forces arrayed on the hill beside the village of Stoke. In all likelihood the young lad was not even paraded before the troops. The commanders probably recognised the futility of putting on public view the frightened child, whose royal blood many of the rebels must have come to question. Doubtless the leaders of the German and Irish contingents sought to inspire their compatriots by appealing to their traditions of valour, their desire for glory and their sense of honour. The earl of Lincoln, too, mustered all his powers of oratory to raise the spirits of the English-speaking troops. It was no hard matter to expatiate again on the slenderness of the claims of Henry Tudor to the throne, and the strength of the title of Edward Plantagenet. Since they were fighting in a just cause, he would have reasoned, there was no doubt that God would strengthen their arms. By way of more immed-

Composite Gothic field armour, made in North Italy c. 1480, (the right gauntlet, tassets and besagues are modern).

iate comfort, he would perhaps have claimed that the royal host, like the army of King Richard at Bosworth, was composed of unwilling conscripts, and hinted at the presence of secret allies who would declare themselves at an opportune time.

With the massive royal host drawn up in battle order, its banners resplendent and its armour shimmering in the morning sunlight, the rebel forces needed all the encouragement that Lincoln and his colleagues could provide. The vanguard alone looked a formidable enough proposition, but behind it there was the main 'battle' with the king's standard unfurled, and beyond that, in all likelihood, a rearguard. It was hard to estimate numbers, then as now, but the royal host must have appeared close to twice the size of the rebel army. The prospect must have churned the stomachs of the less seasoned soldiers, from the Irish kernes whose combat experience was limited to lightly-armed skirmishes to the northern lads who a fortnight ago were tending sheep on the fells. The veterans of European warfare appraised their predicament more coolly, but with no less foreboding. It was clear that, unless there were undeclared allies among the ranks of the enemy, their chances of victory were slim. Of course, as many rebels and their allies knew from first hand experience, upsets did happen. Quite a number of Schwartz's men had served in the Swiss army that trounced Charles the Bold and the pride of Burgundian chivalry at Morat and Nancy, ten years previously, though on both occasions they had enjoyed the advantage of numbers.[17] Rather ironically, Lincoln and his comrades probably drew comfort of a sort from their memories of Bosworth, when twenty-two months ago the small army of Henry Tudor, itself predominantly non-English, had broken and defeated Richard's large host. As in these battles, the strategy now determined upon involved the concentration of the available troops into a single wedge-shaped phalanx, which might not only withstand the charge of superior numbers but also, given the chance, drive itself into the heart of the enemy lines.

It was with mounting dismay, however, that the earl of Lincoln watched the deliberately slow advance, measured yard by yard, of the king's vanguard, and saw interspaced and interlined with the men-at-arms and billmen unit upon unit and row upon row of archers. There was some consolation in his being able to open the tally, as Schwartz's crossbowmen let fly a volley of bolts to check, however momentarily, their progress. Nevertheless, even before the crossbows had been cranked up to unleash another round, the opposing archers were drawing back their longbows and unleashing a hail-storm of steel-tipped arrows. Finding their range almost immediately, the lines of the king's vanguard paused, frustratingly out of reach of the arquebusiers and Irish bowmen, to subject the rebel host to a withering fire. The casualties were awful. Boxed together in a dense mass, the rebels were a sitting target. Without protective clothing of any sort, the native Irish were decimated. According to Polydore Vergil, the heavy punishment inflicted on them sapped the confidence of the whole army.[18] Seeing the devastation wrought by the king's archers, Lincoln and Schwartz could no longer delay ordering the counter-attack, even if it meant forsaking the advantages of the higher ground. Goaded beyond measure, doubtless swearing to sell their lives dearly, the rebels launched their own fierce offensive. Gathering speed and force with the slope, striving to keep in a massed wedge, they came crashing into the royal vanguard.

* * *

John de Vere, Earl of Oxford,
(died 1513), drawing of his
tomb effigy.

King Henry was now watching the battle from some safe vantage-point, perhaps a church-tower or a windmill at Syerston or Elston. The sound of fife and drum was unnerving in its insistent spriteliness. The tension mounted as the rebels gathered momentum down the incline, and did not break until the shrill cries of men on the run broke into the dull thud of line against line. For the English men-at-arms, billmen and archers there was something strangely unnerving, even blood-curdling, in the combination of German discipline and Irish frenzy. It was bad enough to face the steely professionalism of the Germans and Swiss with their twelve-feet pikes, their razor-sharp halberds and their devilish arquebuses. Their Europe-wide repute was clearly deserved. To make matters worse, however, it was necessary to contend simultaneously with the alarming agility and reckless bravery of half-naked Irish tribesmen. Once carried into the press in the wake of their better-armed comrades, they could wreak havoc with their short bows, darts and daggers. Then there were the gallo-glasses, throwing themselves into the thick of the fighting with their awful double-headed axes. The English rebels, whose battle-cry, 'A Warwick, a Warwick', could doubtless still elicit both respect and fear, completed this potent brew.

For a short while at least the battle appeared to hang in the balance. Henry looked on anxiously as his vanguard reeled under the assault of the rebel army. Fortunately he had seen the earl of Oxford withstand a similar attack at Bosworth, and knew well enough that his position now was in most respects far stronger than in his first battle. Most basically, it was he himself, rather than his adversary, who this time had the battalions in reserve. Of course, there was always the danger that such a determined onslaught could break through the front lines, and put to flight the inexperienced levies in the middle ranks. Gazing at the fierce struggle on the fields before him, he could see signs that Oxford's men were feeling the strain, and that the rebels were gaining ground. Furthermore the sheer audacity of the rebels made him uneasy. His main fear was that Lincoln had an understanding with some of the lords and knights in the royal host, and that at a crucial juncture sections might either defect or simply withhold their support. Looking southwards, he could not have been entirely confident of the reliability of the rearguard, most of whose first loyalty was to the house of Stanley rather than the house of Tudor.

On both sides, however, it was known that time would run for King Henry against the pretender. For a while the king's vanguard seemed to crumble before the fierce onslaught, but with each passing moment the prospects of a spill in the ranks of the royal host diminished. Under Oxford's spirited leadership, the front line managed to absorb the shock, and then to hold itself steady. Springing back with vigour, the seasoned troops at the front pressed in around the rebels who had penetrated their lines, hacking and jabbing and crushing them under feet. Through sheer weight of numbers, they began in turn to push back the main body of the rebel army, which now itself was under threat of disintegration. Given room to move and a clear target, the English archers returned to the fray with a vengeance. Cavalrymen from the wings picked off stragglers. With the initiative back in his hands, Oxford launched the vanguard into a full-scale assault on the rebels as they sought to re-group on the high ground. Though fierce fighting continued for an hour, there was not much of a contest. A number of rebel captains were cut down where they tried to rally their men. A great many common soldiers and quite a few gentlemen took to flight, scampering over the hill towards the Trent. According to an old tradition, there was much blood spilled in Red Gutter, a narrow ravine running down the river, where many fugitives were cut off and butchered.[19] Only grim despair and professional vanity kept some of the rebels and their allies fighting. Around their standards, knots of diehard Yorkists and proud landsknechts fought on to the bitter end. If the German and Swiss standard-bearers were worthy of their hire, they died, as was their custom, with their blood-soaked standards draped around their bodies.[20]

*   *   *

By the time King Henry arrived at Burham Furlong, the highest point on the escarpment and the likely site of the rebels' command-post, the carnage was complete. The casualties were appalling. The king's host itself had probably lost hundreds of men, though apparently none of name. Lincoln's army, for its part, had been decimated, with 4,000 or more rebels lying dead in the field, many, according to Molinet, shot through with arrows like hedgehogs.[21] Few of the lightly armed Irish could have survived the merciless rain of arrows and then the relentless harrying of cavalry lances. The English rebels and their German allies also suffered heavy losses, but quite a number seem to have survived the battle to be captured in the field or in flight. An air of mystery surrounds the fate of two of

The Red Gutter, scene of many deaths after the battle.

the leaders. The tale is told that Sir Thomas Broughton made his way back to Furness, where he spent the rest of his days incognito on a sheep-farm in the fells. The disappearance of Viscount Lovell was widely commented on in the chronicles, where it was speculated that he had perhaps been drowned seeking to cross the Trent. A more grisly end was postulated in the early eighteenth century, when a skeleton was discovered walled up in Minster Lovell castle.[22] None of the sources, however, give cause to doubt that the three main commanders, Thomas Fitzgerald, Martin Schwartz, and the earl of Lincoln all perished in the field. According to Polydore Vergil, the king was angered rather than pleased to find Lincoln dead. Wishing to get to the bottom of the whole conspiracy, he had specifically ordered that he should be taken alive. Rather understandably, the soldiers on the ground, seeing him as the focus of resistance, killed him to spare further bloodshed. The boy-king was happily taken alive by an enterprising squire called Robert Bellingham.[23]

The battle was all over in three hours, presumably before noon. The king's standard was firmly planted on the crest of the hill. The victorious but weary troops cheered King Henry, and he in turn congratulated them and led them in prayers of thanksgiving. After briefly looking into the lifeless face of the 'perfidious' Lincoln, he resolved to put as much space as was practicable between himself and the carnage. Molinet claims that he did not even dismount until he was well away from the battlefield. Presumably he left the mopping up operations to some reliable commander. Cavalrymen were dispatched in all directions to run down fugitives, and in the days following several hundred were rounded up. Arrangements were speedily set in train for the burying of the dead. Great trenches were dug in the hot afternoon, into which hundreds of corpses, already stinking and fly ridden, were thrown. The fate of the bodies of chief protagonists is not known. Given the need to pre-empt rumours of his escape from the field, it would have been advisable to put Lincoln's body on display in town, as had been done with Richard's corpse after Bosworth. Legend has it, however, that he was buried, with a willow stave driven through the heart, near where he fell, and that his resting-place at Stoke was long marked by a clump of willow trees.[24]

Sometime in the early afternoon, therefore, the king, his retinue and at least a portion of his victorious army arrived at Newark. Relieved that the war had stopped short of their own door-steps, the townsfolk were happy to fête their triumphant prince and contribute 200 marks to his fighting fund. Henry, for his part, was in high spirits. It was perhaps at Newark that he created additional bannerets, including Sir Edmund Bedingfield, Sir Richard Croft, Sir James Blount and Sir Humphrey Stanley, and knighted a couple of dozen of the young squires, including his standard-bearer Anthony Brown, who had distinguished themselves in the battle. Nonetheless, there was still much business to transact. Letters were dispatched to lords and communities throughout the realm informing them 'how Almighty God had sent the king victory of his enemies and rebels, without death of any noble or gentleman on or part'. The mayor and aldermen of York received tidings at around 3 o'clock on Sunday morning, and immediately proceeded to York minster where the clergy sung the psalm *Te Deum Laudamus*.[25]

After only one night at Newark, Henry led his army to the city of Lincoln, an appropriate place perhaps to celebrate publicly his triumph over the errant earl. There was a suitably splendid reception, though the civic records provide evidence of last-minute concern about the catering. It was originally proposed that there would be six capons, six fat pike and three dozen geese, but the unavailability of geese or any wild fowl at this season led to their being replaced by twenty mutton sheep and two fat oxen. In his description of the clergy of a great church processing out to greet the king, Molinet was probably referring to the canons of Lincoln cathedral. Henry, in his turn, led the citizens in a round of public thanksgivings and celebrations. He saluted the Virgin Mary, and laid a standard before the image of St George. He also sent standards to the shrine of Our Lady at Walsingham, in fulfilment of a vow he had made at Easter. The parsimonious king paid for some at least of the wine that flowed freely at this time. William Bele, a Lincolnshire vintner, later received £42 for wine purchased for the victory celebrations.[26]

King Henry kept together the bulk of his army for a couple of days after Stoke Field. His triumph could not be considered complete until all who had borne arms against him were in his power. Large numbers of rebels captured in the field or in flight were brought to him at Lincoln. The German mercenaries were sent packing. To lose face and go without pay was punishment enough for the proud mercenaries. The surviving Irish and some of the English were hanged. Most English men of name, however, seem to have been spared, though presumably after making full confession, offering excuses and assurances for

Spur found on the battlefield at Stoke.

future behaviour, and making financial composition. Though committed to prison, Lord Scrope of Masham, Edward Frank of Knighton, and Rowland Robinson, yeoman, all kept their lives. The fines paid could be considerable: Thomas Metcalfe had paid the king 1,000 marks by the end of the year, while William Claxton paid 200 marks and Philip Constable of Flamborough £100.[27]

At the same time, in addition to congratulations and affirmations of loyalty, Henry received some disquieting news from various parts of the kingdom. The north remained dangerously disaffected, and a full-scale military expedition was immediately planned for later in the summer. In ordering the muster and array of an army, however, he specifically exempted the men who had served in the Stoke campaign, who were now sent back to their homes.[28] It was perhaps at Lincoln, moreover, that Henry was appraised of the mischief caused in the south by the rumours of his flight or defeat. In London the misinformation had prompted a number of Yorkists and other trouble-makers to sally forth from the sanctuaries of Westminster and Martin le Grand, and, shouting 'Long live Warwick! To King Edward!' to pillage supporters and servants of the king. One item of news, however, brought wry satisfaction to Henry, and was later passed on for the delectation of Pope Innocent VIII. John Swit, one of the rabble-rousers, scoffed at the ecclesiastical censures applied against opponents of the Tudor regime, and crowed that the 'whole anathema' has recoiled on the heads of the men who obtained them from Rome. In the midst of his sneering and jeering, however, he was apparently struck down dead, his face as black as soot.[29] To Henry Tudor, at least, no reasonable person could doubt that God was on his side.

8 The Significance of 1487

It was altogether a strange affair. There was much that the king could not understand, but then there was a great deal that was beyond understanding. After the months of mounting tension, and after the bloodshed of the battle itself, it must have been a curious experience for him to come finally face-to-face with the solemn ten-year-old who had contended for his crown. How the interview proceeded is not recorded. What is known is that, in time at least, Henry came to see a comic side. While Lambert Simnel was imprisoned for a while, first at Newark and later at the Tower of London, he was not treated seriously enough to warrant real punishment. For a time it was proposed, in view of his having been anointed in Dublin, to set him to the priesthood, but the plan came to nothing. Instead the boy remained in the royal household, a living token of the magnanimity of the king and the folly of his opponents. Educated as a Plantagenet prince, young Lambert probably had what it took to advance at court. Over the years he moved from the kitchens to the more exalted status as king's falconer. He probably married and had children. He was still alive in 1525, when he attended the funeral of Sir Thomas Lovell, one of the few knights then alive who had fought at the battle of Stoke.[1]

As the events of 1487 receded in memory, in fact, this tendency to make light of the whole business became general. While the near-contemporary sources are for the most part terse and sober notices of the rebellion and its defeat, most of the later accounts and allusions seem to relish the manifest curiosities of the affair. Fairly soon after the battle of Stoke, Martin Schwartz and his men were gently mocked in the refrain of a popular song. John Skelton in his poem, 'Agaynste a Comely Coystrowne', viewed the Simnel and Warbeck impostures as gross examples of human vanity. For Nicholas, Lord Howth, in his self-promoting narrative, the coronation in Dublin was a matter for jest and merriment. Even the king is alleged to have offered the wry comment that in the end the Irish would finish up crowning apes. In this respect Polydore Vergil, who writes of the whole impersonation as a function of the fickleness and dizziness of the people, is probably only reflecting the view commonly held in the later years of Henry VII's reign. His comments, in turn, became the basis for further moralising and sardonic reflection on human nature on the part of Edward Hall, Francis Bacon and Thomas Gainsford.[2]

Nevertheless the problem remains of assessing the significance of the conspiracy and rebellion. A first approach is to consider their immediate impact on Henry VII's conduct of affairs in 1487. The nature of his response during the critical months most obviously provides important clues as to the degree of seriousness perceived at the time. A broad-ranging survey of the achievement of security and stability in the first decade of his reign, however, is also necessary for a proper understanding of the significance of this early crisis. Generally regarded as the last battle of the Wars of the Roses, Stoke Field naturally merits consideration as a watershed of sorts in English political history. It is certainly worth discussing the impact of the whole episode on the policies of Henry VII and his advisers, and pondering the ways in which the experience of the rising and the circumstances of its suppression prompted or made possible new initiatives in government, and collectively shaped the character of the early Tudor regime.

*　　*　　*

However it was later viewed, the rising of 1487 was, at the time, taken very seriously indeed. For three months, from the middle of February to the middle of May, the conspiracy and the threatened invasion were the main preoccupation of Henry VII and his government. For the best part of the following month the king was in harness and the nation was in arms. Even after the enemy army had been annihilated at Stoke, there was no immediate respite. Throughout the long summer the king moved methodically through areas of possible disaffection. First, he retraced his steps to Coventry and Kenilworth, as if feeling the need to make sure of his ground in Warwickshire and the west midlands before venturing north of the Trent. It was not until the end of July that he advanced from Nottingham into what had been rebel-held territory. He spent the best part of a month in York and other centres, holding court, receiving oaths of loyalty, punishing offenders. It was felt necessary to advance as far as Newcastle upon Tyne before heading back southwards. Even then he moved slowly and cautiously. He spent the second anniversary of the battle of Bosworth on the road between Richmond, whence his first title had been derived, and Jervaulx abbey, where Abbot Haslington sought a general pardon, presumably for his complicity in the rising.[3] From Yorkshire he moved obsessively back to Warwickshire, though perhaps this time largely to be on hand for further intelligence from Ireland. It was not until October that he finally returned to the tasks of civilian government in the capital, and to domestic life to his new 'Richmond' on the Thames.

Fortunately the re-establishment of order was not wholly dependent on the king's presence. Throughout the campaign many lords and gentry committed to the Tudor regime laboured in their own bailiwicks to counter rebel activities and to enforce obedience, and after the victory at Stoke such loyalists presumably worked with greater vigour and more effective co-ordination. The king cannot have had too many anxieties about London. Even when the rumour that he had been slain brought a crowd of Yorkists into the streets, the civic authorities seem to have had little trouble in taking control of the situation. He must have been in some ways consoled, as well, that there had been no break-outs from the Tower of London. Thomas Howard, earl of Surrey, a prisoner since his capture at Bosworth, was given the opportunity to escape to join the rebels, though possibly by an agent provocateur. He wisely declined. Certainly, within a fortnight of his victory, the king felt confident enough to send Lambert Simnel to the capital, and according to an early annalist he and the real Warwick were paraded together at St Paul's on 8 July, Relic Sunday.[4]

By the same token, the king's officers and other elements loyal to the regime had begun the work of pacifying the north before the king crossed the Trent at the end of July. The earl of Northumberland, Lord Clifford and Sir Richard Tunstall, all of whom had made efforts to contain the rebellion, doubtless moved with even greater assurance and expedition to restore order. On 23 June Northumberland wrote to Sir Robert Plumpton pointing out the presence in his bailiwick of numerous gentlemen and commoners who 'hath rebelled against the king, as well in their being at this last field, as in relieving that were against the king's highness', and charging him to find, arrest and imprison at Knaresborough castle, John Pullen and Richard Knaresborough.[5] On occasion there was armed resistance. Thomas Portington, who was accused of aiding the rebels, disregarded letters sent under the privy seal for his surrender, and with drawn sword fought to his death against James Legh, serjeant at arms, and six armed servants.[6] Nevertheless the king's delay in coming north gave plenty of time for local gentlefolk to close ranks, and to put the best possible complexion of their involvement in the rising. The Lords Scrope were both able to argue plausibly that they had been forced by their tenants to take part in the rising, and were dispatched for safe-keeping to castles in southern England. Certainly it was the case that few men of name from Yorkshire were executed or attainted. For the most part the king had to settle for fines and good behaviour bonds, which increasingly kept the lords in thrall but failed to win the hearts of the commons.

The king could do even less about Ireland. A major consideration in his moves to Warwickshire both after the battle and after his visitation of the north was perhaps its suitability as a place from which to monitor developments in Dublin. For some time after the news of Stoke Field was received in the lordship, the earl of Kildare remained defiant, using the resources of the crown to cow loyalist forces. The king could do little more than continue his earlier policy of giving heart to the resistance made by the Butlers and their allies, and towns like Waterford. One of the few positive steps taken was the dispatch of a letter from Kenilworth on 5 July informing the pope of the 'miracle' in London and pressing him to proceed against the archbishop of Dublin and other Irish prelates who had incurred censure by crowning the pretender and assisting the rebels.[7] It was perhaps at Warwick castle, some time in September, that the king finally received news of Kildare's willingness to come to terms.

By this stage King Henry and the court were able to relax somewhat. No one was in a hurry to return to the pestilential air of London, and there was plenty of sport in the Warwickshire woodlands. Henry himself doubtless found it eminently satisfying to have the people of Warwick bear some of the costs of maintaining his swollen retinue. As guardian of the young earl of Warwick, he was already in control of his estates, and was keen to recoup from them some of the heavy expenses of recent times. To his great satisfaction, as well, the wealthy dowager countess of Warwick decided around this time to make the king her heir. As if to mark his conquest of hearts and minds, John Rous of Warwick, the self-appointed champion of the Warwick interest, revised his *Historia Regum Angliae*, replacing his eulogy of Richard III with a vitriolic attack likening him to Antichrist. He then referred to the improved conditions in Ireland, and by cannily noting that Henry was the sixth not the seventh lord of Ireland of this name, he negated at a stroke the force of the Irish prophecies associated with his royal title. He concluded with a fulsome salute to Henry VII and Prince Arthur.[8]

At the languid end of this long summer, however, some members of the king's retinue were growing restless, eager to combine in their own fashion dalliance and fortune-hunting. The most eligible heiress in the vicinity was Margery, daughter of John Beaufitz, now the widow of a wealthy draper from Coventry, and one of the most dashing squires in the royal household was Robert Bellingham, who had recently distinguished himself at Stoke by capturing Lambert Simnel. Quite probably a romance had begun earlier in the summer, but on their return from the north, Bellingham and his friends resolved to abduct the young lady from her father's house at Temple Balsall near Solihull. On 2 September they moved in at supper time, assaulting Beaufitz, ordering other members of the household to 'sit still, for he that stirreth shall die', and carrying Margery off into the night. When the king heard of the affair he was apparently furious, and for some time afterward put the full weight of royal authority behind the prosecution of the men responsible. Bellingham was in prison for a while, but there is much that is mysterious about the whole affair. At least one of his associates was an old Neville retainer, and one of his fellow-prisoners was the attainted rebel, Rowland Robinson. There was a happy ending: Bellingham later achieved distinction in the king's service, and his bride seems to have been happy with the match.[9]

This episode illumines well the tight-rope that the king had to walk in this year of crisis. Obviously he had to deal firmly with the men who had raised rebellion against him. On the other hand, he could not be so severe in his punishments as to alienate whole districts and to provoke diehard resistance. By autumn it was apparent that most deliquent lords and gentlemen would escape not only execution but also attainder. During August royal pardons were granted to a large number of northerners associated in the rising. On 27 August, when friends stood surety that he would not leave Wallingford castle, Lord Scrope of Masham was clearly under the loosest supervision.[10] By the time that parliament met in November, there were only twenty-eight men attainted, few of whom were major landowners. The most notable was the earl of Lincoln, but only his own lands, as opposed to the de la Pole patrimony, were confiscated. What this meant, of course, was that there were few spoils with which to reward the king's own supporters. The contrast between the massive land-transfer after Richard III's suppression of the southern rising of 1483 and the trickle of patronage following the victory at Stoke is most striking.[11] One of the few beneficiaries was Sir John Turberville, knight-marshal, who acquired estates forfeited by Sir Henry Bodrugan and John Mallary.[12] The danger for King Henry, of course, was that in appeasing his enemies he was disappointing his friends. Very probably there were many young men in the royal household who felt aggrieved at not making better pickings, and who made their feelings known in self-help schemes like Bellingham's abduction of the Beufitz heiress, and ultimately in a mysterious plot that came menacingly close to the king's own person.

King Henry, of course, had learned the lessons of the 'tyranny' of Richard III. He was resolved not to appear merely as the leader of a victorious faction, ruling by military might. To this end, he was as severe in imposing discipline on his own followers as he was restrained in exacting retribution from his opponents. It was not enough to proceed with the full penalties of the law against Robert Bellingham. A whole new act was framed to reinforce and extend existing legislation on abduction. The parliament of November 1487, which passed this statute, opened to a schoolmasterly discourse from the chancellor, Archbishop Morton, on the evils of discord. While an important item of business was the act of attainder passed against Lincoln and a score or so of his accomplices, the largely government-directed assembly spent more time dealing with people who thought themselves above the law, predominantly the king's own supporters, than with the rebels. Indeed there is evidence that while parliament was sitting relations between King Henry and some of his servants reached crisis point. A group of malcontents in the royal household gathered on 15 December in a seditious assembly, and conspired to murder certain of the king's counsellors. Parliament was immediately prevailed on to give full statutory authority to a commission, comprising the steward, treasurer and controller of the household, to investigate offences 'occasioned by the envy and malice of the king's own household servants'.[13] Needless to say, these extemporised statutes are very much of a piece with the celebrated but misleadingly named 'Star Chamber Act' of 1487, in which the king's campaign against powerfully-supported and thus politically sensitive lawlessness found most comprehensive expression.

The dangerous year of 1487, however, ended on a more positive note. The coronation of Henry's queen was long overdue. With peace restored to the realm, the ceremony provided a unique opportunity to make further capital from the hackneyed themes of unity and reconciliation. Plans for the coronation were first made at Warwick in September, and in the following month preparations were well in hand for the associated tournaments. King Henry and Elizabeth of York remained at Warwick until late October, perhaps deliberately heightening the drama of their return to the capital for the opening of parliament. When the great moment came, the Londoners staged a spectacular reception for the king who had left the city in such uneasy circumstances seven months earlier. Perhaps for the first time since the death of Edward IV, there was real and well-founded optimism in the air. The parliament of 1487 heartened men who looked to the interests of the 'common weal'. Far from registering a partisan triumph, it launched a broadly-based assault on the arrogance of power. Finally, there was the splendour of the coronation ceremony, watched from a special box by King Henry and his mother. The attendance-list testifies to the broadening base of the ruling elite. The men who won Henry Tudor the crown are still prominent, from the king's uncle to the gallant knights, in four groups of four, who took turns to carry the queen's canopy. The coronation ceremony, however, was very much a national occasion, and the presence of scores of other lords and county notables, many

Seal of Jasper Tudor, Duke of Bedford.

accompanied by their wives, attests a new breadth, rootedness and stability to the Tudor regime.[14]

From the record of events in 1487 it is clear that Henry VII believed that the conspiracy and rebellion presented a formidable challenge to his rule. For some time after his victory at Stoke he remained extremely suspicious and circumspect. Among the slain, it is true, there were the earl of Lincoln, the most impressive of the Yorkist princes, and Thomas Fitzgerald, apparently the most enthusiastic Anglo-Irish conspirator. Yet he could not assume that he had rooted out opposition. The elusive Lovell had vanished, perhaps escaping to fight another day. Richard Harleston, who made his escape to the court of the duchess of Burgundy, was to re-emerge in a later conspiracy.[15] Quite a number of other Yorkist lords and knights, through timely submissions and imaginative excuses, had been allowed to buy their pardons. Their future loyalty could scarcely be depended upon. The king also knew well enough that there were other supporters of the rebellion, now keeping their heads down, who given the chance might well have declared themselves. The whole strategy of the rebels had suggested that there were secret allies, perhaps even in the royal camp. Lincoln certainly had agents behind the royal lines. There were the men spreading rumours of the king's flight, the traitors who acclaimed Edward VI in London, and perhaps the men who tempted the earl of Surrey to escape from the Tower of London.

King Henry's belief that there were secrets that he had still to fathom was obviously a problem in itself. There is reason to suppose that aspects of the authorship and aims of the imposture remained obscure. The ludicrousness of Lambert Simnel notwithstanding, the king certainly had to acknowledge the very real danger that powerfully-backed pretence could present to his rule. In the conspiracy of 1487, fortunately, he had clear advantages. Fairly early on, he seems to have gained some inside information on the plot, and was able to produce the real earl of Warwick, or at least a credible impersonation of him. After capturing the impostor at Stoke Field, Henry wisely refused to allow his government to appear embarrassed by him. Even before the king's return to London, Simnel was put on public display in the capital, at one stage at least with the real Warwick. Thenceforward the boy was a reasonably familiar figure in the royal household. Yet Henry could not expect an end to this sort of trouble. The whole affair highlighted the continued existence of one Yorkist prince in the Tower of London, and there would be further attempts to liberate or impersonate him. At the same time there was the residual problem of the rumoured survival of the sons of Edward IV. As long as their fate remained mysterious, the king would obviously remain vulnerable to men claiming knowledge of them. In the following years there would be several such conspiracies, sometimes even taking root in his own household. While the challenge of Perkin Warbeck would be formidable, however, it would be faced by a monarch better-prepared and more strongly established for his first brush with an impostor.

The rising of 1487, moreover, revealed the tenuous nature of the Tudor regime's hold on many parts of the realm. Even in the Home Counties there were enclaves of intrigue which were difficult to probe. The king had his spies, but in the households of noblemen, in monasteries and colleges, in sanctuaries and the suburbs of towns, plots could be hatched undetected. It was most alarming to discover in 1489 that Abingdon abbey, a major house in Berkshire, had been a centre of Yorkist conspiracy from the outset.[16] The north presented a different kind of threat, less insidious but potentially more dangerous. Even after the king's autumn progress, the region was sullen rather than subdued. In 1489 there was a serious tax-revolt, which had dynastic overtones. Seeking to disperse the rebels, the earl of Northumberland was deserted by his retainers and slain, allegedly, in part, for his 'disappointing' Richard at Bosworth.[17] It is likely, too, that the West Country presented problems of a similar sort. Some Cornish gentlemen had taken part in the rising of 1487, and dynastic and regional issues combined to make the region a major trouble-spot for another decade. Even more out of control were the off-shore lordships. The march of Calais remained loyal during the crucial phases of the rebellion, but there were rumours later in the year that it might be betrayed to the French. The Channel Islands, with the defection of the locally well-regarded Richard Harleston, were in danger of slipping out of the English orbit.[18] Above all, of course, the lordship of Ireland was a major thorn in the government's side. For quite a few months after the defeat of the rising in England, the Great Kildare still defied the government, with only Waterford and a few other towns remaining loyal. It would be a matter of priority to restore, however notionally, the administration in Dublin to its proper allegiance.

Given the weakness of its hold on the realm in 1487, the Tudor regime clearly had reason to fear foreign attack. Wholehearted support for a Yorkist prince by a European power, coupled with a direct attack on its borders or overseas possessions, could well have toppled Henry Tudor. In this respect the king was fortunate. While the rebellion of 1487 was indeed powerfully assisted by the dowager duchess of Burgundy, and that the best troops were her mercenaries, nonetheless her involvement in the movement was very much a freelance operation. Maximilian, king of the Romans, had no interest in supporting the enterprise by open war, and in fact seems to have wished for English friendship. Fully occupied with suppressing revolt in Flanders, recovering border towns lost to the French, and making a bid for the hand of the heiress of Brittany, he was in any case dangerously over-extended. For their part, the rulers of France and Scotland still had hopes of Henry Tudor, whom they had helped to the throne, and were too pre-occupied to turn his weakness to advantage. The French, preparing for the final struggle over Brittany, actually dispatched emissaries to seek English support in June 1487. In Scotland, James III and a group of disaffected lairds were approaching a final showdown. At the time when Henry VII confronted and survived his first great test, he was clearly fortunate that neighbouring princes felt themselves to be approaching crises in their own careers.

*   *   *

At the end of 1487 Henry VII sat much more securely on the throne than at the beginning of the year. From some angles the challenge he had faced might have appeared insubstantial. From other perspectives, however, it had loomed, and continued to loom, menacingly. In the 1490s, as other pretenders and highly-placed conspirators emerged to disturb his peace, it must have seemed as if the triumph at Stoke Field, like his victory at Bosworth, had been of little account. Yet the ordeal he had faced was not in vain. His self-confidence and his stature in the realm inevitably grew from his having passed it. At the same time he had been able to learn a great deal from his trial, which tested so many aspects of statecraft, and which revealed so clearly the strengths and weaknesses of his position. Needless to say, he had not the means to put all his lessons to effect, still less immediate effect. Yet it can perhaps be claimed that from 1487 the seeds of his distinctive political style, evident in some degree from 1485, began to assume recognisable form.[19]

The crisis of 1487 certainly helped King Henry to assess the quality of his ministers and servants. At the outset the inexperienced prince presided over an uneasy coalition, among whom his friends from exile formed the only coherent group. In the first year there were the inevitable shifts and adjustments, but what is remarkable is the emergence in 1486–7 of a team of courtiers, administators and soldiers, that would remain virtually unchanged for a decade or more. The chancellor, keeper of the privy seal and the treasurer in the months leading up to the battle of Stoke, namely Morton, Richard Fox and John, Lord Dinham, would all still be holding their offices in 1500, and their close identification with their respective offices would contribute powerfully to the stability and efficiency of the system.[20] It seems reasonable to imagine, as well, that facing the challenges of 1487 together helped to forge the sort of group identity among the new ruling élite that had previously been the preserve of Henry Tudor's fellow exiles. Moving beyond the inner circle of counsellors and servants, moreover, it is clear that the king's wide-ranging movements and lengthy sojourns in the provinces in 1486–7 accelerated the process by which the Tudor regime took root in the countryside. During this time, most especially in the Stoke campaign and the subsequent northern expedition, Henry met, and established constructive relations with, the leaders of many local communities, and gained the sort of knowledge of people and places for which his father-in-law had won praise. The long list of knights, among whom were the heads of old-established families from all counties of the realm, who attended the queen's coronation in November 1487, is testimony to his success in re-establishing strong ties of interest and co-operation between court and country.[21]

The experiences of this time seem also to have shaped the king's approach to the tasks of administration. For the greater part of 1487, Henry VII was on the move, attending to political and military crises. Inevitably his role in the direction of the campaign developed in him qualities of leadership, habits of command, a broad understanding of government. Remote from the routine processes of government, he became all too painfully aware and intolerant of their cumbersomeness and inflexibility. The acute shortage of ready money at a time when its immediate availability and careful deployment meant the difference between success and failure was an experience he never forgot. The debacle of the Garter feast in 1487 perhaps represented the nadir of his financial fortunes, and the lack of accessible funds must surely have constrained his military planning

Sir Reginald Bray, (died 1503) from the stained glass at Great Malvern Priory.

and operations. His enterprising financial adviser, Reginald Bray, saved the day, raising 6,500 marks in loans on the king's behalf. This money was processed and made available to the king through the royal chamber, and the exigencies of campaigning, if not the logic of recent administrative history, must have revealed to the king the value of this office. From this time onwards, Henry made considerable progress in improving the financial position of the monarchy, not least through a resumption of crown lands in the parliament of 1487, but his most striking achievement was to bring more revenue into the purview of the chamber, where it could be more carefully scrutinised and more sensitively deployed. After the collapse of the rising of 1487, it is significant that the fines paid by rebels and the lands confiscated from them were immediately assigned to the chamber, setting the scene for the revival and expansion of the office's role in royal finance. In this respect it seems apt that the first of the series of surviving books of chamber receipts dates from July 1487, and that its very first entry records the receipt of 200 marks from the town of Newark.[22] All in all, the campaign leading to the battle of Stoke was a rigorous apprenticeship in the craft of personal monarchy.

The experience of moving around his troubled realm, where for generations lawlessness and political instability had seemed to feed on each other, likewise increased Henry VII's resolve to confront the problem of inadequate law-enforcement. With his own troops, he was a firm disciplinarian, clamping down on high-spirited young squires and clearing the camp of unruly elements. More generally, the king was insistent that disturbers of the peace should immediately feel the full weight of the law, and groups of counsellors were doubtless deputed to deal summarily with offenders, however eminent in their own community. In important respects, therefore, his activities on campaign not only revealed the dimensions of the problem but also suggested some approaches to the solution. In the parliament of November 1487 a whole range of laws were passed which addressed, a little scatter-gun style, the age-old evils of riot, maintenance, corruption and abduction. Most especially, he secured the establishment of a regular conciliar tribunal with statutory authority to proceed expeditiously and with the full rigour of common law against serious disturbances of the peace. The court set up under the 'Star Chamber Act' could well have been more active in the early years than has often been supposed. It is noteworthy that among the notables sternly corrected in the associated clean-up were men, like Viscount Lisle, Lord Clifford and Sir Henry Willoughby, who had served the king well at the battle of Stoke. Even if disappointingly few prominent offenders are known to have been brought before the new court, it might well have achieved most simply as a deterrent.[23]

His policies towards the hereditary aristocracy, evident to some degree in 1485, became more explicit in 1487 and the years following. Of course, it is simply not the case that the king was anti-noble. It was perhaps his good fortune rather than his shrewd management that no 'overmighty subject' emerged to cause him strife: neither he nor the queen had brothers, and many of the great lineages of the fifteenth century had become extinct or were headed by minors. At the same time the king was wholly traditional in his view of noblemen as jewels in his crown, and crucial supporters of royal authority and the social order in the provinces.[24] Like his father-in-law, he was content to see loyal peers develop, re-establish or consolidate regional spheres of influence: the duke of Bedford in Wales, the earl of Oxford in East Anglia, and the earl of Derby in the northwest. As regards the north, he seems to have feared, not so much aristocractic power, as the consequences of a political vacuum left after the dismantling of the Neville connection and the waning of Percy influence. After Northumberland's murder in 1489 it is instructive that he rapidly advanced the earl of Surrey as the king's lieutenant in the region. On the other hand, the king seems to have become less tolerant of nobles who were unwilling or incapable of playing a constructive role at court or in their local communities. By the end of his reign, he had ensnared most members of the peerage in a system of bonds and recognisances that meant financial ruin if they stepped out of line. This policy, widely established and well documented after 1502, probably had its roots in the aftermath of Bosworth, when many nobles who fought for Richard III came to terms with the conqueror, and during the crises of 1486–7, when the marquis of Dorset, the Lords Scrope, and others were required to enter bonds for their good behaviour.

This firm grasp of the realities of power can be seen in King Henry's dealings with Ireland and other off-shore lordships. However the king might like to arrange affairs in Dublin, there seems to have been little choice but to deal with the earl of Kildare. It was neither feasible nor desirable to destroy the Fitzgerald paramountcy, which was vital to the maintenance of the Anglo-Irish colony. The negotiations between Henry's chief negotiator, Sir Richard Edgecombe, and the 'Great Kildare' in 1488 are instructive, and not merely for Irish history. In essence, Kildare sought appointment to the governorship of Ireland, and expressed his willingness to do homage in the proper form. What he was not willing to do was to enter a bond for his good behaviour, as some English lords had been forced to do, which might lead to the forfeiture of his lands and offices. Kildare won his point, and a settlement was reached very largely on his terms. Needless to say, it was not King Henry's last word, and Irish involvement in the Warbeck affair led to the dispatch of Sir Edward Poynings on a short but costly experiment in more direct rule. Despite the recall of Poynings, and the inevitable restoration of Kildare in 1496, it is clear that the king's attention to Irish affairs, largely occasioned by the Yorkist conspiracies, marked a revival in royal government in the Pale. It is significant that around the same time, there were interesting attempts to overhaul the administration of the Channel Islands, another area of dubious loyalty in 1487.[25]

Another distinctive feature of Henry VII's statecraft was his European perspective. If he came to the throne a novice in English politics, his long exile had given him a good understanding of foreign affairs. His sense of the importance of international relations was confirmed by the events of 1487, when he was all too aware of how favourable the overall configuration was to the survival of the Tudor regime. On his return from Stoke Field, in fact, he was met at Leicester by a French embassy, seeking his support for their projected annexation of Brittany. The Bretons had a month earlier attempted to send envoys to seek his aid, and Maximilian, king of the Romans, was showing signs of repenting his rash association in the duchess of Burgundy's schemes. The

Sir Richard Edgecombe, (died 1489), painting in his home Cotehele Manor Cornwall, of his tomb at Morlaix, Brittany.

coincidence of his own triumph over the Yorkists with the fast developing crisis over the Breton succession, therefore, enabled the king, in his dealings with European powers, to move rapidly from a largely passive to a cautiously active role. In 1488 an English force under Lord Scales, though allegedly unofficially, would be fighting against the French in Brittany. In his relations with Scotland, Henry likewise re-established the English king's position as senior partner. From the outset, he had been genuinely keen to establish firm peace with the northern kingdom, and during 1486 had hoped to marry off his mother-in-law as well as his sisters-in-law to suitable Scottish princes. A domestic crisis in Scotland, resulting in the slaughter of James III by rebel lords in 1488, temporarily threatened this new understanding, but by the same token ensured that he would not be troubled for a while from this quarter. Even more impressive was his reaching out to establish relations with the Spanish monarchs, Ferdinand of Aragon and Isabella of Castile. The Treaty of Medina del Campo of 1489, and the projected marriage alliance between Prince Arthur and the Infanta Catherine, clearly signified that the house of Tudor had gained acceptance among the ruling families of Europe.[26]

It was certainly a long struggle for Henry Tudor to win total commitment from his subjects, but from the outset he had shown himself adept at harnessing ideology to his cause. His masterly use of his Welsh ancestry and the 'British' tradition is well-documented, but it was really only a limited part of his programme. Less colourful but more significant was his presentation of himself

The 'Burrand Bush' stone.

as the consummate Christian prince. It is in this sphere that most progress is made after 1487. If God had struck down a tyrant and parricide at Bosworth, He had incontestably endorsed the title of his supplanter at Stoke Field. Bernard André, likening Henry to Constantine, even claimed that at a critical moment in the battle God sent a whirlwind to confound the enemy. Even making no allowance for 'miracles', the support of the church proved of inestimable value. Whether the pope had been cajoled, even bribed, into making firm declarations in support of Henry VII's title, his bull threatening spiritual sanctions against opponents of the Tudor regime could well have been crucial in giving malcontents pause in the uncertain months of 1487. The people of Waterford, in their rebuke of the Dubliners, certainly attached importance to the guidance given by the papacy. Favour at the Roman curia assisted in other respects, as over the appointment to bishoprics and the issue of sanctuaries, though as he became better established the king felt less need to oblige the papacy financially. Even the process for the canonisation of Henry VI was allowed to falter. In all sorts of respects, the Tudor regime appears after 1487 to grow more confident of its own righteousness and legitimacy, more ideologically self-reliant.

*   *   *

Lambert Simnel was like a puppet in a shadow-play. Dancing before the lighted screen, his silhouette assumed the proportions of greatness, and his movements seemed portentous. In the flickering light he took the shape of a boy-king, and it appeared, however momentarily, that the fate of nations hung on his life. Of course, the illusion could never be entirely concealed. The machinations of the puppeteers were soon thwarted, and the whole charade destroyed. The puppet was put in a safe place, to be displayed from time to time as a trophy. As a real person, he was banished from history, and his true name and identity remain concealed. Nonetheless the story of Lambert Simnel is an important one, not for what it reveals about the puppet, but for what it reveals about the political culture in which impersonation flourished. Even in 1487 there seem to have been other impostors being groomed, and several others would indeed come to light before the end of the fifteenth century. At one level, of course, the phenomenon of impersonation reflects the increasing corruption of dynastic politics from the Lancastrian usurpation of 1399, through the Wars of the Roses, to the shameful events associated, in the Tudor mind at least, with Richard III. At another level, however, it seems to mark a new beginning, with the implicit recognition that the destinies of nations cannot be left to genealogical chance, and that princes are made as much as born.

Whatever the interest of Lambert Simnel, the drama in which he was unwittingly cast was historically significant. In retrospect, the victory of Henry VII at Stoke in 1487 was a milestone of sort. Of course, the Tudor regime would continue to appear shaky for another decade, and even after that the Tudor succession would not be assured. It is only with the advantage of hindsight that Stoke Field can be seen as the last battle of the Wars of the Roses. More general at the time would be the view that the rising was evidence of a sickness in the body politic, which had afflicted the nation in the 1450s and 1460s, and had taken a new and particularly dangerous turn in the mid-1480s. For a great many it must have been still difficult to know whether Henry Tudor was a symptom of the disease or part of the cure. Yet perhaps the circumstances of 1487 helped settle a lot of people's anxieties. It was apparent to all that this affair marked the nadir of English fortunes. An impostor crowned in Dublin, and brought to England by a small group of factious nobles, German mercenaries and 'wild Irish', could do little for the self-respect of a people justly proud of their political culture and prowess in arms. The success of Henry VII, his self-confidence and his firmness, not only helped to strengthen the personal monarchy, but also to create the climate in which the increase in princely power was accepted. The battle of Stoke would be the last occasion in which he or any other king of England would have to defend his title in the field against a challenger.

APPENDIX

Extracts from Key Sources in Chronological Order

(a) *Proceedings of the convocation of Canterbury*

> DATE: 17 February 1487. AUTHOR: Clerk of John Morton, Archbishop of Canterbury. TEXT: D. Wilkins (ed.), *Concilia Magnae Britanniæ et Hiberniæ, A.D. 466–1718*, 4 vols. (London, 1737), III, p. 618. (Own translation.)

There was brought forward a certain sir William Simonds, priest, twenty-eight years of age, as he asserted, who there in the presence of the said lords and prelates and the clerk, as well as the mayor, aldermen, and sheriffs of the city of London, publicly admitted and confessed that he himself abducted and carried across to places in Ireland the son of a certain organ-maker of the university of Oxford; and this boy was there reputed to be the earl of Warwick; and that afterwards he himself was with Lord Lovell in Furness fells. On those and other things being confessed by him, the said reverend father in God asked the said mayor and sheriffs to lead the said sir William Simonds to the Tower of London, there to be imprisoned on his behalf, because the same said most reverend father held another of the company of sir William, and was only able to hold one person in his mansion at Lambeth.

(b) *Letter of 'King Edward the Sixth' to city of York*

> DATE: 8 June, 1487. AUTHOR: The earl of Lincoln and rebel leaders. TEXT: York City Archives, House Book 6, f. 97. *York Civic Records*, Vol. 2, ed. A. Raine (Yorkshire Archaeological Society, Record Series 103, 1941), pp. 20–1 (English; spelling modernised.)

Trusty and well-beloved we greet you well, and for so much as we been comen within this our realm, not only, by God's grace, to attain our right of the same, but also for the relief and weal of our said realm, you and all other our true subjects, which hath been greatly injured and oppressed in default of non-ministration of good rules and justice, (we) desire therefore, and in righty hearty wise pray you that in this behalf you will show unto us your good aids and favours. And where(as) we and such power as we have brought with us, by means of travail of the sea and upon land, been greatly wearied and laboured, it will like you that we may have relief and ease of lodging and victuals within our city there, and so to depart and truly pay for that as we shall take. And in your so doing you shall do thing unto us of right acceptable pleasure, and for the same find us your good and sovereign lord at all times hereafter. And of your dispositions herein, to ascertain us by this bringer. Given under our signet at Masham the 8th day of June.

(c) *Letter of Henry VII to city of York*

> DATE: 16 June, 1487. AUTHOR: Henry VII or his secretary. TEXT: *York Civic Records*, Vol. 2, ed. A. Raine (Yorkshire Archaeological Society, Record Series 103, 1941), p. 24. (English; spelling modernised.)

Trusty and well-beloved we greet you well. And forasmuch as it hath like our blessed Saviour to grant unto us of His benign grace the triumph and victory of our rebels without death of any noble or gentleman on our part, we therefore desire and pray you, and since this said victory proceedeth from Him, and concerneth not only the weal and honour of us, but also of this our realm, nevertheless charge you, that calling unto you in the most solemn church of our city there, your brethren the aldermen and others, you do lovings and praisings to be given to our said Saviour after the best of your powers. Given under our signet at our town of Newark, 16th day of June.

(d) *Letter of Henry VII to Pope Innocent VIII*

> DATE: 5 July, 1487. AUTHOR: Henry VII or his secretary. TEXT: *Letters and Papers Illustrative of the Reigns of Richard III and Henry VII*, 2 vols., ed. J. Gairdner (Rolls Series, 1861–3), I, pp. 94–6. (Latin: translation from A.F. Pollard, *The Reign of Henry VII from Contemporary Sources*, 3 vols. (London, 1913- 14), III, pp. 156–7.)

Shortly after we had marched an army against our enemies and rebels a report, erroneous and forged, was circulated in London and Westminster, and spread through many other parts of the kingdom, that we had been put to flight and our whole army dispersed. When this was heard some of those who, by reason of their crimes, enjoy the privileges and immunities of Westminster, being of the opinion that after the commission of any nefarious crime soever they could have the free privilege of returning to that sanctuary (as we wrote more at large to your Holiness for the reform of enormities of this sort), took up arms for the purpose of plundering the houses of those whom they knew to be in the field with us, and mustered in a body for the commission of crime.

Amongst their number was one John Swit, who said, 'And what signify censures of church or pontiff? Do you not perceive that interdicts of this sort are of no weight whatever, since you see with your own eyes that those very men who obtained such in their own favour are routed, and that the whole anathema has recoiled upon their own heads?' On pronouncing these words he instantly fell down dead upon the ground, and his face and body immediately became blacker than soot itself, and shortly afterwards emitted such a stench that no one soever could approach it. Verily we give thanks to Almighty God, who, of his ineffable mercy has exhibited in our kingdom so great a miracle concerning the Christian faith.

As some of the prelates of Ireland, namely, the archbishop of Dublin, the archbishop of Armagh, and the bishops of Meath and Kildare, lent assistance to the rebels, and to a certain spurious lad, whom victory has now delivered into our hands, they pretending that the lad was the son of the late duke of Clarence, and crowning him king of England, we implore your Holiness to cite him as having incurred the censure of the church, and proceed against them at law.

(e) *Memoranda of city of York*

DATE: June/July 1487. Author: Clerk of city of York. TEXT: York House Book 6, fos. 98–99d, and in *York Civic Records*. Vol. 2, ed. A. Raine (Yorkshire Archaeological Society, Record Series 103, 1941), pp. 22–4 (English; spelling modernised).

Saturday, the 8th day of June the year of the reign of our sovereign lord King Henry the Seventh, at afternoon of the same day, the chamberlains sent in message unto the Lords of Lincoln and Lovell, and other here before-named, come in at Micklegate Bar, and there showed unto my lord the mayor and other his brethren being present, how the said lords and their retinue was departed on Boroughbridge, and so straight southward, not intending to come near this city to do any prejudice or hurt unto the same. And incontinently after their coming the Lord Clifford sent word unto my lord mayor that he might come in with his folkes and retinue for to assist and support the mayor and the commonalty of this city, if any of the king's enemies would approach unto the same. Whereunto the mayor consented and granted that he should so have his entry, and caused all the street of Micklegate to be garnished with men in harness (to) the number of 600 persons and more, and within the space of 4 hours after, received the said Lord Clifford at Micklegate bar with 400 persons of footmen and horsemen into the said city and sent unto him a present of wine, according to his honour.

And upon Trinity Sunday at noon my Lord Northumberland with many knights and lords of this country came to this city. And the same day at afternoon the Lord Clifford took his journey towards the king's enemies lying upon Bramham Moor, and lodged himself that night at Tadcaster, but the same night the king's enemies lying near to the same town, came upon the said Lord Clifford's folks and made a great skirmish there, into so much that he, with such folks as he might get, returned to the city again. And at that same skirmish were slain and maimed diverse of the said town, and the inhabitants there were spoiled and robbed, and the gardeviances and trussing coffers of the Lord Clifford was taken off the bridge by misfortune, and had unto the other party. Also upon the Tuesday after, the earl of Northumberland, Lord Clifford and many other nobles accompanied with 6,000 numbered, departed southward toward the king's grace at eleven of the clock. And anon after his departure the Lords Scropes of Bolton and Upsall, constrained as it was said by their folks, came on horseback to Bootham Bar, and there cried 'King Edward!', and made assault at the gates, but the commons being watchmen there well and manly defended them and put them to flight. And incontinently the mayor upon knowledge thereupon, accompanied with a 100 persons in harness, made his proclamation throughout the city in the name of King Henry the Seventh, charging all manner of franchised men and other resident within this city, forthwith to be in harness and attend upon the wardens, and that every warden should keep his ward at his jeopardy, and that all manner of strangers in harness should depart forth of the city at the south gate, under the pain of forfeiture of his harness and his body to prison. The earl of Northumberland having knowledge hereof, being within six miles of the city, sent in message unto the mayor and desired him that he might come and enter the city again for diverse considerations and causes him moving. Whereupon the mayor, by the advice of his brethren, sent Master Vavasour, Recorder, and three of his brother-aldermen, with others of the council of this city accompanied with twelve horse, in message unto the said earl, showing how he should be welcome to the said city, and as many as he would undertake were the king's true liegemen, and caused all the street of Mickelgate to be garnished with men in harnesse to the number of 4,000. And incontinently thereupon, the said earl, the Lord Clifford, and other many nobles accompanied with 4,000 men and more, was thankfully received unto the said City, and there continued to Thursday, Corpus Christi day, and the same day at noon hastly the said lords took their journey towards the north parts.

Upon Corpus Christi eve, proclamation was made through the city that the play of the same, for diverse considerations moving my lord mayor, my masters-aldermen and other of the common council, should be deferred unto the Sunday next after the feast of St Thomas of Canterbury. And then after it was deferred to the Sunday next after the feast of Saint Peter called *Ad vincula*, because of the king's coming hither.

The Saturday next after the feast of Corpus Christi, the king lying with a great power divided in three hosts beyond Newark, the vanguard of the same in which the earl of Oxford, the Lord Strange, Sir John Cheney, the earl of Shrewsbury, and many other to the number of 10,000 met with the Lords of Lincoln and Lovell with other many nobles, as well of Englishmen as Irishmen, and others to the number of 20,000, on the moor beyond Newark. And there was a sore battle, in the which the earl of Lincoln and many other, as well Englishmen as Irish, to the number of 5,000 were slain and murdered; the Lord Lovell was discomfited and fled, with Sir Thomas Broughton and many other. And the child which they called their king was taken and brought unto the king's grace, and many other in great number which was judged to death at Lincoln and other places thereabout. And upon Sunday by three of the clock in the morning, tidings came to my lord mayor from the field, how Almighty God had sent the king victory of his enemies and rebels, and thereupon my lord mayor, taking with him his brother-aldermen, with the whole council of this city, upon certain knowledge of the victory forsaid showed by the mouth of a servant of Master Recorder coming straight from the said field, came to the cathedral church of York, and there caused all the ministers of the same to make lovings to our Saviour for the triumph and victory foresaid, singing solemnly in the high choir of the said church the psalm of *Te Deum Laudamus* with other suffrages.

(f)   *Act of Attainder*

DATE: November 1487. AUTHOR: King and council. TEXT: *Rotuli*

Parliamentorum, ed. J. Strachey, 6 vols. (London, 1767–83), VI, pp. 397–8. (English; spelling modernised.)

Forasmuch as the 19th day of the month of March last past John, late earl of Lincoln . . . conspired and imagined the most dolorous and lamentable murder, death, and destruction of the royal person of our said sovereign and liege lord, and also destruction of all this realm, and . . . traitorously departed to the parts beyond the sea, and there accompanied himself with many other false traitors and enemies . . . prepared a great navy for the coasts of Brabant, and arrived in the ports of Ireland, where he, with Sir Henry Bodrugan and John Beaumont, squire, imagined and conspired the destruction and deposition of our said sovereign liege lord. And for the execution of the same there, the 24th day of May last past at the city of Dublin, contrary to his homage and faith, truth and allegiance, traitorously renounced, revoked, and disclaimed his own said most natural sovereign liege lord the king, and caused one Lambert Simnel, a child of 10 years of age, son to Thomas Simnel, late of Oxford, joiner, to be proclaimed, erected and reputed as king of this realm, and to him did faith and homage, to the great dishonour and despite of all this realm. And from thence continuing in his malicious and traitorous purpose arrived with a great navy in Furness, in Lancashire, the 4th day of June last past, accompanied with a great multitude of strangers with force and arms, that is to say, swords, spears, morris-pikes, bows, guns, harness, brigantines, hauberks, and many other weapons and harness defensible, and from thence the same day he, with Sir Thomas Broughton, knight, Thomas Harrington, Robert Percy, of Knaresburgh, in the county of York, Richard Harleston, John Broughton, brother unto the said Sir Thomas Broughton, knight, Thomas Batell, James Harrington, Edward Frank, Richard Middleton, squires; Robert Hilton, Clement Skelton, Alexander Appleby, Richard Bank, Edmund Juse, Thomas Blandrehasset, gentlemen; John Mallary, of Litchborough in the county of Northampton, Robert Mallary, of Fawsley, in the same county, Giles Mallary, of Greens-Norton, in the same county, William Mallary, of Stowe, in the same county, Robert Manning, late of Dunstable, William Kay, of Halifax, gentleman, Roger Hartlington, Richard Hodgeson, John Avintry, Rowland Robinson, yeomen; with many other ill-disposed persons and traitors, defensible and in like warly manner, arrayed to the number of 8,000 persons, imagining, compassing, and conspiring the death and deposition . . . (of) the king, and the subversion of all this realm . . . continually in hostile manner passed from thence, from place to place, to they come to Stoke, in the county of Nottingham; where the 16th day of June last past, with banners displayed, levied war against the person of his sovereign and natural liege lord, and gave to him mighty and strong battle, . . . intending utterly to have slain, murdered, and cruelly destroyed our foresaid liege lord and most Christian prince, to the uttermost and greatest adventure of the noble and royal person of our said liege lord, destruction, dishonour, and subversion of all this realm. For the which malicious, compassed, great and heinous offence, not all only committed against our said sovereign lord, but also against the universal and common weal of this realm, is requisite sore and grievous punishing; and also for an example hereafter that no other be bold in like wise to offend. Therefore be it enacted by our sovereign lord the king by the advice of all the lords spiritual and temporal, and the commons in this present parliament assembled, and by the authority of the same, that the said John, late earl of Lincoln (and the others) be reputed, judged, and taken as traitors, and convicted and attainted of high treason.

(g)   *Poem sent from the city of Waterford to the archbishop of Dublin*

> DATE: Lent, 1488; AUTHOR: Clerk at Waterford. TEXT: T.C. Croker, *The Popular Songs of Ireland* (London, 1839), pp. 318–31. (English; spelling modernised.)

The poem is addressed to Walter, archbishop of Dublin, and sent to him under the names of John Butler, mayor of Waterford, James Rice and William Lyncolle. It exhorts the archbishop and his flock not to persist in their foolish and sinful rebellion against Henry VII. It recalls the former glory of Dublin, and points out that its citizens have strayed from its best traditions in making 'a plain digression from their true liegance unto rebellion.' The centerpiece is a rambling discourse on the validity of King Henry's title, in which most space is given to precedents for the descent of kingdoms through females. Beginning with the laws of Moses, it is even claimed that Jesus, born of the Virgin, was 'by her, true king of Jerusalem.' It is argued that this tradition is especially well established in England, where Stephen and Henry II both became kings by virtue of matrilineage. The most recent precendent is Edward IV, whose title came from Philippa, daughter of Lionel, duke of Clarence, son of Edward III:

> Which title is fallen to our sovereign lady,
> Queen Elizabeth, his eldest daughter lineal;
> To her is come all the whole monarchy,
> For the fourth Edward had no issue male.
> The crown, therefore, and sceptre imperial,
> Both she must have without division,
> For of a monarchy be no particion.
>
> It is so that by Divine purveyance,
> King Henry the Seventh, our sovereign lord,
> And Queen Elizabeth, to God is pleasure;
> Been married both by amiable accord,
> Why should we speak more of this matter a word?
> He is our true king without variance,
> And to him by right we should owe our legeaunce.
>
> Fortune on him have cast her lot and chance,
> That he by God is only provided
> Of England to have the sovereign governance;
> And of the people chosen and elected,
> By grace in battle he have obtained;
> The ancient right of the Britons also,
> Is cast on him with titles many more.
>
> First we say that, by God's provision,
> This noble prince came by this his sceptre;
> Second, by the common election

> Of the lords and commons, he was made sure;
> The queen's title, by fortune's adventure,
> He hath these three; the fourth by victorie;
> And the fifth by the old Britain story.

Furthermore, it is claimed, their title has been confirmed in a papal bull, which imposes penalties for those contesting it and offers indulgences for those defending it. Even if the archbishop is not the 'author of this perversity', he is clearly at fault for not speaking out against it:

> O by what law, custom, or liberty,
> May a king of England be made in Ireland?
> There is no man that have such authority,
> For there was no such act made in this land
> Till now right late, as we understand.
> O fie false land, full of rebellion,
> And with all men had in great dirision!
>
> O God! where was the prudence of reason
> Of you that have your whole common assent,
> That a boy, an organ-maker's son,
> Should be made a king of England, and regent,
> To whom as yet all ye be obedient?
> To your dishonour and evil fame,
> An horrible slander and great shame.
>
> It is great pity that ye be deceived
> By a false priest, that this matter began;
> And that ye his child as a prince receaved
> A boy, a lad, an organ-maker's son,
> Which is now kept in the Tower of London;
> His keepers there, to all men declaring,
> 'This is of Dublin the first crowned king.'

There is a final appeal to the archbishop of Dublin to lead his flock back to the right path. With Lent approaching, it is felt a suitable time for them all to make amends and seek reconciliation.

(h) *Herald's report*

> DATE: c. 1488–90. AUTHOR: A herald or pursuivant at court of Henry VII. TEXT: British Library, Cotton MS. Julius B.XII, fos.27d–29d, amending J. Leland, *Collectanea*, Vol. IV, ed. T. Hearne (Oxford, 1774), pp. 212–15. (English; spelling modernised).

From thence the king proceeded to Coventry, where the bishop of Winchester took his leave and went to the queen and the prince, and the substance of his company waited upon the king, under the standard of his nephew the earl of Devonshire. From Coventry the king removed unto Leicester, where by the commandment of the most reverend father in God, the archbishop of Canterbury, then chancellor of England, the king's proclamations were put in execution, and in especial voiding common women and vagabonds, for there were imprisoned great number of both; wherefore there was more rest in the king's host, and the better rule. And on the morrow, which was on the Monday, the king left there the forsaid reverend father in God and rode to Loughborough; and the said lord chancellor's folks were committed by his nephew, Robert Morton, unto the standard of the earl of Oxford in the foreward. And at Loughborough, the stocks and prisons were reasonably filled with harlots and vagabonds, and after that were but few in the host unto the time the field was done. On Tuesday the king removed and lay all night in the field, under a wood called 'Bonley Rice'. And on the Wednesday the king's marshals and herbingers of his host did not so well their diligence that way, for when the king removed there was no proper ground appointed where the king's host should lodge that night then following. But it was a royal and a marvellous fair and a well-tempered day. And the king, with his host, wandered here and there a great space of time, and so came to a fair long hill, where the king set his folks in array of battle, that is to say, a bow and a bill at his back. And all the foreward were well and warily lodged under the hill to Nottingham ward. And when the king had seen his people in this fair array, he rode to a village three miles on this side Nottingham, on the highway side, where in a gentleman's place his grace lodged. And in that village, and in a bean field to Nottingham ward, lodged all his battle; which evening were taken certain spies, which noised in the country that the king had been fled. And some were hanged on the ash at Nottingham bridge end. And on the morrow, which was Corpus Christi day, after the king had heard the divine service in the parish church, and the trumpets had blown to horse, the king, not letting his host to understand his intent, rode backward to see, and also welcome the Lord Strange, which brought with him a great host, enough to have beaten all the king's enemies, only of my lord his father's, the earl of Derby's, folks and his. And all were fair embattled, which unknown returning to the host, caused many folks for to marvel. Also the king's standard and much carriage followed after the king, unto the time the king was advertised by Garter king of arms, whom the king commanded to turn them all again, which so did them all in battle on the heaf hither side of the great hill on this side Nottingham, unto the time the king came. That night the king's host lay under the end of all that hill toward Nottingham to Lenton ward, and his foreward before him to Nottingham bridge ward. And the earl of Derby's host on the king's left hand to the meadows beside Lenton. And that evening there was a great scry, at which scry there fled many men; but it was great joy to see how soon the king was ready and his true men in array. And from thence, on the Friday, the king, understanding that his enemies and rebels drew towards Newark ward, passing by Southwell and the far side of Trent, the king with his host removed thitherwards, and lodged that night beside a village called Radcliffe, nine miles out of Newark. That evening there was a great scry, which caused many cowards to flee; but the earl of Oxford and all the nobles in the foreward with him, were soon in a good array and in a fair battle, and so was the king and all the very men that there were. And in this scry I heard of no man of worship that fled but rascals.

On the morn, which was Saturday, the king early arose and heard two masses, whereof the Lord John (*recte* Richard) Fox, bishop of Exeter, sang the tone. And the king had five good and true men of the village of Radcliffe, which showed his grace the best way for to conduct his host to Newark, which knew well the country, and showed where were marshes and where was the river of Trent, and where were villages or groves for bushments, or straight ways, that the king might conduct his host the better. Of which guides the king gave two to the earl of Oxford to conduct the foreward, and the remnant retained at his pleasure. And so in good order and array, before nine of the clock, beside a village called Stoke, a large mile out of Newark, his foreward reconnoitred his enemies and rebels, where by the help of Almighty God, he had the victory. And there was taken the lad that his rebels called king Edward, whose name was indeed John, by a valiant and a gentle esquire of the king's house, called Robert Bellingham. And there was slain the earl of Lincoln, John, and diverse other gentlemen, and the Viscount Lord Lovell put to flight. And there was slain of English, Dutch, and Irishmen 4,000. And that day the king made thirteen bannerets and seventy knights, whose names ensueth. These be the names of the bannerets: Sir Gilbert Talbot, Sir John Cheney, Sir William Stonor. These three were made before the battle. And after the battle were made the same day: Sir John Arundel, Sir Thomas Cokesey, Sir John Fortescue, Sir Edmund Bedingfield, Sir James Blount, Sir Richard Croft, Sir Humphrey Stanley, Sir Richard Delabere, Sir John Mortimer, Sir William Troutbeck. The names of the knights made at the same battle: Sir James Audley, Sir Edward Norris, Sir Robert Clifford, Sir George Hopton, Sir Robert Broughton, Sir John Paston, Sir Henry Willoughby, Sir Richard Pole, Sir Richard Fitzlewis, Sir Edward Burgh, Sir George Lovell, Sir John Longville; these noble knights well and liberally paid the whole fees, and these that follow have paid as yet but part: Sir Thomas Tyrell, Sir Roger Bellingham, Sir William Carew, Sir William Troutbeck, Sir Thomas Poole, Sir William Vampage, Sir James Harrington (which is not willing never to do as a gentleman should do, as he saieth as yet; I pray God learn him better), Sir John Devenish, Sir John Sapcote, Sir Thomas Lovell, Sir Humphrey Savage, Sir Anthony Brown, Sir Thomas Grey, Sir Nicholas Vaux, Sir William Tirwhit, Sir Amias Paulet, Sir Ralph Longford, Sir Henry Bold, Sir William Radmill, Sir Thomas Blount (hath truly paid), Sir Robert Cheney, Sir John Windham, Sir John Musgrave, Sir Geroge Neville 'the bastard', Sir James Parker, Sir Edward Darell, Sir Edward Pickering, Sir Thomas Wolton, Sir William Sandes, Sir Robert Brandon, Sir Maurice Berkeley, Sir John Digby, Sir Ralph Shirley, Sir William Littleton, Sir William Norris, Sir Thomas Hansard, Sir Christopher Wroughton, Sir Thomas Lynde, Sir Maurice Burgh, Sir Thomas Monington.

(i) *Chronicles of Jean Molinet*

DATE: c. 1490. AUTHOR: Jean Molinet, historiographer to Burgundian court. TEXT: *Chroniques de Jean Molinet (1474–1506)*, ed. G. Doutrepont and O. Jodogne, 3 vols. (Academie Royale de Belgique. Classe des Lettres et des Sciences Morales et Politiques. Collection des Anciens Auteurs Belges; Brussels, 1935–7), I, pp. 562–5. (French; own translation.)

After the earl of Richmond was crowned king of England and given the title Henry the seventh of that name, by the support and powerful assistance of the king of France, many debates and disputes arose among the English, among whom those most displeased by the coronation were the princes, heirs and successors of the most high and excellent house of York, the which was lately so gloriously raised in triumphant majesty that the renown and the splendour was seen and heard throughout the seven climates of the world, and now was so suddenly fallen, miserably deserted by fortune that one could scarcely see roof, pillar nor foundation which could restore it in royal convalescence. One scion taken from royally born stock, however, had come on splendidly among the fertile and aristocratic shrubs of Ireland, who, when he was full grown, in the flower of manhood, and raised up in force, wished to repair and return to resplendent honour the glorious arch and triumphant house of York, of which he is issue. This most noble scion is Edward son of the duke of Clarence, who by the advice and mature deliberation of the nobles of Ireland and with the favor of a number of barons of England, his well-wishers, decided to have himself crowned king and to expel from his royal throne the earl of Richmond, who then occupied the crown of England to the great prejudice, disparagement and detriment of the said house made up of very high and puissant persons, who had originated, multiplied and prospered under its portals. Then, to realise his high ambition and to have backing for his cause, he made his enterprise known to the most high and mighty lady, Madam Margaret of York, duchess of Burgundy, his aunt, formerly spouse of the most illustrious prince, Monsieur the Duke Charles, whom God absolve. This most high and mighty lady applied herself so diligently on her nephew's behalf to his serene highness, the King of the Romans, her son-in-law, that she raised a company of Germans, some fifteen to sixteen hundred in number, of whom the principal leader and captain was Martin Schwartz. Having made their preparations, the said Germans, loaded with victuals and artillery, clothed and well prepared for all climates, left Holland and arrived in Ireland, where they found the duke of Clarence (*recte* his son) along with the earls of Lincoln and Kildare and some nobles of the land who, with the agreement of all the people, had him crowned king of England by two archbishops and twelve bishops. Then they sent him under the protection of arms to the north country in England, and disembarked at a harbour named Furness and, passing through great mountains without meeting any danger, arrived at 'Scanfort' (Carnforth, Castleford, Stainforth?), where a number of lords from thereabouts made themselves over to his obedience.

This King Edward, newly crowned in Ireland, arrived at 'Scanfort' with large forces. Sir Edward Woodville, Lord Scales, taking the side of King Henry, had come to a town called Doncaster, accompanied by 6,000 men, to seek out King Edward's army, but he was so closely pursued from encampment to encampment and driven back for three days on end that he was forced to fall back in great haste through the forest of Nottingham. The earl of Oxford, the earl of Shrewsbury, called Talbot, the Lord Hastings, Sir John Savage and other great lords, accompanied by 15,000 men, who knowing after Lord Scales's arrival the disposition of King Edward's army, crossed back over the water with all diligence, not daring to await his might, and took to flight. The people of the city of York, informed of the King Edward's coronation in Ireland, of the descent of his army on England, before which the earl of Oxford, the earl of Shrewsbury and others of the King Henry's vanguard had retreated, declared themselves of his party, notably Lord Scrope who for a long time had held the castle of York.

The same day that the said vanguard abandoned Nottingham, Lord Welles, who came to King Henry's service, accompanied by 10,000 men, turned like the others in flight and made his way to London and its environs, and the people there who were in sanctuary in London, seeing this disarray, thinking that all had been won by King Edward, sallied forth from their sanctuaries, pillaged the servants and well-wishers of King Henry living round about, and cried all joyous at the top of their voices, 'Long live Warwick. To King Edward!' King Edward, driving his enemies before him, rode through the forest of Nottingham and, without entering into the town, came to Newark where he crossed the river which is very broad, along which he marched through the country around two or three leagues; and, at the end of a meadow, found King Henry's army, near a village named Stoke, and there was the upset.

King Henry had three 'battles' with two wings. In the rearguard (*recte* vanguard) as leader was the earl of Oxford, accompanied by Lord Stanley, the earl of Shrewsbury, Lord Hastings, the son of the duke of Norfolk (*recte* Suffolk), brother of the earl of Lincoln, and numerous nobles, great and puissant barons of England. In the right wing of the vanguard, as leader, was Lord Scales having 2,000 horse and on the left, Sir John Savage with 1,200 horse in all. In the large 'battle' was King Henry in person, accompanied by noble princes and notable knights, 20,000 in number, and then in the rearguard was Lord Strange, leader of 14–15,000.

The battle formation of King Edward, however, was in one mass, amounting to only 8,000 men, the which, when it came to the joining in battle of the one side against the other, could not withstand the shooting of the English archers, especially the Germans (*recte* the Irish) who were only half-armed; and, although they displayed great bravery, as much, indeed, as their small number and substance allowed, they were routed and defeated, shot through and full of arrows like hedgehogs. There died the earl of Lincoln, most noble and renowned in arms, Sir Martin Schwartz, a most enterprising knight and of greatest courage, along with numerous notable people in such great number that of their whole army only 200 escaped; of whom those, in the two days following, who were found to be Irish and English were hanged, and those who were foreigners were dismissed. And King Edward was taken and made a prisoner in the town of Newark, about four leagues from which place King Henry, joyous of his victory, went, without dismounting, to give thanks to Our Lord for his good fortune. The collegiate clergy of this great church came to meet him in solemn procession; he hailed the Virgin Mary and gave his standard to the image of St George; and, two days later, so completely broke up his army that he had in his company no more than 4–5,000 men.

(j) *Bernard André's 'Life of Henry VII'*

DATE: c. 1500. AUTHOR: Bernard André, French humanist in service of Henry VII. TEXT: B. André, 'Vita Henrici Septimi' in *Memorials of King Henry VII*, ed. J. Gardner (London, Roll Series, 1858), pp. 49–52. (Latin; own translation.)

Concerning the Irish plot. The issue of cruel death of the sons of King Edward flaring up again, behold seditious men hatched another novel evil. In order to veil their plot in deceit, they maliciously put up a certain boy, lowly born, the son of either a baker or a shoemaker, as the son of Edward IV. In conceiving hatred against their king, so great was their boldness that they cared to fear neither God nor men. When the plot had been thus devised among them, therefore, the report went out that Edward's second son was crowned king in Ireland. When this rumour had been brought to the king, he in his great wisdom looked closely into all matters relating to them; namely, by what means, and by whom he was brought there, where he was raised, where he had been for so long, whom he had as friends, and many other matters of this nature he wisely investigated. Diverse messengers were sent on a variety of matters, finally (blank), who asserted that that he would easily learn if the boy was such as he claimed to be, was sent across. The boy, however, instructed now in the evil craft by those who knew the times of Edward replied promptly to all the herald's questions. Then, lest I make long of it, through the false teaching of his coaches he was accepted as Edward's son by many prudent men, and it was believed so firmly that many did not in the least hesitate to meet death on his behalf. Look what follows. In those days such was the folly even of illustrious men, such was the blindness, not to speak of the pride and the malice, that even the earl of Lincoln (blank) likewise did not hesitate to believe it. And since she held it for certain that he was the issue of Edward himself, the Lady Margaret, widow of Charles the most famous duke of Burgundy and Edward's sister, sent letters calling him to her; and he secretly slipping away, with a few accomplices in such a great treachery, speedily set out towards her. And, to cut a long story short, through the doings and advice of this woman, Irishmen and northerners were drawn into the plot. So, having assembled an expeditionary force of Germans and Irish, with the Lady Margaret ever in assistance, they shortly crossed to England, and reached the north coast.

Concerning the second triumph of Henry VII. The king, ever trusting in providence, heard these tidings without trepidation. Rather, with equinimity and distinction he spoke thus to the men on his side: 'Most trusty lords and most valiant comrades in arms, who have experienced with me such great dangers on land and sea, behold again we are assailed against our will in another battle. For the earl of Lincoln, a perfidious man, as you know, without any occasion given him by me, maintains an unjust cause against me. Moreover, as you see, he does not do this surreptitiously, but most brazenly, without any fear of God; not so much that he may trouble us, as that he may follow the advice of a silly and shameless woman, who is not unaware that her dynasty has been destroyed by her brother Richard, but who, because the blood of our line is so hated by her, regarding too little her niece my most illustrious wife, seeks to destroy us and our children. You see, therefore, how often we are provoked by those people, but she will not get away with it unavenged by us. I call God and His holy angels to witness that, while I for my part attend, day and night, to your safety and the general peace, the old enemy opposes. Nonetheless, God, the just, strong, and patient Judge, will apply a remedy to this ill. Meanwhile, I exhort and remind you that this time just heredity will be stronger than their iniquity. Do not doubt but that God Himself, who made us victors in the previous battle, will allow us now to triumph over our enemies. Let us advance against them fearlessly, therefore, for God is our helper.' When he had finished, the earl of Oxford was prepared as before to reply, but because time was pressing, the king proclaimed silence, and ordered attention to exigencies of the time. Rushing headlong, like doves before a black storm, the men grabbed their weapons. And now the royal army approached the mass of barbarians. They were arrayed on the brow of the hill, and were lying in wait for our men. But God, the Lord of Vengeance, avenging their unjustified rage, just as when Constantine struggled against the enemies of the church, with a sudden whirlwind which rose up while they were fighting. And our men, whom they thought were overcome, in the end defeated them. Then suddenly there rose to the sky the shout 'King Henry', and the blaring of trumpets on all sides filled everyone's ears with gladness. Here in this battle was captured a good-for-nothing fellow, that miserable kinglet crowned, as I have said, in Dublin, who having been asked by what effrontery he dared to commit so great a crime, did not deny that he had been forced to it by certain men of his own shameless sort. Afterwards, when interrogated on his family and the status of his parents, he confessed them all to have been common in all respects, and in lowly occupations, unworthy of being inserted in this history. The earl of Lincoln, moreover, came to an end worthy of his deeds, for he was slain in the field, and likewise many others, whose commander and general, Martin Schwartz, a man outstandingly proficient in all the arts of war, fell fighting bravely.

(k)   *Polydore Vergil's 'English History'*

DATE: c. 1503–13, though not published until 1534. AUTHOR: Polydore Vergil of Urbino, in England from 1502, wrote at request of Henry VII. TEXT: *The Anglica Historia of Polydore Vergil, A.D. 1485–1537*, ed. D. Hay (Camden Society, new series 74, 1950), pp. 12–27, incorporating (*in italics*) additional material from later text. (Latin; own translation, often following Denys Hay.)

In the mean time a major disturbance began to arise out of a petty and contrived affair. For indeed from the time when Edward IV, having overthrown Henry VI, arrogated to himself the kingdom of England, men were so nourished on factionalism that they could not thereafter remain quiet, and so confused, by fair means and foul, their divine and human obligations that, blinded by partisan concern, led not by reason but by evil and perverted partiality, they were divided into a thousand factions. This affliction, almost brought under control by Edward after the extinction of almost all the family of Henry VI, was renewed by his brother Richard, who by his example brought to the minds of others the idea of stirring up new divisions and venturing other schemes by which they might gain for themselves power or privileges. Most recently, among other such enterprises, a certain lowborn priest called Richard, whose surname was Simons, a man as subtle as he was shameless, devised a crime of this fashion, by which he might disturb the peace of the kingdom. At Oxford, where he gave himself to study, he brought up a certain boy called Lambert Simnel. He first taught the boy courtly manners, so that if ever he should represent the lad as being born of royal stock, as he had resolved to do, people would the more easily credit it and have certain belief in his great creation. Some time later, since Henry VII, immediately on gaining power, had thrown Edward, the only son of the duke of Clarence, into the Tower of London, and since it was rumoured that Edward had been slain in that place, the priest Richard decided that the time had arrived when he might advantageously execute his planned villainy. He changed the boy's name and called him Edward, by which name the duke of Clarence's son was known, and forthwith departed with him to Ireland. There he secretly summoned a meeting of a considerable number of Irish nobles whom he understood by report to be little disposed to Henry, and having gained their trust, he related how he had saved from death the duke of Clarence's son, and how he had brought him to that land, where he had heard that the name and family of King Edward were ever beloved. The story, readily believed by those men, was soon communicated to others, and was given, without debate, such credit that Thomas Fitzgerald, King Henry's Irish-born chancellor in the island, was among the first to entertain the boy as a scion of royal descent, and to start to give him powerful assistance. First of all calling together his own followers, he informed them of the boy's arrival and how the kingdom of England was his by right as the only male of royal descent, and exhorted them on that account to follow him in restoring the boy to the throne. He then communicated the affair to the rest of the nobles who, accepting his advice, promised their assistance. By this means news quickly spread to all Irish cities, which besides allying themselves to the youth called him king. Then the leaders of the faction sent secret messengers to those in England whom they knew had been followers of King Richard's party, to implore them to remain loyal, and to decide to aid the boy. Other messengers were sent to Flanders to ask the assistance of Margaret, sister of Edward IV and widow of Charles duke of Burgundy.... (Although) she considered the matter to be false, as indeed it was, she not only promised the envoys that she would support it herself, but also assist it by committing certain other English nobles as allies to those already active in the new conspiracy. Furthermore, Francis Lord Lovell, who had come to her in Flanders at this time, encouraged her to undertake a greater role.

When these things were reported to him in England, Henry, as was indeed appropriate, was deeply disturbed that the fraud of a single priest should precipitate so great a war against him. However, because as a rule, he judged it part of good generalship to overcome the enemy by stratagem no less than by force, he wanted to attempt to bring his subjects to their senses without armed conflict. Accordingly, a council of nobles having been convened at the Carthusians' convent near the royal palace which he later named Richmond, he discussed remedies appropriate to the crisis. At the first meeting they all judged it best, before dealing with anything else, that a pardon be extended to all guilty of offences, lest, were this deferred, Sir Thomas Broughton, who had long been in the service of Francis Lord Lovell and was with him at present, and other participants in the new conspiracy, perhaps despairing of a pardon, should persist in the scheme; and, exposing themselves to greater dangers, plunge into open rebellion. Accordingly the king at once by proclamation pardoned and excused from punishment all who were charged with treason or other crimes. Furthermore, after long deliberation, it appeared appropriate to all that the son of the duke of Clarence should be shown to the people, so that thereby the silly notion that the boy was in Ireland would be driven from people's minds.. . . The king, having dismissed his council, came to London and on the following Sunday ordered Edward, the son of the duke of Clarence to be led from the Tower through the middle of the city to St Paul's Cathedral. Here the boy, as he had been commanded, showing himself to everyone, fell to prayer and took part in worship, and at the same time spoke with many notables and especially with those whom the king had under suspicion, so that they might the more readily understand that the Irish had based their new movement on an empty and spurious affair. But this medicine was of no little value for diseased minds. For John earl of Lincoln, the son of John duke of Suffolk and Elizabeth, King Edward's sister, together with Thomas Broughton and many more in his council who were eager for change, joined the conspiracy against Henry, and decided to cross over to Margaret so that they could unite with the other originators of the movement. Therefore, as soon as the council had been dismissed by the king, the earl crossed secretly into Flanders and there busied himself with Margaret and Francis lord Lovell in waging war.

Meanwhile King Henry, who hoped that, after seeing Edward the genuine son of the duke of Clarence, his nobles would remain calm, was applying himself singlemindedly to curbing the rashness of the Irish, when suddenly he learned of the earl of Lincoln's flight. Greatly provoked by this the king determined to prosecute his enemies openly and revenge by force the wrongs they had done him, which he perceived could not be avoided by advice alone. He accordingly ordered musters of soldiers to be held, and he himself, in the mean time, fearful that the earl should draw many nobles into the conspiracy, thoroughly traversed that part of the country closest to Flanders since it was through there that the earl when fleeing to Flanders had earlier made his way. When the king reached Bury St Edmunds, he was informed that Thomas marquis of Dorset was approaching. Suspecting him to be privy to the conspiracy, the king ordered him to be arrested en route by John earl of Oxford and committed to the Tower of London. . . .. Moving thence, the king came to Norwich, where he celebrated the Easter feasts. He then came to the place called Walsingham, where he prayed devoutly before the image of the Blessed Virgin Mary, who is worshipped most reverently there, that he might be safe from the attacks of his enemies. Finally, after he had travelled all around the coastal area and found all quiet, the king returned to the town of Cambridge.

Meanwhile John earl of Lincoln and Francis Lovell, having received from Margaret an army of around 2,000 Germans, whose commander was that most battle-hardened man Martin Schwartz, crossed over to Ireland, and in the city of Dublin made Lambert, the low-born boy, their king, calling him, his name having been changed, Edward, and falsely, as they very well knew, the duke of Clarence's son. After this, having assembled a great number of the beggarly and poorly armed Irish under the leadership of Thomas Fitzgerald, they sailed to England with their new king. They landed according to design on the west coast near Lancaster, putting their trust in the wealth and aid of Thomas Broughton, who was of great authority in that part and who, as was stated above, was one of the conspirators.

King Henry, in truth, anticipating what actually happened, had a little before the arrival of the enemy sent Christopher Urswick to find out whether the ports on the Lancashire coast were able to take large ships; so that if they proved likely to be useful to his adversaries he could at once so position his troops as to deny them the coast. *He dispatched along the west coast companies of horsemen, both to watch for the approach of the enemies and to greet certain people coming from out of Ireland, from whom he might learn his enemies' plans. He himself, having assembled his forces, in command of whom he set Jasper duke of Bedford and John earl of Oxford, set out for Coventry.* Christopher, after he had carried out these orders and learnt from the depth of the bed of the sea that the ports were deep, headed back to the king; but, hearing on route of the sudden landing of the enemy, he sent ahead a messenger to tell the king of the approach of his enemies and he himself, following afterwards, gave a fuller account of the whole matter. The king was at Coventry when he received the messenger, and, abandoning all other business, he determined that he must immediately confront his opponents wherever they might betake themselves, lest time should be given them for assembling greater forces. He marched to Nottingham, and not far from the town, next to a wood which is called Banrys in the vernacular, he made camp, to which there came not long after, accompanied by a great number of armed men, George Talbot earl of Shrewsbury, George Lord Strange, and John Cheney, all distinguished commanders, with many others well versed in military affairs; *for each of the most noble and bold men of the surrounding counties had either been summoned by the king to him, or, in so far as they were able to bear arms, to be as ready as possible to render assistance, if it was needed. In such a way, in one muster of soldiers held near this time, there were gathered great forces, whose leaders were Ralph Longford, John Montgomery, Henry Vernon of the Peak, Ralph Shirley, Godfrey Foljambe, Thomas Gresley, Edward Sutton, Humphrey Stanley, another Humphrey Stanley, William Hugton, William Mering, Edward Stanhope, Gervase Clifton, Brian Stapleton, Henry Willoughby, William Pierpont, John Babington, William Bedyll, Robert Brudenell, John Markham, William Merbury, Edward Burgh, William Tirwhit, John Hussey, Robert Sheffield, William Newport, Roger Ormston, Thomas Tempest, William Knyvet, Henry Willoughby, Edward, Lord Hastings, John Digby, Simon Digby, (James) Harrington, Richard Sacheverell, John Villiers, Edward Fielding, Thomas Pulteney, Nicholas Vaux, Thomas Green, Nicholas Griffin, Edmund Lucy, Edward Belknap, Robert Throckmorton, George Grey of Ruthin, Guy Wolston, Thomas Findern, David Philip, Thomas Cheney, Robert Cotton, John St John, John Mordaunt, Thomas Tyrell, John Rainsford, Robert Paynton, Robert Daniel, Henry Marney, Edmund Arundel. There also joined up at the same time other noblemen and captains from outlying areas, among whom were George Ogle, Ralph Neville, Richard Latimer, William Bulmer, John Langford, William Norris, John Neville of Thornbridge and John William. In this way the king's army was hourly augmented in wonderful fashion.*

The earl of Lincoln meanwhile, entering Yorkshire with the other conspirators, advanced in easy stages, without doing any harm to the inhabitants. Thus he hoped that folk would rally to him. Yet when he saw that few were joining him he resolved none the less to try the fortunes of war, mindful that two years before Henry with a small band of armed men had vanquished King Richard drawn up in the field with a vast host. And although both the Germans and the Irish in the army claimed they had come to restore Edward, the lad recently crowned in Ireland, to the kingdom, nonetheless, the earl, who as has been shown, was the son of Edward's sister, planned to seize the throne himself in the event of victory. Thus trusting to the fortunes of war, he began to make his way out of Yorkshire towards the town called Newark, situated on the bank of the river Trent, so that, having added to his forces there, he could march directly against the king. But before he came to this place, King Henry setting out to block his approach arrived in Newark on the evening of the day preceding the battle. He did not stay there long, but marched three miles beyond the town and there pitched his camp for the night. The earl, having learnt of the king's arrival, continued unabashed on the course he had set out on, until he came the same day to a village near the camp of his enemy, a place they call Stoke, and there made his camp. The following day the king, having formed his whole force into three columns, advanced to the village of Stoke, halted below the earl's camp and, on the level ground there, offered battle. Given the opportunity, the earl drew out his troops and, giving them the single, moved down to the fray. The battle was fought boldly and bitterly on both sides. The Germans, fierce mountainmen, experienced in war, who were in the front line, yielded little to the English in valour; while Martin Schwartz their leader was not inferior to many in his spirit and strength. The Irish, on the other hand, though they fought most spiritedly, were nonetheless slain before the others, being according to their custom devoid of body armour; their slaughter striking no little terror into the other combatants. For some time the contest was even, but at last the royal vanguard, which alone was engaged and sustained the battle, charged the enemy with such impetus that first of all it caused the death of some of the enemy leaders offering resistence in various places, and then put to flight the remainder, who in the course of fleeing were either captured or killed. Indeed it was only then, when the battle was over, that it became all too evident how much boldness there had been in the enemy army; for of their leaders John earl of Lincoln, Francis Lord Lovell, Thomas Broughton, the most bold Martin Schwartz and the Irish captain Thomas Geraldine were slain in that place, which while living they had taken in the fighting. Lambert the false boy-king was indeed captured, with his mentor Richard: but each was granted his life, since the innocent lad was too young to have given offence, and since his mentor was a priest. Lambert is sill alive to this very day, having been made trainer of the king's hawks; for some time before that he turned the spit and did other menial jobs in the royal kitchen.

His enemies defeated, the king was greatly pleased in that he had thus escaped not only the immediate danger, but also the future threat which he feared more. For when he had noticed that his opponents' forces, though much smaller in number and inferior in strength, had come against him with such resolution and had in the end descended into the fray with so little hesitation, he suspected that there must be yet further members of the conspiracy who, at an opportune time and place, would join with the them. Therefore, when he saw the enemy line clearly waver in the battle, he ordered that John earl of Lincoln should not be killed so that he might learn from him more concerning the conspiracy. But it is said that the soldiers declined to spare the earl, fearful lest by chance it would happen that the sparing of one man's life would lead to the loss of many. . . Having gathered the spoils of the slain and committed their bodies for burial, the king proceeded to Lincoln, taking with him a number of captives whom he punished by death. Thence he sent Christopher Urswick with the standard, which he had used against the enemy whom he had defeated, to Walsingham, to give thanks for the victory in the shrine of the Blessed Virgin and to place the standard there as a memorial to the blessing received from God.

LIST OF ABBREVIATIONS

André, *Vita*	B. André, 'Vita Henrici Septimi' in *Memorials of King Henry the Seventh*, ed. J. Gairdner (R.S. 1858)
Bacon, *Henry the Seventh*	F. Bacon, *The History of the Reign of King Henry the Seventh*, F. Levy (Indianapolis, 1972)
Book of Howth	'Book of Howth' in *Calendar of Carew Manuscripts*, V, ed. J.S. Brewer and W. Bullen (London, 1871)
C.C.R.	*Calendars of Close Rolls* (H.M.S.O.)
C.P.R.	*Calendars of Patent Rolls* (H.M.S.O.)
Chroniques d'Adrien de But	*Chroniques relatives 'l'Histoire de la Belgique, sous la Domination des Ducs de Bourgogne. Vol I. Chroniques des Religieux des Dunes*, ed. Kervyn de Lettenhove (Académie Royale de Belgique, Brussels, 1870).
Complete Peerage	G.E. Cokayne, *The Complete Peerage of England, Scotland, Ireland, Great Britain and the United Kingdom*, ed. V. Gibbs, *et al.* 12 vols. (1910–59)
Crowland Chronicle	'Second continuation of Crowland chronicle' in *Ingulph's Chronicles*, ed. H.T. Riley (London, 1893)
D.N.B.	*The Dictionary of National Biography*, 63 vols. (1885–1900)
E.H.R.	*English Historical Review*
Herald's Report	'A short and a brief memory ... of the first progress of our sovereign lord Henry the Seventh ... etc' in J. Leland, *Collectanea*, Vol.IV, ed. T. Hearne (Oxford, 1774), pp. 185–257.
H.M.S.O.	His/Her Majesty's Stationery Office
Letters and Papers	*Letters and Papers Illustrative of the Reigns of Richard III and Henry VII*, ed. J. Gairdner, 2 vols. (R.S. 1861–3)
Materials	*Materials for a History of the Reign of Henry the Seventh*, ed. W. Campbell, 2 vols. (R.S., 1873–7)
Molinet, *Chroniques*	*Chroniques de Jean Molinet (1474–1506)*, ed. G. Doutrepont and O. Jodogne, 3 vols. (Académie Royale de Belgique. Classe des Lettres et des Sciences Morales et Politques. Collection des Anciens Auteurs Belges; Brussels, 1935–7)
Paston Letters	*Paston Letters and Papers of the Fifteenth Century*, ed. N. Davis, 2 vols. (Oxford, 1971–6)
P.R.O.	Public Record Office
R.P.	*Rotuli Parliamentorum*, ed. J. Strachey, 6 vols. (London, 1767–83)
R.S.	Roll Series
Rous, *Historia*	*Joannis Rossi Antiquarii Warwicensis Historia Regum Angliae*, ed. T. Hearne (Oxford, 1716)
Tudor Proclamations	*Tudor Royal Proclamations*, Vol. 1. 'The Early Tudors' P.L. Hughes and J.F. Larkin (New Haven, 1964)

Vergil, Anglica Historia   *The 'Anglica Historia' of Polydore Vergil, A.D. 1485–1537*, ed. D. Hay (Camden Society, new series 74, 1950)

V.C.H.   *Victoria History of the Counties of England*

York Civic Records   *York Civic Records*, Vol.2, ed. A. Raine (Yorkshire Archaeological Society Record Series 103, 1941)

NOTES

1 Prologue: Whitsuntide 1487

1. M.J. Bennett, *The Battle of Bosworth* (Gloucester, 1985), ch. 6; C.F. Richmond, 'The battle of Bosworth', *History Today* 35.8 (1985), pp. 17–22. The controversy over the site of the battle is somewhat overblown, because no historian has ever doubted that it was closer to Dadlington than Bosworth. The projected status of Dadlington as a battlefield chapel, hitherto overlooked by all but local scholars, confirms the drift of my own reconstruction, which placed the main fighting south of Ambien hill, and around the ford: P.J. Foss, *The Battle of Bosworth. Where was it fought?* (Stoke Golding, 1985).
2. C. Wordsworth, *Notes on Mediaeval Services in England* (London, 1898), p. 207
3. *Materials*, II, p. 159.
4. W. Busch, *England under the Tudors, I. Henry VII* (London, 1898) remains the fullest narrative treatment of the reign, but S.B. Chrimes, *Henry VII* (London, 1972), M.V.C. Alexander, *The First of the Tudors. A Study of Henry VII and His Reign* (London, 1981), and R.A. Griffiths and R.S. Thomas, *The Making of the Tudor Dynasty* (Gloucester, 1985) provide more up-to-date guides to the establishment of the Tudor regime.
5. M.T. Hayden, 'Lambert Simnel in Ireland', *Studies. An Irish Quarterly Review* 4 (1915), 622–38; *Book of Howth*, pp. 188–9. The pretender is referred to as 'Edward VI' at York: (York City Archives, House Book 6, f.97), not 'Edward V' as appears erroneously in *York Civic Records*, pp. 20–1.
6. A. Cosgrove, *Late Medieval Ireland, 1370–1541* (Dublin, 1981), esp. ch. 4; M. Hicks, *False, Fleeting, Perjur'd Clarence. George, Duke of Clarence* (Gloucester, 1980), pp. 14, 23, 42, 74–5, 169.
7. T. Gainsford, 'The True and Wonderful History of Perkin Warbeck, proclaiming himself Richard the Fourth (1618)' *Harleian Miscellany*, ed. W. Oldys and T. Park (London, 1810), pp. 545–6.
8. D. Bryan, *Gerald Fitzgerald. The Great Earl of Kildare (1456–1513)* (Dublin, 1933)
9. *Tudor Proclamations*, pp. 12–13.
10. Bacon, *Henry the Seventh*, p. 95.
11. *Materials*, II, pp. 148–9; Vergil, *Anglica Historia*, pp. 16–19; Bacon, *Henry the Seventh*, pp. 87–8.
12. D. Wilkins (ed.), *Concilia Magnae Britanniae et Hiberniae, A.D. 466–1718*, 4 vols. (London, 1737), III, p. 618; *Letters and Papers*, I, pp. 94–6; R.P., VI, pp. 397–400.
13. *Materials*, II, pp. 130–9; *Tudor Proclamations*, pp. 12–15; *C.P.R. 1485–1494*, pp. 170–1, 191, 193, 197, 199, 209, 227; P.R.O., E101/413/2/1.
14. P.R.O., C142/23, no.200; *Acts of Court of the Mercers' Company 1453–1527*, ed. L. Lyell (Cambridge, 1936), p. 303. I am most grateful to M.M. Condon and Dr Alison Hanham for providing these references.
15. J.O. Haliwell (ed.), *Letters of the Kings of England*, Vol. 1. (London, 1846), p. 171;

York Civic Records, pp. 20–1; *Paston Letters*, II, p. 453; *York Civic Records*, p. 21; T. Stapleton (ed.), *Plumpton Correspondence* (Camden Society, original series 4, 1839), pp. 54–5.

16. *York Civic Records*, esp.pp. 6–29
17. British Library, Cotton MS. Julius B.XII, fos.8d–66; *Herald's Report*, pp. 185–257. When the report of affairs in 1486 and 1487 assumed its final form, the death of Sir Edward Woodville in 1488 was known, whereas the earl of Northumberland's death in 1489 was not similarly anticipated.
18. R.F. Green, 'Historical notes of a London citizen', *E.H.R.* 96 (1981), 585–9; *Crowland Chronicle*, p. 514; Rous, *Historia*, p. 219.
19. *The Great Chronicle of London*, ed. A.H. Thomas and I.D. Thornley (London, 1938), pp. 240–1; B. André, *Vita*, pp. 49–54.
20. Molinet, *Chroniques*, I, pp.562–5.
21. Vergil, *Anglica Historia*, pp. 12–27.
22. *Book of Howth*, esp. p. 189; Edward Halle, *The Union of the Two Noble Families of Lancaster and York* (London, 1550) (Facsimile, 1970); Raphael Holinshed, *Chronicles of England, Scotland and Ireland*, ed. H. Ellis, 6 vols. (London, 1807–8); Bacon, *Henry the Seventh*, pp. 82–95.
23. Vergil, *Anglica Historia*, pp. 22n–23n.
24. Bodleian Library, Oxford, MS. Lat. misc. c.66, f.104.
25. The refrain, 'Martin Swart and his men, sodledum, sodledum / Martin Swart and his men, sodledum bell' appears in W. Wager, The Longer Thou Livest The More Fool Thou Art (c.1568), lines 92–3. There is an earlier allusion to 'Martin Swart and all his merry men' in Skelton's 'Agaynste a comely coystrowne': *John Skelton: The Complete English Poems*, ed. J. Scattergood (Harmondsworth, 1983), pp. 391, 37.
26. Gainsford, 'Wonderful History of Perkin Warbeck', pp. 545–6; *Complete Peerage*, VIII, p. 225; *Chroniques de Jersey, 1585, par an auteur inconnu*, ed. A. Mourant (Jersey, 1858), pp. 22–9; *Book of Howth*, pp. 189–90.
27. T.C. Croker, *The Popular Songs of Ireland* (London, 1839), pp. 310–40; R. Brooke, *Visits to Fields of Battle in England of the Fifteenth Century* (London, 1857), pp. 185, 188–9.
28. Vergil, *Anglica Historia*, pp. 24–5; Wilkins, *Concilia*, III, p. 618. I would like to thank Dr Christopher Harper-Bill, editor of the forthcoming Canterbury and York Society edition of Morton's register for confirming details of this entry, and sending me the relevant extract (item 89) from his calendar.

2 Blood and Roses

1. J. H. Huizinga, *The Waning of the Middle Ages*, transl. F. Hopman (Harmondsworth, 1965), p. 25 and passim. See P. Burke, 'Huizinga, prophet of "blood and roses"', *History Today* 36.11 (1986), 23–8.
2. C. Ross, *The Wars of the Roses. A Concise History* (London, 1976), ch. 1.
3. J.R. Lander, *Conflict and Stability in Fifteenth-Century England* (London, 1969); J. Gillingham, *The Wars of the Roses. Peace and Conflict in Fifteenth-Century England* (London, 1981), esp. chs. 1 & 2; C.A. Sneyd (ed.), *A Relation of the Island of England* (Camden Society, old series 37, 1847).
4. C.A.J. Armstrong, 'The piety of Cicely, duchess of York: a study in late medieval culture' in D. Woodruff (ed.), *For Hillaire Belloc. Essays in Honour of his*

Seventy-First Birthday (New York, 1942), pp. 68–91; P.M. Kendall, *The Yorkist Age. Daily Life during the Middle Ages* (London, 1961), esp. pp. 423–6.

5. *Complete Peerage*, XII, pt. 2, pp. 544–7.
6. B. Wilkinson, 'The deposition of Richard II and the accession of Henry IV' *E.H.R.*, 73 (1958), 583–613.
7. G.P. Cuttino and T.W. Lyman, 'Where is Edward II?', *Speculum* 53 (1978), pp. 522–44.
8. M.J. Bennett, *Community, Class and Careerism. Cheshire and Lancashire Society in the Age of 'Sir Gawain and the Green Knight'* (Cambridge, 1983), p. 39; J.H. Wylie, *The Reign of Henry the Fifth*, Vol. 1. (Cambridge, 1914), ch. 27.
9. R.A. Griffiths, *The Reign of Henry VI. The Exercise of Royal Authority, 1422–1461* (London, 1981), ch. 22.
10. R.A. Griffiths, 'The sense of dynasty on the reign of Henry VI' in C. Ross (ed.), *Patronage, Pedigree and Power in Later Medieval England* (Gloucester, 1979), pp. 13–36; R.A. Griffiths, 'Duke Richard of York's intentions in 1450 and the origins of the Wars of the Roses', *Journal of Medieval History* 1 (1985), pp. 187–209.
11. R.L. Storey, *The End of the House of Lancaster* (London, 1966); Griffiths, *Reign of Henry VI*, chs. 21–4.
12. Kendall, *The Yorkist Age*, pp. 423–6.
13. D. Mancini, *The Usurpation of Richard III*, ed. C.A.J. Armstrong (Oxford, 1969), pp. 60–3.
14. Hicks, *False, Fleeting, Perjur'd Clarence*, ch. 2.
15. C. Ross, *Edward IV* (1974), ch. 7; Hicks, *Clarence*, ch. 3.
16. Hicks, *Clarence*, ch. 4 and appendix 1.
17. *R.P.*, VI, pp. 193–5; Hicks, *Clarence*, ch. 4. Stillington was arrested in 1478 for 'some utterance prejudicial to the king', but there is no clear connection with Clarence's treason: Hicks, *Clarence*, pp. 163–4. Perhaps Stillington had been less than discreet with colleagues at Wells, one of whom had passed on the allegation to Clarence.
18. C.L. Scofield, *The Life and Reign of Edward IV*, 2 vols. (London, 1923), II, pp. 205, 299.
19. C. Ross, *Richard III* (London, 1981), ch. 4; Armstrong, 'Piety of Cicely, duchess of York', pp. 68–91.
20. J. Gairdner, *History of the Life and Reign of Richard III* (Cambridge, 1898), pp. 189–90; A.R. Myers, 'Richard III: a correspondence', *History Today* 4 (1954), 709; P.M. Kendall, *Richard III* (London, 1955), p. 332.
21. Armstrong, 'Piety of Cicely, duchess of York', pp. 87–8, 74–6.

3 The Tudor Interlude

1. *Crowland Chronicle*, pp. 505–6; D. Palliser, 'Richard III and York' in R. Horrox (ed.), *Richard III and the North* (Hull, 1986), pp. 68–9.
2. Bennett, *Battle of Bosworth*, esp. ch. 7.
3. A. Goodman, 'Henry VII and Christian renewal' in *Religion and Humanism*, ed. K. Robbins (Studies in Church History 17, 1981), pp. 121–2.
4. Molinet, *Chroniques*, I, p. 432.
5. *Materials*, I, pp. 282–3.
6. A.F. Pollard, *The Reign of Henry VII from Contemporary Sources*, 3 vols. (London, 1913–14), I, p. 21.
7. Goodman, *Wars of the Roses*, pp. 98–9; A.L. Rowse, 'The turbulent career of Sir

Henry de Bodrugan', *History* 29 (1944), pp. 17–26.

8. Bryan, *Kildare*, pp. 96–8; S.G. Ellis, 'The struggle for control of the Irish mint, 1460–*c.* 1506', *Proceedings of the Royal Irish Academy (Section C)*, 78 (1978), pp. 29–30; A.J. Eagleston, *The Channel Islands under Tudor Government, 1485–1642. A Study in Administrative History* (Cambridge, 1949), pp. 5–7; *Chroniques d'Adrien de But*, p. 665; C.S.L. Davies, 'Bishop John Morton, the Holy See, and the Accession of Henry VII', *E.H.R.*, 102 (1987), 26. (I would like to thank Dr Davies for allowing me to see this article in advance of its publication.)

9. *Tudor Proclamations*, p. 3.

10. *Plumpton Correspondence*, p. 49.

11. *Plumpton Correspondence*, p. 50. Irish prophecies hostile to Henry VII can be inferred from Rous, *Historia*, p. 219, who turned them on their head by insisting that Henry Tudor was only the sixth lord of that name of Ireland.

12. André, *Vita*, p. 38; *Plumpton Correspondence*, p. 48. Davies, 'Morton, the Holy See and Henry VII', pp. 1–29, discusses Morton's role in preparing the way for papal support for the royal marriage.

13. Bryan, *Kildare*, pp. 98–9.

14. *Herald's Report*, pp. 185–203; S. Anglo, *Spectacle, Pageantry and the Early Tudor Polity* (Oxford, 1969), ch. 1.

15. *Plumpton Correspondence*, p. 50; *Letters and Papers*, I, pp. 234–5.

16. *Herald's Report*, p. 185.

17. *Herald's Report*, pp. 185–6; C.H. Williams, 'The rebellion of Humphrey Stafford in 1486', *E.H.R.*, 43 (1928), 181–9.

18. *Herald's Report*, pp. 186–7; Bennett, *Battle of Bosworth*, p. 171.

19. Vergil, *Anglica Historia*, pp. 10–11; *Herald's Report*, 186–7; *Crowland Chronicle*, pp. 513–14; *York Civic Records*, pp. 3–5.

20. *Herald's Report*, pp. 188–92.

21. *C.P.R. 1485–1494*, pp. 106–7; Williams, 'Rebellion of Humphrey Stafford', 181–9.

22. *C.P.R. 1485–1494*, p. 112; Williams, 'Rebellion of Humphrey Stafford', 183.

23. *C.P.R. 1485–1494*, pp. 21, 110, 112.

24. *Select Cases in the Council of Henry VII*, ed. C.G. Bayne and W.H. Dunham (Selden Society 75, 1958 for 1956), p. 8.

25. *Herald's Report*, 196; *Select Cases in Council of Henry VII*, p. 8; *Tudor Proclamations*, I, pp. 6–7.

26. *Herald's Report*, pp. 204–7.

4 The Lambert Simnel Mystery

1. C.E. Mallet, *A History of the University of Oxford. Vol. 1. The Mediaeval University and the Colleges founded in the Middle Ages* (London, 1924), pp. 344–7, 386–7.

2. A.B. Emden, *A Biographical Register of the University of Oxford to A.D. 1500*, 3 vols. (Oxford, 1957–9), III, 1841–3

3. Vergil, *Anglica Historia*, pp. 12–17.

4. Williams, 'Rebellion of Humphrey Stafford', 183; *Plumpton Correspondence*, p. 54. It was believed at Dunkirk that many Londoners, irritated by Henry VII's confirmation of the privileges of the Hanseatic merchants, conspired in favour of Warwick: *Chroniques d'Adrien de But*, p. 665.

5. Molinet, *Chroniques*, I, pp. 562–3; André, *Vita*, pp. 49–50.

6. Wilkins, *Concilia*, III, p. 618.

7. Bacon, *Henry the Seventh*, p. 95. It is in noting the priest's disappearance that Bacon refers to the king 'as loving to seal up his own dangers'.

8. *R.P.*, VI, p. 194. Allegedly Clarence 'willed and desired the abbot of Tewkesbury, Master John Tapton, clerk, and Roger Harewell, esquire, to cause a strange child to have been brought into the castle of Warwick, and there to have been put and kept in likeliness of his son and heir, and that they should have conveyed and sent his said son and heir into Ireland or into Flanders, out of this land, whereby he might have gotten him assistance and favour against our said sovereign lord, and for the execution of the same sent one John Taylor his servant, to have had deliverance of the said son and heir', but the abbot and the others refused.

9. Molinet, *Chroniques*, I, pp. 562–5. It is possible that Molinet was writing a little tongue-in-cheek.

10. Wilkins, *Concilia*, III, p. 618; R.P., VI, p. 397; *Herald's Report*, p. 214; Vergil, *Anglica Historia*, pp. 24–5.

11. M.J. Bennett, 'Spiritual kinship and the baptismal name in traditional European society' in *Principalities, Powers and Estates. Studies in Medieval and Early Modern Government and Society*, ed. L.O. Frappell (Adelaide, 1979), 1–13; *Crowland Chronicle*, pp. 494, 506.

12. This rare practice can be documented, coincidentally, in the case of a child called Lambert: in 1448 the daughter of John Lambert of Lancaster granted a burgage to Lambert Stodagh, probably her son: *C.C.R. 1447–1454*, p. 34.

13. *D.N.B.*, XVIII, pp. 261–2.

14. British Library, MS. Cotton Julius B.XII, f.29.

15. British Library, MS. Cotton Julius B.XII, fos. 28d (where mistake stands) and 25d (where emendation is made).

16. W. Prevenier and W. Blockmans, *The Burgundian Netherlands* (Cambridge, 1986), pp. 310–11.

17. Wilkins, *Concilia*, III, p. 618; *R.P.*, VI, p. 397; Croker, *Popular Songs of Ireland*, p. 328.

18. *Calendar of Papal Registers relating to Great Britain and Ireland*, Vol. XIV (H.M.S.O., 1960), pp. 307–8; André, *Vita*, pp. 49–50, 52; Bacon, *Henry the Seventh*, p. 82.

19. H. Ansty (ed.), *Munimenta Academica*, 2 vols. (R.S., 1857), II, p. 710; Mallet, *History of University of Oxford*, I, p. 401.

20. *C.P.R. 1485–1494*, pp. 139, 141. The rumour, however, was that Warwick was in Guernsey not Jersey: Williams, 'Rebellion of Humphrey Stafford', p. 183.

21. *Plumpton Correspondence*, p. 54; P. Holmes, 'The great council in the reign of Henry VII', *E.H.R.* 101 (1986), 852–3; *Chroniques d'Adrien de But*, p. 665.

22. Vergil, *Anglica Historia*, pp. 16–19; Bacon, *Henry the Seventh*, pp. 83–4.

23. Vergil, *Anglica Historia*, pp. 12n–13n; J. Gairdner, *History of the Life and Reign of Richard the Third* (Cambridge, 1898), pp. 266–7; C. Roth, 'Perkin Warbeck and his Jewish Master', *Transactions of the Jewish Historical Society of England* 9 (1918–20), pp.143–62. C. Roth, 'Sir Edward Brampton: an Anglo-Jewish adventurer during the Wars of the Roses', *Ibid.*, 16 (1945–51), 121–7. While both acknowledged that during his time in Brampton's service, Perkin could have learned about the life of the prince he was later to impersonate, neither Gairdner nor Roth accord Brampton any witting part in preparing the imposture, principally because when the conspiracy broke he was back in favour with Henry VII. Some of the oddities of this case could be resolved, however, if it were assumed that an imposture centring on Warbeck had begun by 1487, but was overtaken by a more widely-supported plot centring on Simnel, and that Brampton, breaking with his Yorkist allies at this point, was later, when Warbeck's pretence was given support, in a position to disclose to Henry VII biographical details of his former protégé.

24. J.A.F. Thomson, 'John de la Pole, duke of Suffolk', *Speculum* 54 (1979), pp. 528–42, esp. 537.

25. In 1489 it was alleged that John Sant, abbot of Abingdon and others on 1 January 1487 sent John Mayne abroad with a sum of money to aid the earl of Lincoln: *R.P.*, VI, pp. 436–7.
26. Halliwell, *Letters of Kings of England*, Vol. 1, p. 172.
27. *The Registers of Robert Stillington, Bishop of Bath and Wells, 1466–1491, and Richard Fox, Bishop of Bath and Wells, 1492–1494*, ed. H.C. Maxwell-Lyte (Somerset Record Society 52, 1937), pp. ix–xiii. According to Commines, Richard III at some stage planned to marry Elizabeth of York to the son of Bishop Stillington, but the latter young man was captured by the French and died in captivity (xiv–xv).
28. *Paston Letters*, I, pp. 652–3. Hextall received a pardon on 4 May: *C.P.R. 1485–1494*, p. 172.
29. *York Civic Records*, pp. 3–6.

5 The Gathering Storm

1. Croker, *Popular Songs of Ireland*, pp. 318–31.
2. M.A. Hicks, 'Dynastic change and northern society: the career of the fourth earl of Northumberland, 1470–89', *Northern History* 14 (1978), pp. 78–107. For his brief attendance at the council at Sheen and his return northwards, see *Paston Letters*, I, pp. 652–3.
3. *Paston Letters*, I, p. 654.
4. The herald and Polydore Vergil both relate episodes from the tour: *Herald's Report*, p. 209, and Vergil, *Anglica Historia* , pp. 20–1. The large number of Lancashire gentlemen in the king's retinue, anticipated by William Paston (*Paston Letters*, I, p. 654), illustrates the dependence of the royal household on the military resources of the palatinates of Chester and Lancaster, and the correspondingly influential brokerage of the house of Stanley. On 23 September 1486 Henry retained in his service over 100 knights and squires from Lancashire and Cheshire, with annuities totalling almost £1,000: P.R.O., DL42/21, fos. 49–50, 108–108d.
5. R. Virgoe, 'The recovery of the Howards in East Anglia, 1485–1529' in E.W. Ives, R.J. Knecht and J.J. Scarisbrick (eds.), *Wealth and Power in Tudor England. Essays presented to S.T. Bindoff* (London, 1978), pp. 1–20. J.P. Collier (ed.), *The Household books of John, Duke of Norfolk and Thomas, Earl of Surrey* (Roxburghe Club, 1844), pp. 493–501; *Paston Letters*, II, pp. 452–3.
6. *Materials*, II, pp. 135, 143, 136–7.
7. *Herald's Report*, p. 209; *York Civic Records*, pp. 10–11.
8. *Materials*, II, pp. 152–3.
9. *York Civic Records*, pp. 13–14.
10. C.f. the problems posed by adverse weather to the fleet launched against England from the Netherlands in 1688: J. Carswell, *The Descent on England. A Study of the English Revolution of 1688 and Its European Background* (London, 1969), ch. 12.
11. R.H. Ryland, *The History, Topography and Antiquities of the County and City of Waterford* (London, 1824), pp. 142–3.
12. Molinet, *Chroniques*, I, pp. 444–51, 524–8. See in general F. Redlich, *The German Military Enterpriser and his Work Force. A Study in European Economic and Social History*, 2 vols. (Vierteljahrschrift fur Sozial- unde Wirtschaftsgesichte 47 & 48, Wiesbaden, 1964–5), I, pp. 16–20, 107.
13. E.M. Nokes and G. Wheeler, 'A Spanish account of the battle of Bosworth', *The Ricardian* 2, no.36 (1972), pp. 1–5; A. Goodman and A. MacKay, 'A Castilian report on English affairs, 1486', *E.H.R.* 88 (1973), pp.92–9; Molinet, *Chroniques*, I, p. 521.

14. André, *Vita*, p. 50.
15. Molinet, *Chroniques*, I, pp. 562–3. In July 1487 some 15,000 men were sent to Brittany under the Bastard Baldwin of Burgundy: B.A. Pocquet du Haut-Jussé, *François II, Duc de Bretagne et L'Angleterre (1458–1488)* (Paris, 1929), p. 278.
16. *Acts of Court of Mercers' Company*, pp. 300–1. I am grateful to Dr Alison Hanham for providing me with this reference.
17. *R.P.*, VI, pp. 436–7.
18. *Letters and Papers*, I, pp. 382–3.
19. *Chroniques de Jersey*, p. 29.
20. Rowse, 'The career of Sir Henry de Bodrugan', 17–26, accepts as 'a likely enough story' (26) the claim that Bodrugan was in Ireland visiting relatives.
21. In general see Cosgrove, *Late Medieval Ireland*, chs. 3 & 4; Bryan, *Kildare*, pp. 1–97.
22. Hayden, 'Simnel in Ireland', 622–38; Bryan, *Kildare*, pp. 99–119; *Book of Howth*, pp. 188–9; P.R.O., PROB 11/8, fos. 60d–61; Croker, *Popular Songs of Ireland*, pp. 310–17
23. Bacon, *Henry the Seventh*, p. 91; An expedition to Ireland was under consideration around the middle of May: Halliwell, *Letters of Kings of England*, vol. 1, p. 171; *Paston Letters*, II, p. 432.
24. Bryan, *Kildare*, pp. 52–3, 81–2; K. Nicholls, *Gaelic and Gaelicised Ireland in the Middle Ages* (Dublin, 1972), pp. 84–90.
25. Bryan, *Kildare*, p. 114.

6   The Struggle for the Kingdom

1. *Letters of Kings of England*, I, p. 171. In general see *Herald's Report*, pp. 209–10.
2. F.C. Dietz, *English Government Finance 1485–1558* (Urbana, 1920), p. 52; *Paston Letters*, II, p. 453.
3. *York Civic Records*, pp. 16–18.
4. Vergil, *Anglica Historia*, pp. 20–3.
5. *Tudor Proclamations*, pp. 12–13.
6. *V.C.H. Lancaster*, VIII, pp. 310–11.
7. C. Ross, *Richard III* (London, 1981), pp. 25–6, 53–4.
8. *V.C.H. Lancaster*, VIII, 403; Vergil, *Anglica Historia*, pp. 10–11, 16–17, 20–1.
9. *Materials*, II, pp. 99–100; Vergil, *Anglica Historia*, pp. 20–3; *The Register of Thomas Rotherham, Archbishop of York 1480–1500*, Vol.1., ed. E.E. Barker (Canterbury and York Society 69, 1976), pp. 220–3. In October 1487 the abbot of Furness compounded with the king to the tune of 400 marks, PRO, E101/413/2/1, f.9d.
10. *V.C.H. Lancaster*, VIII, p. 287. The tradition might have arisen from the belief that Swarthmoor was named after Martin Schwartz.
11. P.R.O., D101/413/1/2. f.9.d. Molinet, *Chroniques*, I, p. 563; Goodman, *Wars of Roses*, p. 257n; C. Fleury, *'Time-Honoured Lancaster'. Historic Notes on the Ancient Borough of Lancaster* (London, 1891), p. 138.
12. Goodman, *Wars of Roses*, pp. 97–9; *V.C.H. Lancaster*, VIII, p. 194; *V.C.H. Lancaster*, V, p. 90; W.E. Hampton, *Memorials of the Wars of the Roses. A Biographical Guide* (Upminster, 1979), pp. 101–2.
13. R. Davies (ed.), *Extracts from the Municipal Records of th City of York during the Reigns of Edward IV, Edward V and Richard III* (London, 1843), pp. 303–4; *V.C.H. Lancaster*, VIII, pp. 126–7.
14. *R.P.*, VI, p.398; *Materials*, II, p. 184. Skelton, Appleby and Musgrave had all been involved in Fitzhugh's rising in 1470: *C.P.R. 1467–1477*, pp. 214–15, 277. Hampton, *Memorials*, pp. 26–7.

15. Goodman, *Wars of the Roses*, pp. 67–9, 74; A.J. Pollard, 'The Richmondshire community of gentry during the Wars of the Roses' in C. Ross (ed.), *Patronage, Pedigree and Power in Later Medieval England* (Gloucester, 1979), pp. 37–59; A.J. Pollard, 'The tyranny of Richard III', *Journal of Medieval History* 3 (1977), 147–65.

16. *Complete Peerage*, V, pp. 429–31. In 1485 Fitzhugh rapidly came to terms with Henry VII: *C.P.R. 1485–1494*, pp. 16, 39.

17. *York Civic Records*, pp. 20–1.

18. *Tudor Proclamations*, p. 13

19. *Herald's Report*, p. 210.

20. *Tudor Proclamations*, pp. 14–15; *Herald's Report*, pp. 210–11.

21. *Herald's Report*, p. 212; *Materials*, II, p. 157.

22. *Herald's Report*, p. 212.

23. Molinet, *Chroniques*, I, p. 563.

24. Palliser, 'Richard III and York', pp. 51–81.

25. *York Civic Records*, pp. 9–15.

26. *York Civic Records*, pp. 20–2.

27. *York Civic Records*, p. 22.

28. *York Civic Records*, pp. 22–3.

29. Molinct, *Chroniques*, I, p. 563. There is no English evidence that York eventually declared for the rebels, though, since the York house book was written up some weeks after the failure of the rising, its silence on the matter is to be expected.

30. *Herald's Report*, p. 212. Vergil, *Anglica Historia*, pp. 22–3, refers to a camp at 'Banrys'.

31. *Herald's Report*, p. 212; P.R.O., E 101/412/19.

32. *Herald's Report*, p. 213. Other sources refer to false reports of the king's flight or defeat, though it cannot be assumed that they all relate to this particular episode: *Letters and Papers*, I, pp. 94–5; Molinet, *Chroniques*, I, pp. 563–4; *Great Chronicle of London*, p. 241.

33. *Herald's Report*, p. 213.

34. *Three Books of Polydore Vergil's 'English History'*, ed. H. Ellis (Camden Society, old series 29, 1844), pp. 217–18. It is possible that Vergil mistakenly attributed to the Bosworth campaign an episode from the Stoke campaign.

35. *Herald's Report*, p. 213.

36. *Herald's Report*, esp. pp. 214–15; Vergil, *Anglica Historia*, esp. pp. 22n–23n.

37. *Herald's Report*, p. 213; Vergil, *Anglica Historia*, pp. 22–5. A.H. Burne, *More Battlefields of England* (London, 1952), pp. 151–6, makes a convincing resolution of the matter.

38. *Herald's Report*, p. 213.

39. *Chroniques de Jersey*, p. 29.

40. Wager, *The Longer Thou Livest*, lines 92–3.

41. While the men attainted in 1487 (*R.P.*, VI, pp. 397–8) presumably fought against the king at Stoke, the degree of culpability of Yorkists who sued for pardons in the aftermath of the rebellion is impossible to establish (*C.P.R. 1485–1494*, pp. 170–1, 191, 193, 197, 199, 209). Fortunately, in the case of at least two persons pardoned, Sir Edmund Hastings and John Pullen, there is independent evidence of their participation in the rising: *Register of Thomas Rotherham*, p. 136; *Plumpton Correspondence*, pp. 54–5.

42. Hampton, *Memorials*, pp. 50–1.

43. There is no evidence other than tradition for this crossing. Molinet implies that the rebels passed through Newark (Molinet, *Chroniques*, p. 564), which might explain

the town's payment of 200 marks to the king shortly after the battle: P.R.O., E101/413/2/1. f.1).

7 The Battle of Stoke

1. C. Brown, *A History of Newark-on-Trent, being the Life Story of an Ancient Town*, 2 vols. (Newark, 1904, 1907).
2. *Lincoln Diocese Documents 1450–1544*, ed. A. Clark (Early English Text Sociey 149, 1914), pp. 256–9; *Register of Thomas Rotherham*, p. 213.
3. Gillingham, *Wars of the Roses*, pp. 161, 192
4. Shilton, *Battle of Stoke-Field*, p. 54, provides details of the Trent's fordability at Fiskerton in 1825 and 1826. All the indications, not least the poverty of the subsequent harvest, are that the summer of 1487 was hot and dry. I would like to thank Hugh Aixill for sharing his thoughts on this matter.
5. The 'sources' for the actual conduct of the battle are restricted to a few observations in Molinet, André and Vergil, inferences drawn from military tactics of the time, and local tradition. Burne, More Battlefields of England, ch. 14, is the most reliable guide.
6. *Complete Peerage*, XI, pp. 544–6.
7. *Chroniques de Jersey*, pp. 21–7; Pocquet du Haut-Jussé, *François II, Duc de Bretagne, et L'Angleterre*, pp. 113, 169, 260.
8. The numbers involved remain guesswork. The York house book claims that Lincoln had 20,000 men in arms, with 5,000 slain (*York Civic Records*, p. 23). The act of attainder of 1487 and Molinet, with unwonted sobriety, both record 8,000 (*R.P.*, VI, p. 397; Molinet, *Chroniques*, I, p. 564). Lovell's attainder in 1495 refers, austerely, to only 5,000 (R.P., VI, 502–3). The herald records that 4,000 rebels were slain (*Herald's Report*, p. 214), while Robert Fabian suggests that the rebels behaved in battle as if they had 20,000 more men than they actually did (Great Chronicle of London, p. 241).
9. P. Contamine, *War in the Middle Ages* (Oxford, 1984), pp. 132–7; Redlich, *The German Military Enterpriser*, I, pp. 1–21. J.R. Hale, 'The soldier in Germanic graphic art of the Renaissance', *Journal of Interdisciplinary History* 17 (1986), 85–114, esp. 87n. See also M. Vale, *War and Chivalry. Warfare and Aristocratic Culture in England, France and Burgundy at the End of the Middle Ages* (London, 1981), ch. 4.
10. C. Falls, *Elizabeth's Irish Wars* (London, 1950), ch. 4, provides an illuminating discussion of traditional Irish weapons and tactics.
11. Molinet, *Chroniques*, I, p. 564.
12. André, *Vita*, p. 52; Vergil, *Anglica Historia*, pp. 24–5.
13. *Herald's Report*, pp. 213–14.
14. The numbers in the royal army were assuredly large. Molinet's figures imply a total of at least 40,000 men (Molinet, *Chroniques*, I, p. 564). The York account refers to a vanguard of 10,000 men (*York Civic Records*, p. 23), while the herald implies that the Stanleyites forces alone were more than a match for the rebels (*Herald's Report*, 213). For battle-formation, see *Herald's Report*, pp. 210–15, and for Stanleyites in vanguard, see Molinet, *Chroniques*, I, p. 564 and *York Civic Records*, p. 23.
15. *Herald's Report*, pp. 214–15.
16. André, *Vita*, p. 51, where Henry is presented, anachronistically, as referring to his 'children'.
17. Contamine, *War in the Middle Ages*, pp. 228–37.
18. Vergil, *Anglica Historia*, pp. 24–5. See also Molinet, *Chroniques*, I, p. 564.

19. Shilton, *Battle of Stoke-Field*, p. 68.
20. Hale, 'Soldier in Germanic graphic art', 87.
21. Molinet, *Chroniques*, I, p. 564.
22. *Herald's Report*, p. 214; *York Civic Records*, II, p. 23. Both the early accounts record the flight of Lovell and Broughton, but Vergil claims them as casualties (*Anglica Historia*, pp. 24–5). For traditions regarding the fates of the two latter men, see *Complete Peerage*, VIII, p. 225n; *V.C.H. Lancaster*, VIII, p. 403.
23. Vergil, *Anglica Historia*, pp. 26–7; British Library, Cotton MS. Julius B.XII, f.29 (*Herald's Report*, p. 214). Adrien de But at Dunkirk, however, believed that, once the heavy odds against the rebels became apparent, 'Warwick' had been taken from the field and brought to Guines: *Chroniques d'Adrien de But*, pp. 674–5.
24. Molinet, *Chroniques*, I, pp. 564–5; Shilton, *Battle of Stoke-Field*, p. 68n.
25. *Herald's Report*, pp. 214–15; *York Civic Records*, II, pp. 23–4.
26. 'Manuscripts of the Corporation of Lincoln' *Historical Manuscripts Commission, Fourteenth Report*, Appendix, Part VIII (H.M.S.O., 1895), p. 35; Molinet, *Chroniques*, I, pp. 564–5; Materials, II, p. 158.
27. Molinet, *Chroniques*, I, p. 564; *York Civic Records*, p. 23; *C.P.R. 1485–1494*, pp. 238–9. After being captured in the 'Lincoln battle', Edward Frank was committed to the Tower of London: C.A.J. Armstrong, 'An Italian astrologer at the court of Henry VII' in E.F. Jacob (ed.), *Italian Renaissance Studies* (London, 1960), p. 443; P.R.O. E101/413/2/1.
28. See commission to earl of Oxford in eastern counties, 21 June: *Household Books of Duke of Norfolk*, pp. 501–3, 493.
29. *Letters and Papers*, I, p. 95; Pollard, *Reign of Henry VII*, III, p. 157.

8 The Significance of 1487

1. *D.N.B.*, XVIII, pp. 261–2.
2. *John Skelton: Complete Poems*, pp. 397, 36–41; *Book of Howth*, p.190; Vergil, *Anglica Historia*, pp.12–13; Bacon, *Henry the Seventh*, pp.81–2, 95; T. Gainsford, 'Wonderful History of Perkin Warbeck', pp. 539–41.
3. *Materials*, II, pp. 157–63, 184–9.
4. M.J. Tucker, *The Life of Thomas Howard, Earl of Surrey and Second Duke of Norfolk, 1443–1524* (The Hague, 1964), pp. 49–50; Green, 'Historical notes of London citizen', 589.
5. *Plumpton Correspondence*, p. 54.
6. *R.P.*, VI, pp. 413–14.
7. Bryan, *Kildare*, pp. 118–19; Pollard, *Reign of Henry VII*, III, pp. 156–7
8. Rous, *Historia*, p. 219.
9. E.W. Ives, '"Agaynst the taking awaye of women": the inception and operation of the abduction act of 1487' *Wealth and Power in Tudor England*, ed. Ives, Knecht and Scarisbrick, pp. 26–30. Ives make no mention of Bellingham's military exploits, in which the anonymous herald took a special interest (*Herald's Report*, pp. 214, 247), nor does he remark on the Neville associations of some of his associates (*CPR 1485–1494*, p. 239).
10. *Materials*, II, p. 291.
11. *R.P.*, VI, pp. 397–400. Cf. Pollard, 'Tyranny of Richard III', 157–62.
12. *Materials*, II, pp. 186–7.
13. Ives, 'Ageynst the taking away of women', pp. 21–30; *R.P.*, VI, pp. 402–3; Green, 'Historical notes of London citizen', 589.
14. *Herald's Report*, pp. 216–33.

15. *Chroniques de Jersey*, pp. 28–9; *R.P.*, VI, pp. 503–7.
16. *R.P.*, VI, pp. 436–7.
17. Hicks, 'Dynastic change and northern society', pp. 78–107.
18. Green, 'Historical notes of London citizen', 590; Eagleston, *Channel Islands under Tudor Government*, pp. 6–7.
19. For what was new and distinctive about politics in the reign of Henry VII, see A. Grant, *Henry VII. The Importance of His Reign in English History* (London, 1985).
20. Chrimes, Henry VII, pp. 104–9; N. Pronay, 'The chancellor, the chancery and the council at the end of the fifteenth century' in *British Government and Administration, Studies presented to S.B. Chrimes*, eds. H. Hearder and H.R. Loyn (Cardiff, 1974), p. 101.
21. *Herald's Report*, pp. 229–33.
22. *Materials*, II, pp. 158–9; W.C. Richardson, *Tudor Chamber Administration 1485–1558* (Baton Rouge, 1952), esp. pp. 107–8; P.R.O., E101/413/2/1.
23 Chrimes, *Henry VII*, ch. 10; Pronay, 'Chancellor, chancery and council at end of fifteenth century', p. 99; A. Cameron, 'The giving of livery and retaining in Henry VII's reign', *Renaissance and Modern Studies* 18 (1974), pp. 29–30; Grant, *Henry VII*, pp. 32–3.
24. M. Condon, 'Ruling élites in the reign of Henry VII' in *Patronage, Pedigree and Power*, ed. Ross, pp. 114–21.
25. Cosgrove, *Late Medieval Ireland*, chs. 5 & 6; Eagleston, *Channel Islands under Tudor Administration*, pp. 9–16. S. Ellis, 'Crown, community and government in the English territories, 1450–1575', *History* 71 (1986), pp. 187–204, provides a convincing new framework for understanding the relations between the crown and the overseas lordships, though curiously he neglects the Channel Islands.
26. R.B. Wernham, *Before the Armada. The Growth of English Foreign Policy 1485–1588* (London, 1966), chs. 2 & 3; Pocquet du Haut-Jussé, *François II, Duc de Bretagne et L'Angleterre*, pp. 279–80; A. Conway, *Henry VII's Relations with Scotland and Ireland 1485–1498* (Cambridge, 1932), pp. 9–20.
27. Griffiths and Thomas, *Making of Tudor Dynasty*, ch. 13; Goodman, 'Henry VII and Christian renewal', pp. 115–25; André, *Vita*, p. 52; Davies, 'Morton, the Holy See and Henry VII', 1–29; Croker, *Popular Songs of Ireland*, p. 329.

INDEX

Abingdon, abbey of 50, 112
Abingdon, abbot of see Sant, John
Agincourt, battle of 19
Allerton Mauleverer 55
Altoft, William 3
Ambion hill 1
André, Bernard 1, 10, 12, 35–6, 43, 47, 61, 94–5, 119, 131–3
Anglica Historia see Vergil, Polydore
Anne (Neville), queen of England 30
Anne, duchess of Brittany 112
Appleby, Alexander 74, 125
Arderne, John 88
Armagh, archbishop of, see Palacio, Octavian del
Arundel, Edmund 136
Arundel, Sir John 129
Ashton under Lyne 73
Ashton, Sir Ralph 73
Atherstone 3
Audley, Sir James 129
Augsburg 64
Avintry, John 125

Babington, Sir John 136
Bacon, Sir Francis 8, 11, 47, 67, 105, 144n
Baldwin, bastard of Burgundy 147n
Ballads – *Bosworth Field* 11; *Battle of Stoke* 11
Banbury 22
Bank, Richard 125
'Banrys' 136
Barkswell 38
Barnet, battle of 22
Barnsdale 37
Barton, John 88
Battell, Thomas 125
Baugh Fell 74
Baynard's Castle 24
Beauchamp, Anne, countess of Warwick 108
Beaufitz, John 108
Beaufitz, Margery 108
Beaufort, house of 77
Beaufort, Edmund, duke of Somerset 19
Beaufort, Edmund, duke of Somerset (d.1471) 22
Beaufort, Joan, duchess of Westmorland 17
Beaufort, John, earl and duke of Somerset 19
Beaufort, Lady Margaret, countess of Richmond 4, 22, 30
Beaumont, John 64, 125
Bedford, dukes of, see Plantagenet, John; Tudor, Jasper
Bedingfield, Sir Edmund 59, 83, 101, 129
Bedyll, William 136
Bele, William 102
Belknap, Edward 136
Bellingham, Robert 101, 108, 129, 150n
Bellingham, Sir Roger 129
Berkeley, Sir Maurice 129
Berkhamsted 17, 24–5
Berkshire 112

Birmingham 38
Blandrehasset, Thomas 125
Blount, Sir James 83, 101, 129
Blount, Sir Thomas 129
Bodrugan, Sir Henry 33, 35, 64, 125, 147n
'Bonley Rice' 128
Boroughbridge 79, 123
Boru, Brian 8
Bosworth, battle of 1, 3, 25, 27, 30–1, 37, 41, 58, 61, 66, 71, 76, 82, 95, 97–8, 101, 106, 113, 119, 148n see also Market Bosworth
Bowness 74
Brabant 59–60, 125
Brackenthwaite 74
Bramham Moor 79, 81, 123
Brampton, Sir Edward 51, 54, 61, 145n
Brandon, Sir Robert 83, 129
Bray, Reginald 69, 114–15
Bristol 39
Brittany 63, 112, 116–17 See also Anne, duchess of Brittany
Broughton, John 71, 125
Broughton, Sir Robert 129
Broughton, Sir Thomas 71, 91, 101, 125, 134–6, 150n
Broughton Tower 71
Brown, Sir Anthony 83, 101, 129
Brudenell, Robert 136
Bruges 60
Brussels 60–1
Buckingham, dukes and duchesses of see Stafford, Humphrey; Neville, Anne
Bulmer, William 136
Bunny 81
Burgh, Sir Edward 129, 136
Burgh, Sir Maurice 129
Burgundy, dukes and duchesses of, see Charles the Bold; Margaret of York; Mary of Burgundy; Philip of Habsburg
Burham Furlong see Stoke, battle of
Bury St Edmunds 58, 135
But, Adrian de 50, 150n
Butler, house of 65–7, 107
Butler, John, mayor of Waterford 126
Butler, Thomas, earl of Ormond 33, 65
Butler, Thomas 67
Butler, William 67

Cade, Jack 20
Calais 33, 56, 61, 63, 112
Cambridge 25, 36, 59, 135
Cambridge, university of 41
Cambridge, earl of, see Plantagenet, Richard
Canterbury, archdiocese of 45, 121
Canterbury, archbishop of, see Morton, John
Carew, Sir William 129
Carlisle 74
Cartmel 72–3
Cartmel, priory of 72–3
Castleford 81, 130
Catherine of Aragon 117

Channel Islands 33, 39, 49, 57, 61, 63–4, 112, 116 See also Guernsey; Jersey
Charles VIII, king of France 130
Charles the Bold, duke of Burgundy 23, 47, 61, 97, 130
Chaucer, Geoffrey 7
Cheney, Sir John 38, 83, 95, 124, 129, 136
Cheney, Sir Robert 129
Cheney, Thomas 136
Cheshire 77, 84, 146n
Chester 21
Chilterns 16
Clarence, dukes and duchesses of, see Plantagenet, George; Plantagenet, Lionel; Neville, Isabel
Claxton, William 86, 103
Clifford, Henry, Lord Clifford 37, 74, 79, 81, 107, 123–4
Clifford, Sir Robert 83, 129
Clifton, Sir Gervase 83, 136
Cloyne, bishop of see Roche, William
Cokesey, Sir Thomas 129
Colet, John 63
Commines, Philippe de 146n
Connaught 8
Constable, Philip 103
Conway, Hugh 36
Cornwall 57, 64, 114
Cotehele 114
Cotton, Robert 136
Courtenay, Sir Edward, earl of Devon 75, 83, 127
Courtenay, Piers, bishop of Winchester 76, 127
Coventry 1, 9, 21, 59, 69, 75–6, 89, 108, 127, 136
Croft, Sir Richard 101, 129
Crowland, abbot of see Fossedyke, Lambert
Crowland Chronicle 10, 30, 38
Crown hill 1
Culham 38
Cumberland 74
Cumbria 57, 71, 74

Dadlington 1, 76, 141n
Daniel, Robert 136
Darcy, Lord of Platen 6
Darell, Sir Edward 129
David Thomas 61
Delabere, Sir Richard 129
De La Pole, house of 55, 58, 85, 108
De La Pole, Edward 24, 51
De La Pole, John, duke of Suffolk 7, 51, 58, 60, 131, 135
De La Pole, John, earl of Lincoln 5, 7, 11, 24, 30, 33, 37, 39–40, 43, 50–1, 53–5, 57–8, 60, 63–4, 71, 73–4, 79, 81, 84–6, 91–2, 94–5, 97, 101–2, 108, 121, 123–6, 129–38, 149n
De La Pole, William, duke of Suffolk 19
Derby, earl of see Stanley, Thomas
Derbyshire 84
Desmond, earl of, see Fitzgerald, James
Devenish, Sir John 129

Devereux, Walter, Lord Ferrers of Chartley 29
Devon, earl of, *see* Courtnay, Edward
Digby, Sir John 129, 136
Digby, Sir Simon 136
Dinham, John, Lord Dinham 113
Doncaster 37, 54, 81, 130
Dorset, marquis of, *see* Grey, Thomas
Dover 54, 57
Dublin 4–9, 20, 33, 35, 47–51, 55, 59–61, 63–8, 105, 107, 112, 116, 119, 125–6, 133, 135 – Christchurch cathedral 5, 66 – Hoggen Green 66 – St Sabviour's church 65
Dublin, archbishop of *see* Fitzsimons, Walter
Dunkirk 144n, 150n
Dunstable 85, 125

Ebranc 38
East Bridgford 86, 94
East Stoke 86, 91 *see* also Stoke
Edgecote, battle of 22
Edgecombe, Sir Richard 37, 64, 116
Edward I, king of England 18
Edward II, king of England 18
Edward III, king of England 7, 17–18, 126
Edward IV, king of England 3, 6–7, 21–5, 30–1, 45, 49, 51, 53–4, 63, 65, 74, 77, 90, 109, 111, 126, 132–5
Edward V, king of England 24–5, 32, 53
'Edward VI', pretended king of England 4, 44, 55, 65–6, 68, 70, 91, 111, 121, 130, 141n *see also* Simnel, Lambert and Plantagenet, Edward, earl of Warwick
Elizabeth Woodville, queen of England 9, 22, 40, 50–1, 54
Elizabeth of York, princess and queen of England 3–4, 9, 15, 28–32, 35, 40, 53, 57, 66, 109, 146n
Elston 91, 94, 98
Ely, bishop of, *see* Morton, John
Essex 45
Ewelme 51
Exeter, bishop of *see* Fox, Richard

Fabian, Robert 149n
Fame, George 35
Fawsley 125
Ferdinand, king of Aragon 117
Ferrers, Lord, of Chartley, *see* Devereux, Walter
Fielding, Edward 136
Findern, Thomas 136
Fiskerton 86, 91, 149n
Fitzalan, Thomas, Lord Maltravers 60
Fitzeustace, Roland, Lord Portlester 67
Fitzgerald, house of 65–8
Fitzgerald, Gerald (Garret Mor), earl of Kildare 5–8, 33, 35, 65–8, 107, 112, 116, 130
Fitzgerald, James, earl of Desmond 65
Fitzgerald, Thomas 66, 68, 91, 101, 111, 134–5, 137
Fitzhugh, Henry, Lord Fitzhugh 74
Fitzhugh, Richard, Lord Fitzhugh 30, 37, 74, 85
Fitzlewis, Sir Richard 129
Fitzsimons, Walter, archbishop of Dublin 5, 47, 66, 107, 123, 126–7

Flanders 24, 43, 60–1, 112, 134, 145n
Foljambe, Godfrey 136
Fortescue, Sir John 129
Fosse Way 36, 84, 90–1, 94
Fossedyke, Lambert, abbot of Crowland 44, 48
Fotheringhay 20, 23
Foulney Island 70–1
Fox, Richard, bishop of Exeter 45, 94, 113, 128
Flamborough 103
France 17, 19, 22, 91, 112, 116–17
Franco-Breton war 91, 117
France, king of *see* Charles VIII
Frank, Edward 74, 103, 125, 150n
Furness 71–2, 78, 101, 125, 130
Furness, abbey of 71–2, 147n
Furness Fells 50, 101, 121

Gainsford, Thomas 105
Gascoigne, Sir William 38
Gascony 19
Gaunt, John of, *see* Plantagenet, John
Geraldine, Thomas, *see* Fitzgerald Thomas
Germany and Switzerland 60
troops from 10–11, 60–2, 74, 85, 91–4, 98–9, 102, 130–1, 135, 137
Gloucester, duke of, *see* Richard III
Great Chronicle of London 10
Great Malvern, priory of 114
Green, Thomas 136
Greens Norton 125
Gresley, Thomas 136
Grey, Edward, viscount Lisle 3, 75, 83, 95, 115
Grey, George (of Ruthin) 136
Grey, Henry, Lord Grey of Codnor 65
Grey, John, Lord Grey of Powys 83
Grey, Sir John 22
Grey, Thomas, marquis of Dorset 6, 23, 32, 51, 54, 58, 116, 135
Grey, Sir Thomas Grey 129
Griffin, Nicholas 136
Grosmont, Henry of, *see* Plantagenet, Henry
Guernsey 145n
Guildford, Sir Richard 59
Guines 150n

Halifax 85, 125
Hall, Edward 11, 105
Hamond, William 85
Hansard, Sir Thomas 129
Hanseatic League 144n
Harleston, Richard 11, 49–50, 64, 85, 91, 112, 125
Harrington, family of 33, 73–4
Harrington, Sir James 33, 35, 73, 91, 125
Harrington, Sir James (of Northamptonshire) 129, 136
Harrington, Sir Robert 73
Harrington, Thomas 125
Hartlington, Roger 125
Harwich 59
Haslington, William, abbot of Jervaulx 106
Hastings, Sir Edmund 81, 86, 148n
Hastings, Edward, Lord Hastings 3, 75, 83, 131, 136
Henry II, king of England 126
Henry III, king of England 18
Henry IV (Henry of Bolingbroke), king of England 18, 64, 77

Henry V (Henry of Monmouth, prince of Wales), king of England 18–19
Henry VI, king of England 3, 19–22, 30, 36, 57, 77, 119, 133
Henry VII (Henry Tudor, earl of Richmond), king of England 1–4, 8–12, 15–16, 22, 25, 27, 29–33, 35–40, 48–51, 53–5, 57–60, 63, 65–7, 69–70, 72, 75–9, 81–4, 89, 94–5, 97–9, 101–3, 105–9, 111–13, 115–17, 119–20, 122–38, 143n, 144n, 145n, 146n, 148n, 149n
Henry VIII (Henry, prince of Wales) 11, 45
Herald's report (British Library, Cotton MS. Julius B.XII) 10, 45–7, 82, 84, 94, 127–9, 149n
Hereford 21
Hest Bank 50
Hextall, Edward 54
Heysham 73
Hilton, Robert 125
Hodgeson, Richard 125
Holinshed, Raphael 11
Holland 59–60, 130
Holme 89
Hopton, Sir George 83, 129
Hornby (castle) 33, 73–4
Hoveringham 84
Howard, house of 58
Howard, John, duke of Norfolk 29, 131
Howard, Thomas, earl of Surrey 33, 58, 107, 111, 116
Howth, Book of 11
Howth, Lord, *see* St Lawrence, Nicholas; St Lawrence, Robert
Huddleston, family of 71
Hugton, William 136
Huizinga, Johan 15
Hull 55–6, 85
Huntingdon 59
Hussey, John 136

Imola, bishop of *see* Pasarella, Giacomo
Innocent VIII, pope 39, 103, 119, 122–3
Ireland 1, 4, 8, 11, 20, 23–4, 33, 35, 43–4, 50, 53, 55, 60, 63–8, 107, 112, 116, 121, 125–7, 130, 132, 134–5, 144n, 145n, 146n *troops from* 68, 85, 92, 98–9, 102, 135, 137
Isabella, queen of Castile 117
Italy 18

James III, king of Scotland 23, 112, 117
Jersey 49, 64, 85
Jervaulx, abbey of 74, 106, 145n *see* Haslington, William, abbot of Jervaulx
Juse, Edmund 125

Kay, William 85, 125
Keating, James, prior of Kilmainham 66–7
Kelham 89
Kendal 72–3
Kendall, P.M. 25
Kenilworth 3–4, 59, 69–70, 75, 78, 108
Kent 59
Kent river 73
Kilberry 67

Kildare, bishop of see Lane, Edmund
Kildare, earl of, see Fitzgerald, Gerald
Kilmainham, prior of, see Keating, James
Kirkby Muxloe 3
Knaresborough 81, 107
Knaresborough, Richard 107
Knyvet, William 83, 136

Lambert, Elizabeth ('Jane Shore') 45
Lambert, John (of Lancaster) 145n
Lambert, John (of London) 45
Lambeth 121
Lancashire 33, 43, 58, 69, 71–4, 77, 84, 125, 136, 146n
Lancaster, duke of, see Plantagenet, John
Lancaster, earl of, see Plantagenet, Edmund 'Crouchback'
Lancaster, house of 18–19, 22, 29–31, 35, 40, 57, 64–5, 77, 119 see also Plantagenet
Lane, Edmund, bishop of Kildare 66, 123
Langford, John 136
Langley, Edmund of, see Plantagenet, Edmund
Latimer, Richard 136
Leconfield 78
Legh, James 107
Leicester 1, 29, 31, 76–7, 116, 127 Greyfriars 1, 77 St Mary's church 77
Leicestershire 1, 3–4
Leinster 8
Leland, John 10, 45, 47, 127
Lenton 82, 128
Liège 47–8
Lincoln 36, 89–90, 102–3, 124, 138
Lincoln, bishop of, see Russell, John
Lincoln College, see Oxford university
Lincoln, earl of, see De La Pole, John
Lincolnshire 64, 85
Lionel of Antwerp, duke of Clarence, see Plantagenet, Lionel
Lisle, Viscount, see Grey, Edward
Litchborough 125
Littleton, Sir William 129
London 8–9, 16, 21–2, 24, 29, 31–2, 35–6, 38, 43, 45, 55, 58, 69, 77, 89, 107, 109, 111, 121–2, 131, 135, 144n Martin le Grand 103 St Pauls 107, 135 Tower of London 6, 23, 25, 32, 43, 51, 106–7, 111, 121, 134–5, 150n Tyburn 38
London, chronicles of see Great Chronicle of London
Longford, Sir Ralph 129, 136
Longville, Sir John 129
Lonsdale 74
Loughborough 81, 128
Lovell, Francis, Viscount Lovell 5, 11, 30, 33–9, 43, 50, 58, 63–4, 71, 74, 79, 84–8, 91, 101, 111, 121, 123–4, 129, 134–5, 137, 149n, 150n
Lovell, Sir George 129
Lovell, Sir Thomas 105, 129
Low Countries see Netherlands; Flanders
Lucy, Edmund 136
Ludlow 21
Lune river 74 see also Lonsdale
Lyncolle, William 126
Lynde, Sir Thomas 129

Macclesfield 83
Malines 61
Mallary, Giles (of Greens Norton) 85, 125
Mallary, John (of Litchborough) 85, 125
Mallary, Robert (of Fawsley) 85, 125
Mallary, William (of Stowe) 85, 125
Maltravers, Lord, see Fitzalan, Thomas
Manning, Robert 85, 125
Mansfield 85
March, earl of see Mortimer, Edmund
March, earldom of 19
Margaret of Anjou, queen of England 21–2, 77
Margaret of York, duchess of Burgundy 43, 47, 52–4, 61, 63–4, 95, 111–12, 116, 130, 132, 134
Market Bosworth 1, 76 see also Bosworth, battle of
Markham, John 136
Marney, Henry 136
Mary of Burgundy 23, 61
Masham 74, 79, 85, 122
Mauleverer, Sir Thomas 37, 55, 85
Maximilian, of Habsburg, regent of Netherlands, king of Romans, later emperor 61, 63, 112, 116, 130
Mayne, John 146n
Meath 8
Meath, bishop of see Payne, John
Medina del Campo, treaty of 117
Merbury, William 136
Mering, William 83, 136
Mersey river 71
Metcalfe, Thomas 74, 103
Middleburg 60
Middleham (castle and lordship) 38, 74, 85
Middleton, family of 74
Middleton, Richard 125
Millom 71
Minster Lovell 50, 101
Molinet, Jean 10, 12, 46, 63, 73, 81, 94, 99, 101, 129–31, 145n, 148n, 149n
Monington, Thomas 129
Montagu, house of 17
Montgomery, John 136
Montorgueil 91
Morat, battle of 95
Mordaunt, John 136
Morlaix 117
Mortimer, Edmund, earl of March 18
Mortimer, Sir John 129
Morton, John, bishop of Ely, archbishop of Canterbury 9, 12, 35–6, 43, 66, 75, 81, 113, 121, 128
Morton, Robert 81, 128
Munster 8
Musgrave, Sir John 129
Musgrave, Nicholas 74

Nancy, battle of 95
Netherlands 1, 45, 47, 51, 53–4, 59–61, 63
Neville, house of 17, 30, 38, 58, 74, 78, 107–8, 116, 150n
Neville, Anne, duchess of Buckingham 21
Neville, Anne see Anne, queen of England

Neville, Cecily, duchess of York 16–17, 19–22, 24–5
Neville, Sir George 129
Neville, Isabel, duchess of Clarence 6
Neville, John (of Thornbridge) 136
Neville, Ralph, earl of Westmorland 17–18
Neville, Ralph 136
Neville, Richard, earl of Salisbury 17, 20–1
Neville, Richard, earl of Warwick 6, 17, 20–3, 39, 71, 74, 78,
Newark 9–10, 36, 86, 89–91, 94, 101–2, 105, 115, 122, 124, 129, 137, 148n
Newby Bridge 72
Newcastle upon Tyne 106
Newport, William 136
Norfolk 59
Norfolk, duke of, see Howard, John
Norris, Sir Edward 83, 129
Norris, Sir William 129, 136
Northampton 59
Northampton, battle of 21
Northamptonshire 123
Northumberland, earl of, see Percy, Henry
Norwich 58, 135
Nottingham 4, 36–9, 59, 75, 81–6, 90 Castle 36–8, 81
Nottinghamshire 81, 85, 125
Nuthall 85, 125

O'Connor, clan of 68
Ogle, George 136
Ormond, earl of, see Butler, Thomas
Ormston, Roger 136
O'Toole, St Lawrence 5
Otter, Thomas 38
Oxford, earl of, see Vere, John de
Oxford 41–3, 48, 50, 53, 125 St Mary's church 41
Oxford, university of 24, 41–2, 48–9, 53, 121, 133 All Souls college 41 Lincoln college 41 Magdalen college 41, 48–9
Oxfordshire 51

Palacio, Octavian del, archbishop of Armagh 64, 66
Paris 19
Parker, Sir James 83, 129
Pasarella, Giacomo, bishop of Imola 35
Paston, Sir John 83, 129
Paston, William 58, 146n
Paulet, Sir Amyas 129
Payne, John, bishop of Meath 6, 66, 123
Paynton, Robert 136
Pembrokeshire 71
Pennines 33, 74–6
Percy, house of 17, 116
Percy, Henry, earl of Northumberland (d.1455) 17
Percy, Henry, earl of Northumberland (d.1489) 4, 9, 29–30, 32, 37, 39, 55, 58, 77–9, 81, 107, 112, 116, 123–4, 142n, 146n
Percy, Robert 125
Percy, Sir Robert (of Scotton) 81, 86
Philip, David 136
Philip of Habsburg, duke of Burgundy 61
Philpot, John 89

Pickering 81
Pickering, Sir Edward 129
Piel, castle of 70
Pierpont, William 83, 136
Pilkington, Sir Thomas 73
Plantagenet, house of 6, 15, 57
Plantagenet, Blanche 77
Plantagenet, Bridget 24
Plantagenet, Cecily, duchess of York, *see* Neville, Cecily
Plantagenet, Edmund ('Crouchback'), earl of Lancaster 18, 30
Plantagenet, Edmund (of Langley), duke of York 18
Plantagenet, Edmund (son of Richard, duke of York) 20
Plantagenet, Edward, *see* Edward I
Plantagenet, Edward, *see* Edward II
Plantagenet, Edward, *see* Edward III
Plantagenet, Edward, duke of York 19
Plantagenet, Edward, *see* Edward IV
Plantagenet, Edward, *see* Edward, prince of Wales, *see* Edward V
Plantagenet, Edward, prince of Wales (d.1471) 22
Plantagenet, Edward, earl of Warwick 4, 6–7, 25, 30, 33, 39, 43–5, 48–50, 53–5, 57–8, 63–4, 107, 111, 121, 130, 134, 144n, 150n *see also* 'Edward VI', Simnel, Lambert
Planagenet, Edward (of Middleham), earl of Salisbury, prince of Wales (d.1484) 24–5
Plantagenet, Elizabeth, duchess of Suffolk 7, 24, 64
Plantagenet, Elizabeth *see* Elizabeth, queen of England
Plantagenet, George, duke of Clarence 6–7, 20, 22–5, 29–30, 51, 53, 57, 63–5, 123, 126, 130, 134, 143n, 145n
Plantagenet, Henry, *see* Henry II
Plantagenet, Henry, *see* Henry III
Plantagenet, Henry (of Grosmont), duke of Lancaster 77
Plantagenet, Henry (Henry of Bolingbroke), *see* Henry IV
Plantagenet, Henry, *see* Henry V
Plantagenet, Henry, *see* Henry VI
Plantagenet, Henry (son of Richard, duke of York) 20
Plantagenet, Humphrey, duke of Gloucester 19
Plantagenet, John (of Gaunt), duke of Lancaster 18, 22, 31, 77
Plantagenet, John, Duke of Bedford 19
Plantagenet, Lionel (of Antwerp), duke of Clarence 7, 18, 126
Plantagenet, Margaret, *see* Margaret of York, duchess of Burgundy
Plantagenet, Philippa 126
Plantagenet, Richard, *see* Richard II
Plantagenet, Richard, duke of Gloucester *see* Richard III
Plantagenet, Richard, duke of York 6–7, 18–21, 23–4, 65
Plantagenet, Richard, duke of York (son of Edward IV) 24–5, 32
Plantagenet, Richard, earl of Cambridge 18–19
Plumpton, Sir Robert 35, 107
Plunket, Edward Og 68
Pole, Sir Richard 83, 129
Pontefract 37, 39, 81

Poole, Sir Thomas 129
Pope, *see* Innocent VIII
Portington, Thomas 107
Portlester, Lord, *see* Fitzeustace, Roland
Portugal 54
Poynings, Sir Edward 116
Princes in the Tower *see* Edward V; Plantagenet, Richard, duke of York
Pullen, John 107, 148n
Pulteney, Thomas 136

Raby 16–17
Radcliffe on Trent 84, 86, 91, 94, 129
Radmill, Sir William 129
Rainsford, John 136
Redesdale, *see* 'Robin of Redesdale'
Redhill 82
Redman, Richard, bishop of St Asaph 74
Rhys ap Thomas 75, 83
Ribble river 71
Rice, James 126
Richard II, king of England 17–19, 64–5
Richard III, king of England 1, 3–4, 6–7, 12, 22–5, 27, 29–33, 36–7, 41–2, 51, 59, 61, 63–5, 71, 73–4, 76–8, 81, 97, 101, 108–9, 112, 116, 119, 133, 146n
Richard 'Strongbow' 5
Richmond (Yorkshire) 106
Richmond (Surrey) 106, 134
Richmond, countess of, *see* Beaufort, Margaret
Richmond, earls of, *see* Henry VII; Tudor, Edmund
Rivers, earl, *see* Woodville, Anthony; Woodville, Richard
Roche, William, bishop of Cloyne 66
Rome 31, 39, 103
'Rose of Raby', see Neville, Cecily
Rotherham, Thomas, archbishop of York 72, 89
Rouen 20, 24
Rous, John and *Historia Regum Angliae* 10, 108, 144n
Ruddington 82
Rugeley 9
Russell, John, bishop of Lincoln 36, 39, 89

Sacheverell, Richard 136
St Albans, battle of 20
St Asaph, bishop of, *see* Redman, Richard
St John, John 136
St Lawrence, Nicholas, Lord Howth 11, 66, 105
St Lawrence, Robert, Lord Howth 66
St Osith, abbey of 45
Salazar, Juan de 61
Salisbury, earls of, *see* Neville, Richard; Plantagenet, Edward
Sandeford 1
Sandes, Sir William 129
Sant, John, abbot of Abingdon 63, 146n
Sapcote, Sir John 129
Savage, Sir Humphrey 129
Savage, Sir John 83, 95, 131

Savage, John 38
Scales, Lord, *see* Woodville, Sir Edward
Scarborough 78
Schwartz, Martin 11, 60–1, 63–4, 73, 85–6, 91–2, 97, 101, 105, 130–1, 135, 137, 142n, 143n
Scotland 18, 30, 91, 112, 117 *See also* James III
Scotton 81
Scrope, John, Lord Scrope of Bolton 30, 37–9, 74, 79–80, 85–6, 91, 107, 116, 123, 131
Scrope, Thomas, Lord Scrope of Masham and Upsal 30, 37, 74, 79–80, 85–6, 91, 103, 107, 116, 123, 131
Sea, Sir Martin of the the 37
Sedbergh 72–4
Shap, abbot of, *see* Redman, Richard
Shap, abbey of 74
Sheen 9, 39, 51, 58, 146n *See also* Richmond (Surrey)
Sheffield, Robert 136
Sheriff Hutton (castle) 6, 25, 31
Sherwood Forest 37, 85, 90, 130
Shirley, Sir Ralph 129, 136
Shore, Elizabeth ('Jane'), see Lambert, Elizabeth
Shrewsbury, earl of, *see* Talbot, George
Simnel, Lambert 4, 8–9, 11–13, 41–51, 53–5, 57, 63, 105–7, 119–21, 125, 127, 129, 132–5, 137, 145n
Simnel Richard 45
Simnel, Thomas 47–8, 125
Simonds, Richard (alias William) 12, 42–4, 47–50, 63, 121, 133–4, 137, 144n
Skelton, Clement 74, 125
Skelton, John 105
Solihull 108
Somerset, dukes and earls of, *see* Beaufort, Edmund; Beaufort, John
Somerset, Charles 83
Southwell 85, 91, 128
Stafford, Edward, earl of Wiltshire 37, 83
Stafford, Humphrey, duke of Buckingham 17
Stafford, Humphrey 37–8
Stafford, Thomas 37–8
Staffordshire 9
Stainforth 81, 130
Stanhope, Edward 83, 136
Stanley, house of 33, 71, 73, 75, 77, 82, 95, 99, 146n, 149n
Stanley, George, Lord Strange 75, 77, 82, 124, 128, 136
Stanley, Sir Humphrey 101, 129, 136
Stanley, Humphrey 136
Stanley, Thomas, Lord Stanley, earl of Derby 3, 29, 33, 37–8, 69, 75, 77, 82, 116, 128, 131
Stapleton, Sir Brian 136
Stephen, king of England 126
Stillington, Robert, bishop of Bath and Wells 24, 53–4, 143n, 146n
Stodagh, Lambert 145n
Stoke (Stoke Field), battle of 9–12, 45–6, 85–6, 89–103, 108, 111, 113, 115–16, 118–20, 124–5, 129, 131–3, 136–8, 148n –*Red Gutter* 99–100; *Burham Furlong* 91, 94, 99 *See also* East Stoke

Stoke Bardolph 84, 86
Stonor, Sir William 95, 129
Stowe 125
Strange, Lord, *see* Stanley, George
Suffolk 58
Suffolk, duke and duchess of, *see* De La Pole, John; Plantagenet, Elizabeth
Surrey, earl of, *see* Howard, Thomas
Sutton, Edward 136
Swarthdale 74
Swarthmoor 72, 147n
'Sweating sickness' 4, 33, 36, 41, 44
Swit, John 103, 122
Switzerland *see* Germany
Swynford, Catherine 30
Syerston 91, 94, 98

Tadcaster 79, 81, 123
Tait, James 54–5
Talbot, George, earl of Shrewsbury 37, 75, 83, 95, 130–1, 136
Talbot, Sir Gilbert 95, 129
Tapton, John 145n
Taylor, John 145n
Tempest, Thomas 136
Temple Balsall 108
Tewkesbury 22
Tewkesbury, abbot of 145n
Thetford 59
Thornbridge 136
Throckmorton, Robert 33, 136
Tiptoft, John, earl of Worcester 65
Tirwhit, Sir William 129, 136
Todd, William 78
Towton, battle of 21, 77, 91
Trent river 15, 37, 81–2, 84–6, 89–91, 94, 99, 101, 106, 128–9, 131, 137, 149n
Troutbeck, Sir William 129
Tudor, house of 15, 77, 99, 117
Tudor, Arthur, prince of Wales, 4, 40, 42, 51, 108, 117
Tudor, Edmund, earl of Richmond 30
Tudor, Henry, *see* Henry VII
Tudor, Henry, *see* Henry VIII
Tudor, Jasper, earl of Pembroke, duke of Bedford 3, 33, 36, 38, 58, 69, 75, 83, 110, 116, 136
Tunstall, Sir Richard 78–9, 107

Tyler, Sir William 37, 39
Tynemouth 57
Tynemouth, prior of 55
Tyrell, Sir Thomas 129, 136

Ughtred, Sir Robert 37
Ulster 8
Ulster, earldom of 19
Ulverston 72
Urswick, Christopher, dean of Windsor 11, 39, 69, 72, 75, 136, 138

Vampage, Sir William 129
Vaux, Sir Nicholas 129, 136
Vavasour, Master 124
Vere, John de, earl of Oxford 3, 9, 22, 31, 37–8, 58–9, 75, 83, 90, 94–5, 98–9, 116, 124, 128–31, 136
Vergil, Polydore and *Anglica Historia* 11–12, 37, 42–5, 47–8, 53, 82, 94, 97, 101, 105, 133–8, 148n, 149n, 150n
Vernon, Henry (of Haddon) 84, 136
Villiers, John 136

Wainfleet, William, bishop of Winchester 41
Wakefield, battle of 21, 65, 77
Wales 36, 71, 117 *See also* Plantagenet, Edward, Henry; Tudor, Arthur
Walsingham 59, 103, 138
Warbeck, Perkin 12, 51, 54, 105, 111, 116, 145n
Wars of Roses 21–3, 61, 90, 106, 119
Warwick 1, 10, 107–8, 145n
Warwick, countess of *see* Beauchamp, Anne
Warwick, earls of, *see* Neville, Richard; Plantagenet, Edward
Warwickshire 1, 4, 33, 38, 49, 59, 69, 85, 107–8
Waterford 8, 11, 47, 57, 60, 66, 107, 112, 119, 126–7
Waterton, Sir Robert 19
Wells 24, 143n
Welles, John, Viscount Welles 77, 131
Welles, William 78

Wensleydale 38, 72, 74, 79
Westminster 32, 103, 122
Westmorland, earl of, *see* Neville, Ralph
William, John 136
Willoughby, Sir Henry 83, 115, 129, 136
Willoughby, Henry 136
Willoughby, Sir Robert 31
Wiltshire, earl of, *see* Stafford, Edward
Winchester 40
Winchester, bishop of, *see* Wainfleet, William; Courtenay, Piers
Windham, Sir John 129
Windsor 54, 66
Wolston, Guy 136
Wolton, Sir Thomas 129
Woodville ('Wydeville'), house of 23
Woodville, Anthony, earl of Rivers 23
Woodville, Sir Edward, 'Lord Scales' 75, 81–2, 95, 117, 130, 142n
Woodville, Elizabeth, *see* Elizabeth Woodville, queen of England
Woodville, Richard, earl of Rivers 37
Worcester 39
Worcester, earl, *see* Tiptoft, John
Worcestershire 38
Worksop 85
Wroughton, Sir Christopher 129

York 4, 10, 12, 27, 37–8, 54–5, 59, 69, 75, 77–81, 85–6, 101, 106, 121, 123–4, 130–1, 148n, 149n Bootham Bar 78–80, 123 Micklegate bar 123–4
York, archbishop of, *see* Rotherham Thomas
York, duchy of 19
York, duke of, *see* Plantagenet, Richard
York, house of 1, 6–7, 23–4, 29–31, 33, 36, 40, 50–1, 53, 57, 61, 64–5, 77–8, 111, 130 *See also* Plantagenet
York, Elizabeth of, *see* Elizabeth of York, queen of England
York, Margaret of, *see* Margaret of York, duchess of Burgundy
York, Richard 78
Yorkshire 38, 55, 74, 77–8, 81, 85, 106–7, 136